Beyond unity-in-tension

Edited by

Thomas F. Best

Beyond unity-in-tension

Unity, renewal and the
community of women and men

Faith and Order Paper No. 138
WCC PUBLICATIONS, GENEVA

Cover design: Rob Lucas

ISBN 2-8254-0889-1

© 1988 WCC Publications, World Council of Churches,
150, route de Ferney, 1211 Geneva 20, Switzerland

Printed in Switzerland

Contents

Preface

The study on "The Community of Women and Men in the Church" found its preliminary conclusion at a WCC international consultation held in 1981 in Sheffield, England.[1] The recommendations of this conference urged the different sub-units of the World Council of Churches to continue work — in the context of their own mandates — on the issues which had emerged in the course of the Community study and at the Sheffield consultation. The Faith and Order Commission of the WCC, which had been co-responsible for the Community study, has responded positively to the request for a follow-up of the study.

This response is being made in the framework of the new Faith and Order project on "The Unity of the Church and the Renewal of the Human Community". Two areas were selected which should serve as concrete examples for the task of theologically inter-relating the concerns for the visible unity of the church and for Christian witness and service in addressing the divisions and brokenness within the human community: the churches' involvement in (1) promoting justice, and in (2) furthering and realizing a true community between women and men in church and society.

It was decided that four international consultations should deal with these two areas. The first consultation in relation to the Community issue took place in 1985 at Prague, Czechoslovakia. A second international

● Rev. Dr Günther Gassmann (Lutheran) is Director of the Commission on Faith and Order, World Council of Churches.

consultation on this issue will take place in Africa in late 1988. The participants in the Prague meeting recommended that the papers and reports of this consultation, which struggled considerably with conflicting approaches and positions, should be made available to a wider public. We are now able to implement this recommendation and I am grateful to all who helped to make this publication possible.

Geneva, November 1987   *Günther Gassmann*

NOTE

[1] Cf. Constance F. Parvey, ed., *The Community of Women and Men in the Church*, WCC, Geneva, 1983.

Editor's Introduction

This strong and diverse collection makes an important contribution to the ecumenical discussion on issues of women and men. It contains the papers and report from the Faith and Order Prague consultation — the second within its study programme on "The Unity of the Church and the Renewal of Human Community" — on the Community of Women and Men and issues of unity and renewal.[1]

The consultation focused upon the ongoing significance of the World Council of Churches' Community of Women and Men in the Church Study (1977-1981), new approaches to biblical analysis and interpretation incorporating perspectives of women, basic traditional and confessional perspectives, and specific examples of Christians, in different confessional and cultural contexts, working towards more complete community of women and men in the church. In keeping with the methodology of the Unity and Renewal programme as a whole, it sought to combine traditional theological work with reflection upon the experience of Christians in concrete situations today.

Thus the volume includes two important reviews of the Community of Women and Men Study and its ongoing significance; a realization, both unequivocal and constructive, of a feminist hermeneutic as applied to the New Testament; two concrete accounts of Christians struggling for new community of women and men within the church, in contexts as diverse as India and Berkeley, California; and two accounts of the Orthodox position, one exploring the Orthodox vision of the equality of women and men, the other offering an incisive critique of ecumenical methodology in this area. At Prague three working groups reflected upon the material of the consultation; their reports illuminate, in different ways, complementary aspects of our theme. Following a personal theological and ecclesiological reflection upon the material and the process of the meeting, the consultation material concludes with the offical report. The appendices include a list of participants, an additional Orthodox statement, and an overview of the programme elements of the Unity and Renewal Study as a whole. The collection begins with a modest attempt to counteract the dreaded "loss of ecumenical memory", by recovering certain material from Faith and Order's own "tradition".

The themes dealt with in Prague were at once fundamental and existential, general and deeply personal. There were differing experiences and perceptions of the issues *and of the meeting itself.* It should perhaps be emphasized that, in the several signed articles and statement, the respective authors speak only for themselves.

And what of the ecumenical *future*? With respect to the Unity and Renewal study, the Prague consultation will be followed by another on issues of women and men (to be held in Africa), and has already been complemented by two consultations on the ecclesiological significance of the churches' involvement in issues of justice, one in the Asian[2] and one in the Latin American context.[3] These will be brought together with the other elements of the Unity and Renewal Study programme, namely the text on "The Church as Mystery and Prophetic Sign"[4] and the results from local groups around the world using the recently-published Unity and Renewal Study Guide.[5] The combination of these diverse approaches and methods — all valid, but traditionally claimed by different groups within the ecumenical movement — is the genius and challenge of the Unity and Renewal programme. Further information on the programme, and on other aspects of the work of Faith and Order, is available from the Commission at 150 route de Ferney, 1211 Geneva 20, Switzerland.

Official thanks to our hosts and colleagues, thanks to the churches with whom we worshipped while in Prague, an appreciation of the beauty and historic significance of our setting, and something of the dynamics of the meeting, are all included in the consultation report and elsewhere in this volume. I add here simply my personal note of gratitude to the Czechoslovak Ecumenical Council, especially its then president, Dr Anezka Ebertova, for its invitation; to the staff and students at the Comenius Faculty and the Hus-Seminary, and particularly to Josef Smolik and Jaroslav Ondra, for their efforts to make our work comfortable and productive; and to the Faith and Order consultation staff who worked, under the usual unusual conditions of such meetings, with such commitment to support the search for a deeper and more complete community of women and men.

Thomas F. Best

NOTES

[1] "The Community of Women and Men and the Unity of the Church and the Renewal of Human Community", Prague, 25 September-2 October 1985.

[2] This consultation was held in Singapore, 19-26 November 1986. Its report, "Unity and Renewal: the Ecclesiological Significance of the Churches' Involvement in Issues of Justice" (F/O 87:13), is available from the Faith and Order Commission, 150 route de Ferney, 1211 Geneva 20, Switzerland.

[3] On "The Ecclesiological Significance of the Churches' Involvement in Issues of Justice", 13-20 November 1987. The consultation report is available from Faith and Order at the above address.

[4] See "The Unity of the Church and the Renewal of Human Community: the Church as Mystery and Prophetic Sign" (FO/85:4), available in its latest form for study and comment from the Faith and Order Commission. The original version (from the first Unity and Renewal consultation, Chantilly, France, January 1985) is printed in "Church, Kingdom, World: the Church as Mystery and Prophetic Sign", ed. Gennadios Limouris, *Faith and Order Paper No. 130*, Geneva, WCC, 1986, appendix 2, pp.163-175.

[5] "Unity and Renewal: a Study Guide for Local Groups", *Faith and Order Paper No. 136*, Geneva, WCC, 1987.

Beyond Unity-in-Tension
Prague: the Issues and the Experience in Ecumenical Perspective

THOMAS F. BEST

> Words strain,
> Crack and sometimes break, under the burden,
> Under the tension, slip, slide, perish,
> Decay with imprecision, will not stay in place,
> Will not stay still.[1]

For one remarkable week thirty persons wrestled in Prague with issues of the deepest significance for the self-understanding and life of the church.[2] Meeting within the Faith and Order programme on "The Unity of the Church and the Renewal of Human Community",[3] and drawn from many confessions and some fifteen countries, they focused upon the significance of new understandings of the community of women and men, in both church and world, for the unity and renewal of the church. They explored the continuing significance of the WCC programme on the Community of Women and Men in the Church, new approaches to Bible study from the perspective of women, and the experiences of churches from contexts as diverse as India and Berkeley, California, and considered fundamental ecclesiological and confessional perspectives.

There was a search for words, for language which would enable us to move forward in areas which are among the most pressing and challenging facing the church today. It seemed at times that we reflected — to use a phrase which has been with Faith and Order at least since 1974 — a "unity in tension".[4] This was hardly surprising; the issues included those

---

● Rev. Dr Thomas F. Best (Disciples of Christ) is on the staff of the Commission on Faith and Order, World Council of Churches.

with which the Faith and Order movement has struggled over many years, in some respects from its very beginning at Lausanne in 1927. And yet as the issues were sharpened and defined, at points clues emerged for a possible way ahead, a way *beyond* "unity in tension". These clues came in three areas of theological and ecclesiological reflection, but equally in terms of the "style" of our work and its human dimensions.

Scripture and Tradition

Three theological and ecclesiological issues in particular were at the heart of the discussion and interaction in Prague. The first was the interpretation of scripture and of Tradition, and the question of their interrelationship. Reflection in this area within Faith and Order had found classic expression at its fourth, most recent world conference in Montreal (1963):

> But this Tradition which is the work of the Holy Spirit is embodied in traditions (in the two senses of the word, both as referring to diversity in forms of expression, and in the sense of separate communions). The traditions in Christian history are distinct from, and yet connected with, the Tradition. They are the expressions and manifestations in diverse historical forms of the one truth and reality which is Christ. [5]

It is essential to note that Montreal affirmed not only the Tradition, but equally the need for *interpretation* of both Tradition and scripture: indeed, the ecumenical affirmation of tradition was possible precisely because of a readiness to wrestle with the question of interpretation. And it is striking that the development of *Tradition* was understood as, fundamentally, a process of the developing interpretation and renewed understanding of the *Bible* through the ages and in differing contexts:

> The Tradition in its written form, as Holy Scripture (comprising both the Old and the New Testament), has to be interpreted by the Church in ever new situations... A mere reiteration of the words of Holy Scripture would be a betrayal of the Gospel which has to be made understandable and has to convey a challenge to the world. [6]

Thus it was affirmed that the constant tradition must be reinterpreted and understood anew within the conditions and circumstances of each successive historical era (and, though in 1963 this was not emphasized as it is today, in different social and cultural settings). In a word, Faith and Order's view of both scripture and tradition was *contextual*.

This was a "breakthrough" on behalf of Tradition as being fundamentally important for the ecumenical movement as a whole. As often happens, in answering old questions some new ones were posed: what then is the nature of "interpretation", and what are its guiding principles? What are its limits? Thus at its Commission meeting in Bristol (1968), Faith and Order wrestled with the issue of hermeneutics (the principles and practise of interpretation). It affirmed that the tools of modern historical-critical scholarship are important if the biblical text is to speak with full power and meaning today:

> There is a generally accepted process of scholarly exegesis which is the practice of biblical scholars, upon which the church is to a considerable extent dependent and to which it is deeply indebted... we therefore hold that the literary-critical method is a necessary one... We therefore hold that the historical-critical method is a necessary one.[7]

This was, in effect, a recognition of the vital and positive role that modern biblical scholarship had played in the Montreal "breakthrough". It was not just that biblical scholars had given, through their development of hermeneutical principles, a conceptual framework for dealing with questions of interpretation. Far more significant, by showing that the New Testament itself reflected a "traditioning" process, that it had within itself a diversity of texts and tendencies which could be seen developing through their use within the life of the early Christian community, it enabled the Faith and Order movement as a whole to adopt a more positive attitude towards tradition. It is significant that papers from both a Protestant (Ernst Käsemann) and a Roman Catholic (Raymond Brown) New Testament scholar were fundamental in this discussion at Montreal.[8]

To return to the question of contextual interpretation, Bristol spoke not only of "questions arising out of the text" but also "questions put to the text,"[9] questions seeking guidance from "the" biblical or "the" Christian position about contemporary ethical and social issues. It was recognized that this was sometimes a complex process; there could be no fundamentalist approach since not every question had been anticipated, literally and in its modern form, by the biblical writers:

> The more these questions were already in the field of vision of the biblical writers, the more direct will be the answers which we receive. When, however, we approach the Bible with questions which come to us from our situation but which were foreign to the writers, the Bible will give us indirect answers, or sometimes no answers at all.[10]

This perspective was extended and deepened through reflections at the Faith and Order Commission meeting at Louvain (1971). There is, it was noted, "interpretation" within the Bible itself. We observe the Pauline churches, or the Johannine community, understanding the significance of

God's revelation in Christ in complementary ways relevant to their own social, cultural and philosophical backgrounds. As the development of "traditions" within the Bible had been seen, at Montreal, as a model for the traditioning process within the early church, at Louvain the process of interpretation already visible within the Bible itself was understood as a model for our own interpretation of the scriptures today:

> ...the process of contemporary interpretation is seen as the prolongation of the interpretative process which is recognizable in the Bible... Just as the biblical writers responded to a particular situation, so contemporary interpretation is also determined by our own situation... The reports of the groups make it quite clear that such situation-conditioned hermeneutic perspectives are inescapable. They should not be branded as bias but understood rather as a method of relating to contemporary situations. [11]

This view is reflected in the current Unity and Renewal programme (to be discussed in detail later on). The report of its first consultation (on "The Church as Mystery and Prophetic Sign", Chantilly, France, 1985) noted that: "Some contemporary events and issues are not the subject of direct references in the scriptures; some of them lead the Christians who are involved in them to fresh insights from the witness of the scriptures and the tradition for our time." [12]

It is important to note two things at this point. First, the recognition of our modern context as the locus for our reading of the Bible did not mean a biblical subjectivism, as if we could read any desired or "fashionable" meaning out of the text. The point is that our own situation forms the inescapable arena within which we read the text and have to apply it. Second, there was no "modernism" in the sense of an uncritical acceptance of modern thought-forms as a norm of judgment over against the biblical (or Traditional) witness. There was no rush simply to translate the Bible into modern terms and thought-forms, but a carefully-nuanced awareness that the Bible both speaks to all contexts and is also "foreign" to each, standing over against and challenging each. It was recognized that the categories of thought of our own era are also conditional, imperfect, and problematic, and are challenged by the word of God. And yet we do face, just as previous ages have faced, the inescapable responsibility of proclaiming the truth of the faith within the language and thought-forms of our own time:

> ...the Church not only speaks to the world outside, but receives from the world outside categories of thinking which it must use to understand and express its own message. The conscious study of these categories may enable

us to prevent them from becoming dominant in a harmful way, and may also make it possible to translate our thought from one system of philosophical categories into another...[13]

It is very important to note that this was an hermeneutical approach to the *whole* tradition: it included not only the Bible but also and equally the church fathers. There was also at Bristol a serious attempt to explore the implications of a contextual hermeneutic for the understanding, interpretation and appropriation of the fathers, using Basil of Caesarea's text *De Spiritu Sancto* as an exemplary case. It was affirmed that "the patristic period has both constitutive and paradigmatic significance for the Church today";[14] at the same time it was recognized that

> *The particular significance of the patristic period does not exclude critical examination and confrontation. Rather it demands it since we must hear the Fathers against the background of the apostolic work which they wanted to transmit in their own time.* [15]

What were the implications of a contextual hermeneutic for the reading of the church fathers? It was understood that it was not sufficient simply to read Basil, any more than simply to read the New Testament; this led in both cases to a fundamentalism which imprisoned the text within its own time-period and conceptual framework, preventing it from speaking its word of truth to the present day. Rather one must speak of the "re-actualization of Basil's decision"[16] regarding the Holy Spirit in the context of modern life. To do this one must take full account of the historical and spiritual context in which Basil wrote:

> Each text has an historical framework which conditions it, on the one hand, and offers a key to a more exact understanding of it, on the other. It must not be removed from this framework; otherwise there is the danger that irrelevant presuppositions will be brought into the interpretation and that the original content will be lost.[17]

Several factors were identified as especially important "for the historical and biographical situation of the composition of *De Spiritu Sancto* (375)", including: the historical situation; the ecclesiastical and theological situation, including the theological controversies of the day, particularly the conflict with Eustathius of Sebaste; and the cultural and intellectual situation, including the influences of Hellenistic philosophy, particularly Neoplatonism.[18]

Any "re-actualization" of Basil's decision would, of course, have to take account of the thought-forms and expressions of today — again, not because these are ontologically superior to those of Basil's time, but because we live, think and act today not in Basil's thought-world but in that of our own time. And we must take serious account of the differences between his world and ours:

> Although Basil's dogmatic decision has permanent significance, this does not imply that the cognitive presuppositions which led to it can also claim permanent and binding validity. The thought forms and idiom of that time raise particular difficulties for interpretation. [19]

This line of thought culminated in Bristol in the following statement:

a) A schematizing distinction between a permanent content and a changing form is an extremely problematic undertaking, theologically and historically, in which the historicity of the church and its proclamation are not taken into account.

b) It is much more important to understand the appropriateness of the theological statements in their historical conditionedness. If the appropriateness of the statements about the divinity of the Holy Spirit is so recognized, the dogmatic considerations which Basil formed in his concrete situation can acquire new significance, basically as well as exemplarily, for the doxology, the proclamation of the trinitarian God, and the theological reflection of the present time. [20]

This did not deny the reality of a permanent truth to which both Bible and Tradition point. But it does insist that we know, experience, relate to, and act upon this truth within the context of our own time and consciousness, which is inevitably shaped by the presuppositions and thought-forms of our age, and by our philosophical, social and cultural background. It warns that any effort to abstract the "permanent truth" from its historical rooting leads to the danger of so idealizing it as to remove it from life altogether, of so abstracting the gospel from life that we deny its reality: the point of a contextual hermeneutic is not to deny the permanent truth of the gospel but to take seriously its *incarnational* nature.

Of course today's hermeneutical context is again different from that of the late 1960s. Faith and Order faces a new situation in both church and world, a situation marked by a new global consciousness, a sense of the fragility of "spaceship earth" and the disastrous and irreversible character of many of our assaults on the world of nature, and a sharpened sense of issues of justice and peace, all made the more insistent by a growing awareness of the interconnectedness of these issues as well as the interdependence of all peoples. Besides movements to recognize "rights" of nature — for example, the right of a species not to be made extinct for human convenience or pleasure — there is a growing sense of the right of all peoples and groups to a part in shaping their own destiny. Often this is accompanied by a more flexible attitude to traditional societal roles, with a corresponding sense of new personal possibilities, which one may have a "right" or even obligation to exercise and explore.[21] These changes bring problems as well as positive results; but in any case the personal and social "breakthroughs" of one generation, such as the principle of equal pay for men and women for the same work, are understood as commonplace rights, as one's due, by the next generation.[22] The positive aspects of such developments have been affirmed frequently by the member churches of the World Council of Churches.[23]

Traditional "Western" biblical studies and theology — which are found, of course, not only in "Western" countries — have been shaken by the need to take seriously the challenges from this new world situation. Nor has this been purely from outside the churches, as a solely secular intrusion upon them. There have also been challenges from within the household of faith as indigenous theologies claim the right to express the gospel in new forms, each appropriate for its distinctive social and cultural context. The dominant theological traditions of the past centuries have been accused by liberation theologies of perpetuating an abstract, academic approach to the Bible which fragments the text, entombs it in the winding-sheets of academic jargon, and removes it from living contact with the people of God; and of claiming as "universal" a theology which is, in fact, also local and contextual: a Western theology which baptizes Western, white, male experience and values in the name of the gospel. With this comes an appeal for a new sensitivity to the insights of "the people," often in the form of communitarian or group reflection and discussion of the biblical text on the basis of the experiences of everyday life.[24]

Perhaps the most fundamental challenge has come from feminist theologians and biblical scholars. This is a large and very diverse movement, most stereotypes of which are inaccurate; but in general it expresses a new consciousness on the part of women, a fundamental refusal on their part to be defined any longer as "the other",[25] passive over against men and determined by them. One characteristic of this movement is that it tends to proceed from a deep analysis of culture and society as determined by patriarchy, i.e. by a

> group organization in which males hold dominant power and determine what part females shall and shall not play, and in which capabilities assigned to women are relegated generally to the mystical and aesthetic and excluded from the practical and political realms.[26]

From these developments has come an important shift in the discussion of hermeneutics and contextual interpretation. When in the 1960s we established that the interpreter's historical, social and cultural context was an inevitable aspect of our understanding of the Bible and the Tradition, it was still "our" (Western) context which was considered the norm. And this is precisely what is challenged today: the Western, male, white and middle-class context and perspective, whose thought forms have shaped the interpretation and understanding of both Bible and Tradition, is challenged from many sides as not being the only one from which to view Bible and Tradition. It is said, more radically, that this Western perspective sometimes *distorts* the intention of Jesus' message — that is to say, it distorts the Tradition, properly understood — and that such distortions need to be identified and corrected.

Scripture and Tradition: issues and challenges

What these challenges mean for the work of Faith and Order is not yet clear. Its task is not the construction of new theologies, however exciting and "relevant" they might appear, but work towards overcoming present differences in theology and practice which divide the churches. It is not so much a question of adopting this or that new approach as of taking the present Christian situation seriously, of giving full and appropriate weight to these new factors in theology, the life of the churches, and the ecumenical movement. The fundamental theological and ecclesiological issues involved here are the relation between the truth of scripture and its historical formulation in first-century categories; the relation of Tradition to both scripture and to the history of the church; and the criteria for interpreting both scripture and Tradition in the present cultural and religious situation. Clearly further ecumenical work is needed in the field of hermeneutics — as applied to both scripture and to the church fathers — and on the question of the authority of both scripture and Tradition.

Scripture, Tradition, traditions... and experience

The second area of theological focus emerging at Prague was the validity and proper role of experience in doing theology, and the relation of experience to both scripture and Tradition. In one sense, of course, all theology is the result of *someone's* experience; scripture reflects the experience of the first disciples with Jesus, or Paul's experience with the communities of Corinth or Philippi, and Tradition can be said to enshrine the experience of the men (and women!) of the early church as they encountered the gospel message and wrestled with its meaning for their own day. In the same light, it is possible to understand the language and thought-forms of liturgy also as not just "poetic hyperboles" — as if remote and abstracted from experience — but as liturgical words and deeds which "reflect the existential experience of the church's worship and belief in the resurrection and the presence of the Spirit in its midst". [27] Tradition, in this sense, is codified experience. But there must also be an appropriation of the truth contained in Tradition within the lives of individual Christians; the experience of earlier believers, codified as Tradition, must interact with my own unique, personal experience, if that tradition is to be not just an abstract principle from the past but is to become a living, vital spring of faith and action in my life today. [28] It is this dynamic interaction of Tradition and present experience which is at issue.

Again it is important to note that this was hardly a new theme for Faith and Order; it had been developed, particularly in two aspects, during the 1960s and 1970s. First was an attempt to link the more traditional Faith and Order theological work to reflection upon the present experiences of Christians from different concrete contexts. This was done through the so-called "inter-contextual method" which had already aroused within Faith and Order, as John Deschner put it at Louvain (1971), a "marked interest". [29] He noted that in the study programme using this method — "The Unity of the Church and the Unity of Mankind", a predecessor of the present study on "The Renewal of the Church and the Renewal of Human Community" — Faith and Order had

> ...found both the process and the theme "extremely helpful and productive... as a means of relating traditional Life and Work concerns directly to traditional Faith and Order issues". In effect we said: This problematic must be a permanent addition to our work. [30]

Indeed, at the Louvain meeting Deschner went so far as to say that there should be "a permanent commitment to inter-contextual work in planning all our Faith and Order studies..." [31] This was, in effect, an appeal to expand the Montreal "trilogy" to include a fourth element, so that we would speak of Scripture, Tradition, traditions *and experience*. It is important to clarify the term "inter-contextual" because it is so fundamental to the methodology of the Unity and Renewal Study. Again in the words of John Deschner,

> ...there has been a widespread misunderstanding that it means nothing more than contextual theology. But it means something much more. It must be related to its own ground and problematic, method and authority. This is no

mere case of permitting the world to set the Faith and Order agenda, or of misunderstanding "situation" as a "source" for theology. And it is certainly no repudiation or even reflection upon the importance and urgency of the classical Faith and Order agenda.

"Inter-contextual method" aims to relate the two sets of problems in a much more careful and disciplined way. Two movements are required. On the one hand, it means bringing a specific problem of human division into the context where church unity is the central interest, in order to learn what new insight we are stimulated to gather about *church unity* — drawing upon its own proper theological sources in so doing. On the other hand, it also means asking what light the principles of church unity can throw upon those basic human problems as we bring the former into the latter context.[32]

A second new factor was a new awareness of the importance of the people of God as a *whole* people, of the need to listen not only to those in the official structures of the churches or to professional theologians, but to be more open to the insights and reflection of the broadest possible range of persons within the churches — and not only groups which have been marginalized and excluded from from the discussion so far, but also the mass of everyday church members who simply have been silent. This new awareness was expressed by some through the term "whole theology," a theology which is "possible only when the whole people become a part of its process",[33] and for which pluralism, as a recognition of the richness and diversity of God's people,[34] is a positive constituent element:

> ...one can only speculate at this point on what a whole theology can become. But of one thing we may be sure: It cannot come out of one group or one sex or one nation or one culture speaking for the whole, any more than men have been able to speak for the whole. A whole theology would envision all the people speaking out of their own experiences into the process and towards full humanness.[35]

In practical terms this led Faith and Order already at its Accra meeting (1974) to an increased sensitivity to input from the various regions of the world,[36] and to a methodology of receiving input from local study groups in the various regions — for example, the various "Hope Groups" who brought statements to the Faith and Order Commission meeting in Bangalore (1977) from Africa, Asia, East Europe, Latin America, the USA, and Western Europe.[37]

This double concern — for taking seriously the present experience of men and women in the churches today, and for incorporating the views of a broad range of the people of God within the work of Faith and Order — was at the heart of the studies on "Unity of the Church — Unity of

Humankind",[38] as well as several other Faith and Order studies through the 1970s. Each dealt with an issue confronting the church today: the relationship between theology and racism,[39] questions of church and state,[40] the question of the full inclusion of the handicapped in the life of the church.[41] These "prismatic" studies[42] each illuminated, from a distinctive perspective, the relationship between theology and an issue of burning concern within the human community. They had in common that they sought to take, more intentionally and seriously than had been done in the past, the experience and witness of groups on the margins of the life of the church.

These concerns had a gradual but profound effect upon Faith and Order by challenging it to broaden the base of its theological reflections. This "prophetic" quality of the work in this area was expressed most powerfully by John Deschner, in summing up the significance of the "Unity of the Church — Unity of Humankind" studies:

> I suspect it will not be wrong, one day, in retrospect to call this study something of a turning point in the history of the Faith and Order movement: from a classical ecumenism which considered traditional denominational divisions as the central issue in the church unity problem to a more contemporary focus which also takes into account the human divisions which invade and divide the church. The two approaches are not alternative but complementary.[43]

The most consistent application of these principles by Faith and Order in its work was the Study on the Community of Women and Men in the Church (1977-1981), conducted jointly with the Women's Sub-unit of the World Council of Churches but "lodged" in Faith and Order, and culminating in the famous international consultation at Sheffield, England.[44] From the beginning this Study insisted both upon the inclusion of concrete experience and on the need for broad involvement in the overall study process. These factors were expressed in the desire to establish local study groups around the world:[45]

> It is hoped that women and men of all church traditions and cultures will find ways to participate in this study... All groups must feel free to react to this study according to the cultural patterns in which they find themselves and which vary greatly from country to country and church to church... wherever possible the groups may be set up in an ecumenical way and include as many confessional, racial and ethnic categories as possible. There may also be good reasons for limiting participation to one or two confessional groups... the context of each particular history and culture should be carefully taken into account.[46]

One fruit of the insistence on a broad range of experience was the inclusion of *men* within the focus of the Community Study! One of the motivations of the Study was a desire to recover, celebrate and learn from, after so many centuries of neglect, the distinctive experience of women. We cannot here discuss the issues of distinctive women's experience,[47] whether women are more "intuitive"[48] etc. than men — issues as important as they are controversial — but simply note that, while seeking to incorporate women's experience as fully as possible, the Community Study insisted that it was a study of and for the *whole* church, men as well as women, and refused to focus on issues that would limit its scope only or primarily to concerns of women.

The Community Study, as one of the most broadly-based and best known projects of the WCC and of Faith and Order, further affirmed the importance of drawing upon the broadest possible range of experience within the whole people of God. This has had significant implications for the WCC in general; it is surely symptomatic that recommendations from the Community Study presented at the Dresden WCC Central Committee meeting (1981) included the study of "the recent *experience* of women with regard to power, authority, and structure in Church and society" and "the manner in which our *experience* of power and authority and the character of our structures either express or obscure the community life of the gospel".[49] With respect to Faith and Order, it can be said that the use of a broad range of experience is now part of our approach, and not as a "concession to contextualism" but as a necessary and integral aspect of our theological work:

> The recent history of Faith and Order suggests that the "profile" of the Commission is changing in a way that gives recognition to the need for as broad and diverse a community as possible to reflect upon the Commission's classical agenda... And in the search for visible unity of the Church it is the experience of the widest community that has to be brought into that identifying of the "faith of the Church through the ages". Many will recognize this as a sign of renewed strength and hope for the future, others may see it as a threat.[50]

All of these developments formed the background for a new focus for the work on themes of unity and renewal, now brought under the heading "The Unity of the Church and the Renewal of Human Community" and launched at the Faith and Order Standing Commission meeting in Crete (1984).[51] The study picks up John Deschner's comment about the need to consider not only the "traditional denominational divisions" but also "the human divisions which invade and divide the Church" (see note 43, above). It affirms that churches today are divided not only over the traditional theological issues of transubstantiation or the proper age and forms for baptism but also, and often with more tragic results, by the alienation between ethnic groups, social and economic classes, and the sexes: the divisions of the world are, insofar as the church is a human institution, church-divisive realities. This did not mean that Faith and Order was shifting its attention to "non-theological" factors, but a new awareness that sexism and racism raise precisely theological and ecclesiological issues, and that work towards greater visible unity of the churches must also take account of these realities.

The point is that the search for Christian unity, and the struggle to overcome the brokenness of the human community (a brokenness which leads to divisions within the church as human institution), are part of one and the same response to the gospel of Jesus Christ. The two must not be left to different "wings" of the ecumenical movement, thus reinforcing the old, destructive, tragic and false division between "theologians" and "activists". Nor is this a new theme for Faith and Order, but the direct response to a challenge already sounded in its By-Laws:

> The Functions of the Commission are: (a) To study such questions of faith, order, and worship as bear on this task [to call the churches to the goal of visible unity...] *and to examine such social, cultural, political, racial and other factors as affect the unity of the Church.* [52]

Within the newly-shaped Unity and Renewal Study the commitment to taking seriously the element of present experience was affirmed; the moderator of the study, Paul A. Crow, Jr, spoke rhapsodically about

> ...the richly diverse experiences in diverse situations from which God's people bring their yearnings, their life situations, and their thoeological reflections. As we have listened to these local witnesses we have come to realize that some of the most theological issues come to light in the encounter between God and God's people in concrete experiences and situations. [53]

And it has been noted — correctly, I believe — that "without the acceptance of such a methodology [e.g. the inclusion of experience as a critical component] as a valid way of reflecting theologically, the programme on the 'Unity of the Church and Renewal of Human Community' fails to interest or convince". [54]

As for the concern for input from a broad variety of women and men within the churches, this became the basis for a mandate, issued by the Faith and Order Plenary Commission at Stavanger (1985), that the Unity and Renewal programme include work by local study groups around the world. This would draw upon the methodology of the Community of Women and Men Study, as well as the earlier "Hope Groups" (see note 37, above); what is "studied" would not be an "official" theological position of Faith and Order, but precisely the *experience* of women and men at the local level. In keeping with the orientation of Faith and Order, however, the *unity of the church* would be a primary focus for each area of reflection. The local study process would gather insights and reflection from local contexts for interaction with the other elements of the Unity and Renewal Study.[55]

But alongside this was a renewed commitment to more traditional forms of theological reflection and, in particular, a stronger and more explicit commitment to the ecclesiological elements and significance of the unity and renewal programme. The study, it was affirmed, would "require an *integrated* theological approach"[56], combining reflection upon the experience of a broad range of the people of God with the "deductive" approach more traditional to Faith and Order.[57] And issues such as the churches' involvement in work for justice, the community of women and men, the challenges and opportunities of an interfaith context, would all be approached as "prisms" through which to view the reality of brokenness within the church, and its call to be a "prophetic sign" for the healing of these divisions in the human community as a whole.

Thus it is recognized that present experience must not be emphasized at the expense or neglect of Tradition; rather both elements must be brought into a creative dialogue. The question of scripture is important at this point as well. Here the Unity and Renewal Study has been instructed by earlier Faith and Order work, and most recently by biblical reflections from the Community Study. Thus one of the specialized consultations prior to Sheffield, building upon the results of Montreal, Bristol, and Louvain, affirmed that:

> Interpretation occurs in the encounter of the biblical text, embedded as it is in its historical context, with readers who are also embedded in a particular historical moment. A fully "objective" interpretation of scripture is therefore impossible because no interpreter, or community of interpreters, can be divorced from the prejudices that accompany his/her immersion in time. Interpretation, then, involves a constant dialogue between the experience of the text and the experience of those who interpret. This interpretation does not rule out the operation of the Holy Spirit in understanding scripture; rather, it locates this operation precisely in the ever new encounter of contemporary context and historical text.[58]

The result is that

> Our experience constitutes a vital partner in the unending dialogue with
> God's living word... We discover the meaning and authority of scripture as it
> lives among us, challlenges us, and takes shape incarnationally through and
> with our experience. [59]

This interaction, then, of Tradition, scripture and personal experience
is at the heart of the Unity and Renewal Study. While the methodological
issues which it raises were discussed in the programme outline for the
study coming from Crete, [60] the most nuanced and substantial consideration of them was given in a preparatory paper for the Faith and Order
Commission meeting at Lima (1981):

> The theological method... was based on the conviction that our experience
> of life — whoever we are, wherever we live, whatever church we belong to —
> is vital raw raterial for understanding Christian truth and for our vision of the
> community we seek. But such experience has always to be measured against
> the Christian tradition which has come down to us through the centuries and
> which is given to us in and through the teaching, life and witness of the
> Christian communities to which we belong. That inherited tradition must
> judge and speak to our experience. But, in its turn, reflection upon our
> experience as women and men in community helps us to perceive ever fresh
> and creative insights in that tradition we receive in and through the Church to
> which it is entrusted and in which it is embodied. This theological method of a
> continual interplay between experience and tradition and between tradition
> and experience lay at the basis of the Community Study. Here was a double
> dynamic at work in which, on the one hand, examination of our experience of
> being women and men, in relationships and in community, put critical
> questions to the Christian tradition and, on the other, the tradition pointed to
> new evaluations of our experience... [61]

Note that this excludes any idea of a simple "judging" of either
scripture or Tradition *by* present personal experience, much less the
ready "rejection" of scripture or Tradition because it does not appear to
conform *to* present personal experience. This is a critical point; the
effort to take scripture, Tradition and present experience seriously led to
an intense discussion at Prague as to whether experience was being
elevated "above" Tradition, leading to a "subjectivism" which
threatened the role of Tradition in theological work. Is this charge
justified?

Now indeed at some points in the unity and renewal discussion the
language of putting "critical questions to the Christian tradition" [62] is used,
as is the language of "testing" the tradition:

...The conviction that the Christian Tradition expresses revealed truth includes the conviction that the tradition will past the test of relevance in every context: "I will prove to you, then, that the Son of Man has authority on earth to forgive sins". So he said to the paralyzed man, 'Get up, pick up your bed, and go home!'" (Matt. 9:6).

Equally, the claim to effective expression of God's saving purpose in each context, the prophetic claim that God is at work here and now, must be tested by the normative self-revelation of God in Christ: "do not believe all who claim to have the Spirit, but test them to find out if the spirit they have comes from God" (1 John 4:1).

This dual process of testing is at the heart of an approach appropriate to this study of unity and renewal.[63]

Certainly it is true that — as the programme outline from Crete itself says — "a better way of describing the methodological issues must... be developed as part of the unity/renewal study process..."[64] But it is important to understand the language in light of the continuing Faith and Order discussion of the issue; for example, already at Louvain it had been said that "the situation [in which one reads the Bible today] with its given elements and open problems determines the perspective within which the biblical witness must be read and interpreted".[65] The point here was not to limit the authority of the biblical witness, but to acknowledge that it speaks and works not as an abstract, distant text, but in and through the lives of men and women who are inspired by the word, and who through the Spirit seek to apply the biblical message to life in our world today.

And what of the statement, quoted above from the programme outline at Crete, that "the tradition will past the test of relevance in every context"? Is there not a legitimate sense in which we can say that the Christian message "proves" itself in each generation — not in the sense that its truth must be, ontologically as it were, established ever anew, for the message is eternal, true and sure — but in the sense that women and men, in concrete situations, *do* apply the message and seek to live it, and *do* find that it offers a word of truth and power for today. Nor is this process a modern invention, the product of a frenzied search for "relevance". As Louvain pointed out:

> The biblical writers sought to speak and act in response to the challenges of their own times. The supreme challenge was the message itself but besides this there was also the confrontation with contemporary movements, such as syncretism, the emperor cult, gnosticism and so on. *The message had to prove itself in the midst of constant controversy.*[66]

From one theological perspective, ontologically and ultimately speaking the truth of the message is established for all time; from another it is precisely this "proving" of the message — as it speaks again and again its word of power, liberation, judgment and reconciliation to ever-new contexts — which *is* the revelation, embodiment and demonstration of this eternal truthfulness. And as Christians today we *do* have the confidence that the word will continue to speak its word of truth. Thus Louvain affirmed that

> The Bible begins to speak most effectively when it is read in the context of the corresponding controversies of our own times. It has, therefore, to be exposed to the challenge of the situation existing at any given time. [67]

— precisely in order that, we might add, the message may bring its word of power into the situations of life and death within which Christian men and women struggle to be faithful.

Experience: issues and challenges

In looking to the future, one important question will be how seriously we can deal with the calls for a new approach and understanding of the Tradition in light of the experience of various groups today — for example, the claim that patriarchal elements in both scripture and Tradition have diverted the original intention of Jesus' teaching. [68] Here it will be helpful to remember that, however sensitive such an issue may be, the fundamental theological and ecclesiological issues are closely related to those which the ecumenical movement has faced before in other forms, for example in dealing with the "traditional" threefold pattern of ministry (handled in "Baptism, Eucharist and Ministry") or as we ask ecumenically the question, "Is there a God-given structure of the church?" (which is a prominent theme in the second phase of the International Roman Catholic-Reformed dialogue.) These issues are: How does the present experience of Christians — which sometimes brings new and challenging insights — relate to both scripture and Tradition? What are the criteria for evaluating present experience? What constitutes the proper interpretation of scripture, and what in the teaching and history of the church is, in fact, Tradition, and how is this determined, and by whom? Here work is needed on both the criteria for evaluating experience and the relation of experience to scripture and the Tradition of the church.

Christian community as the "human face" of ecclesiology

The third issue emerging from the discussion at Prague was the nature of the community we seek. We discerned that efforts to work towards more complete Christian community are hampered by a lack of common understanding about what elements this would contain, and how such new visions of community would relate to the institutional structures of the church.

The biblical witness is clear that Christian life is fundamentally a life in *community*. Among Jesus' first public acts was his forming the community of his disciples and followers (already at Mark 1:16ff., Matt. 4:18ff.); and Paul knows not individual Christians so much as Christians within the community of believers (note that for Paul the test of individual spiritual gifts is whether they serve not only the individual but also the community as a whole: 1 Cor. 14:1-19). The image of the "solitary" Christian has its place only within, and subject to correction by, the larger framework of the people of God as a whole; otherwise it is prey to individualistic distortions (which have indeed characterized much Western theology). Furthermore, Jesus and Paul insisted that the Christian community be marked by love, justice and reconciliation; and Christians recognize that the gospel message should, in so far as is possible, be embodied in and through the institutional churches. The church as human institution has the task and responsibility of not only challenging the world with its proclamation of the gospel, but itself "living" the message of liberation and reconciliation which it preaches.

The churches considered as historic, human institutions do not fully realize this goal and hope. This has been a common theme of WCC Assemblies from the first at Amsterdam in 1948, where it was said:

> Within our divided churches, there is much which we confess with penitence before the Lord of the Church, for it is in our estrangement from Him that all our sin has its origin. It is because of this that the evils of the world have so deeply penetrated our churches, so that amongst us too there are worldly standards of success, class division, economic rivalry, a secular mind. Even where there are no differences of theology, language or liturgy, there exist churches segregated by race and colour, a scandal within the Body of Christ. We are in danger of being salt that has lost its savour and is fit for nothing. [69]

The Nairobi Assembly (1975) said frankly: "Sometimes the institutional structures of the churches themselves are oppressive and dehumanizing; often they uncritically reflect the values of their own culture."[70] And such admissions are part of the self-critical, honest realism of many churches as they examine their own institutional life.[71]

This raises, to be sure, profound and difficult issues of ecclesiology, in particular the nature of the church in relation to its historical and institutional expression. Intense discussion at Prague centred on this issue, and on the use of the term "renewal" with respect to the church. For some this is an impossible concept because the church is itself already perfection, incapable by definition of "renewal", particularly if "renewal" is used in its common sense, implying "improvement". But for others the term "church" may be used quite specifically of the historic, human institution, and the language of "renewal" is a challenging and helpful way of pointing to the need for a more complete realization of the gospel in its institutional life.

Clarification of this issue is essential for ecumenical progress. Those who understand the church primarily in terms of its eternal reality will inevitably feel that others, with their readiness to speak of "change" and "renewal", are compromising the "ontological dignity" of the church; those who, from another perspective, speak of reform or growth in the life of the church will feel blocked by a refusal to take seriously the historical, institutional aspects of the church, or the reality of human sinfulness. Language must be found to enable these groups to talk to each other. Perhaps the language of "mystery" and "sign" already developed in the Unity and Renewal Study[72] will be useful here, or perspectives may emerge from an approach such as this:

> ...unity and renewal are concerns both for the church and for the human community. Renewal is a condition of unity, and unity is the result of renewal. This should apply both to the church and to human community. It is this unity-renewal dynamic that suggests theological perspectives of the study at the initial stage. This may lead to a reconstruction of theology of the church and human community in a fundamental way.[73]

But the Unity and Renewal programme is not interested only in the universal church; its commitment to taking seriously the experience, insights and reflection of a broad range of persons within the church today leads it to focus also upon life in the local congregation. For it is here that the love, justice, reconciliation and "new being" offered by the gospel should be available; it is here that ecclesiology ceases to be an abstract system, and takes on a "human face", that its theological categories and truths become embodied in Christian sisters and brothers who incarnate God's challenging, enabling love and redeeming grace. It is not too much to say that the "quality of Christian life" within a Christian community is the primary test of its faithfulness to the gospel, more important than tests of doctrinal "correctness" (cf. Matt. 25:31-46, 7:21-23, cf. Luke 6:46-49!).

It must be clear that this is not simply a "social" or "sociological" concern, but is deeply theological and ecclesiological. To take a specific example, the Nairobi Assembly of the WCC (1975) affirmed that "the unity of the Church requires that women be free to live out the gifts which God has given to them and to respond to their calling to share fully in the life and witness of the Church".[74] Why is the full participation of all God's people in the life of the Church required precisely for the *unity* of the church? Because our churches as human institutions are often affected and afflicted by the divisions of the human community; because, as Paul experienced in his congregations (cf. 1 Cor. 11:17-22), so also in ours the divisions of class, gender, and race, rather than being overcome and transformed by the judging and reconciling power of the gospel, may impose themselves upon the life of the congregation, alienating men and women from each other and denying the reality of the gospel in that place.

Work to overcome such brokenness and division is not ancillary to the gospel but an expression of it; the search for new and deeper forms of Christian community arises from the desire to enable the "gifts" of all (1 Cor. 12:1-14:33) to come to creative expression. As the Asian regional consultation prior to Sheffield expressed it,

> ...the equality of women and men in church and society is understood as both a theological and spiritual issue. Because of sin the relationship of "being one flesh" is broken. The task of the Christian community is to heal this distortion and alienation of women and men from each other and bring them to their authentic identity in interdependence and mutuality.[75]

But what does this mean in practice? How do we embody these goals in actual communities? Clearly it is necessary to gain a better understanding of the proper elements of new or renewed Christian community. There have been many attempts to define such elements, including some within the Community Study and Unity and Renewal programmes; and undoubtedly much interesting material on community will come from the reflections of the local study groups around the world on unity and renewal issues.[76]

Again it will be necessary to find language enabling differing traditions and cultures to speak together. The language of "equality" and "participation" which figures in many visions of new community is unacceptable to some, who see here thought-forms from Western liberal culture which may not fit in other contexts; but others will regard the refusal to move in this direction as an excuse to continue old patterns of domination. With a greater agreement on the *elements* of Christian community we might do better at seeing how they can be embodied in different traditional and cultural contexts. Here it is striking that the Asian consultation mentioned above did not use the Western liberal-democratic language of equality and participation but rather the language of "interdependence" and "mutuality" — language equally rooted in the hunger for deeper community.

A further critical issue here is the relation of new or renewed Christian community to the institutional church. In church-historical terms much of the work on and in community has an ambivalent relationship to the institutional church: frequently it is done by self-consciously *alternate* communities, drawing upon elements from scripture and Christian tradition, and frequently claiming to be re-establishing "primal" forms of New Testament Christianity (with particular reference to such "reversal" passages as Mark 10:35-45 and Matt. 18:1-4); but such communities are often — with their utopian elements of participation, shared decision-making, and alternate visions of society — deeply challenging to established church structures. It can be argued that the most effective movements for reform and renewal are those coming from within rather than outside of the church; this requires a commitment on the part of new communities to the church as institution, and the churches' willingness to take seriously the visions of new community which are offered from such groups.

Finally, it is important to avoid triumphalism in the search for new and renewed forms of community. History is replete with "reforms" and "renewals" which, not having come to terms with the underlying issues and problems, only perpetuate many of the old injustices under a new ideology and vocabulary.[77] It is striking, for example, that even in "renewed" or "liberated" communities change in the status of women does not happen without careful planning and insistent and persistent work. A recent study of Basic Christian Communities in the Philippines indicates that unless improving the position of women is explicitly on the agenda it will simply not happen, no matter how much the goals of the group are oriented to "liberation" and "equality" *as abstract ideals*:

> ...although the BCCs [Basic Christian Communities] have been successful in improving certain aspects of the welfare level of their members, they have not had an effect on the status of women as such because they have not set out explicitly to do so...women's concerns will not be addressed comprehensively as integral aspects of community development without first making their attainment *explicit goals* of the BCCs.[78]

Community: issues and challenges

It is clear that *intentional* work towards specific goals is essential for genuine and lasting renewal; otherwise old attitudes and patterns of behaviour inevitably reassert themselves. This brings us once more to our initial point — that we lack a common understanding about the nature of the community which we are seeking. Here the theological and ecclesiological issues at stake are the nature and elements of distinctive Christian community; the criteria for determining this, and who decides; the limits of diversity within Christian community; and the relationship of particular communities to the larger church. Thus what is urgently needed is ecumenical work on the elements of renewed community, and the relation of these to both the biblical witness and the Tradition of the church, including the many and diverse forms of community which have been a legitimate and creative part of Christian history.

Unity-in-tension

These three theological and ecclesiological issues of scripture and Tradition, experience, and community provoked intense discussion at Prague. The participants, and the churches from which they came, were committed to drawing closer together; but, as was said above, we sometimes reflected a state of "unity-in-tension". What is the background of this term, and what does it indicate? It emerged at the Faith and Order meeting at Accra (1974), as the title of a formal "Statement of the Conference" which was then submitted to the Fifth Assembly of the WCC at Nairobi (1975) under the heading "What Unity Requires".[79] Accra insisted that church unity should serve not only the churches themselves, but must be understood within God's design for justice, reconciliation and renewal of the human community as a whole. In this context Accra reaffirmed the statement of the Fourth Assembly of the WCC at Uppsala (1968): "The Church is bold in speaking of itself as the sign of the coming unity of mankind."[80] But at Accra the question was the possible tension between the commitment to church unity and the commitment to justice and reconciliation: as Christians struggled towards these goals in the world, they might find themselves on opposing sides of certain issues, thus leading to further differences within the church. In this context a warning was issued against an "easy" church unity, bought at the price of one's Christian commitments to justice and reconciliation. On the contrary, it was said, to admit and deal with genuine differences between Christians is a sign of the health of the ecumenical movement — as already the Faith and Order By-Laws had indicated in noting that, as all traditions and positions "are invited to share reciprocally in giving and receiving... Differences are to be clarified and recorded as honestly as agreements."[81]

In this context the essential thing is that greater visible unity of the churches must remain an explicit, intentional goal even as we struggle with issues of brokenness in church and world; otherwise the search for church unity will be relegated to second place, or left only to specialized "ecumenical" theologians or professional ecumenists — who may then be branded as "elitist" and "irrelevant".

Here the crucial theological point is that unity is not something which we have to create, but is a reality given already by God; our work is to enable the structures of the churches better to reflect and manifest this unity — rather than obscuring it, as they often seem to at present. To begin from the unity given by God has profound consequences for our relations with other Christians, precisely those from whom we differ most profoundly. It means that we must see such differences within the overall context of God's uniting, just and reconciling purpose for both the church and the world. It is the uniting power of the Spirit, and our commitment to the one body of Christ, that enables us to reject an "easy unity", and to bear the honest differences which we may have with Christian sisters and brothers. As Accra put it:

> We must resolutely refuse any too easy forms of unity, or any misuses of the "sign", that conceal a deeper disunity. At the same time, we may believe in and give witness to our unity in Christ, even with those from whom we may, for his sake, have to part. This means to be prepared to be a "fellowship in darkness" — dependent on the guidance of the Holy Spirit for the form which our fellowship should seek and take; and a "unity in tension" — dependent on the Spirit for the strength to reconcile within the one body of the Church all whom the forces of disunity would otherwise continue to drive apart. For there is no "fellowship in darkness" without some sign of the reconciling judgment and love of Christ. [82]

As we have moved into the 1980s the differences between churches — and sometimes between Christians within the same church — on issues of women and men have proved to be equally sensitive and complex as those in other areas of justice and reconciliation prominent in the 1970s at Accra and Nairobi. The "Accra principle" of the need for acceptance and continuing dialogue between representatives of differing positions, churches and traditions, in the face even of serious differences of belief and practise, is equally necessary in the 1980s as we seek for ecumenical understanding on issues of women and men. As one Faith and Order commissioner has written, picking up the language of Accra quoted above:

...[In the face of our differences with respect to the roles of women and men within the church] we have to discover new ways of offering our experience and doctrinal understanding to each other, ways that uphold and do not deny the other. We must find unity in tension and fellowship even in the darkness of unknowing. [83]

In this area too the refusal to find an "easy unity" at the cost of one's Christian commitments must be balanced by a commitment to a deeper understanding of Christian unity — a unity which comes not from avoiding one's differences but precisely through facing and working through them together. This is not to say this is easy; indeed this is arguably the most complex and problematic area on the whole ecumenical agenda. Whenever issues of women and men have been addressed at anything more than a superficial level, or in more than purely abstract and theoretical terms, they have given rise to intense, sometimes difficult debate. This was true, for example, at the WCC Central Committee meeting at Dresden in 1981, where many thoughtful and important recommendations from the Sheffield Community Study meeting were lost in the the outrage over one suggestion regarding balanced representation. [84] And it was true at the Sheffield Community Study meeting itself, where serious differences in perspective and priority arose between "first-world" and "third-world" women. [85]

As we look towards future ecumenical work in this area it is important to reflect on why these issues have proved difficult to handle. We are dealing with deeply-held convictions, hallowed by centuries of Tradition and understood, by all parties, as reflecting the witness of scripture. And it is surely significant that issues of women and men are, in their nature, deeply personal. In this area, perhaps more than any other, it is difficult to remain within the abstract categories in which so much theology and ecumenical discussion have been conducted. Considerations of ecclesiology, anthropology and the status and functions of women and men very quickly involve issues of power and authority, of deeply-rooted roles in society and the church, of the nature and function of the family, and of personal identity at the deepest level, including sexual identity.

Although this last issue was not on the agenda at Prague, it is worth noting that it has always been a particularly difficult subject for the ecumenical movement — standing as it does at the intersection of vastly different cultural, social and religious traditions — to tackle openly and constructively. Along with positive factors church history includes, as many have recently pointed out, numerous examples of a destructive and distorted approach to human sexual potential. [86] At present there seems to be a theological attempt to recover a more positive understanding of creation, including the sexual dimension of personality, and clearly the churches need to work together towards greater understanding in this area. But we are only beginning to learn how to talk about it helpfully. Philip Potter had noted already in 1974:

> Of course, it is also true that, even in my time as a student and student pastor, we hardly every discussed "sex" as such. It was almost a taboo subject. No doubt it was because of this failure to come to terms with the issues of sex that we men easily fell into the patterns of sexist discrimination once we left university. [87]

While this may be an oversimplification, it does point to important truths: that unclarified attitudes towards sexuality will inevitably influence one's attitude towards issues of women and men in the broadest sense, and often negatively; and that these attitudes may work unconsciously even as we seek to be "objective" in our reflection and discussion.

Beyond unity-in-tension

To return to the discussion and interaction at Prague: besides the usual and inevitable differences of theological position, and the sensitive nature of the subject matter, there were differences over deeply-held values, and of expectations about the role of scholarship and biblical study in ecumenical discussion. There was even discussion about what subjects were discussable: for some an academic, "objective" presentation of "positions" was the only suitable approach, while others considered this impossible, indeed a violation of the subject matter — which, they felt, inevitably includes a subjective dimension. Given the complexity, sensitivity, and fundamental character of the issues which surfaced, and the history of the ecumenical movement's efforts in this area, it is scarcely surprising that the discussion proved difficult at times, and that the meeting will be remembered rather for its strong presentation of basic positions than for specific suggestions for ways to move forward. But if Prague reflected a "unity in tension" there were yet clues from our experience there for the content, method, and "style" of Faith and Order work, clues that may help us to move forward, to find a way beyond unity-in-tension.

In the area of *content*, as we have seen, three theological and ecclesiological areas were identified, along with fundamental issues and the ecumenical work needed in each. First was the area of scripture and

Tradition, involving the relation between the truth of scripture and its historical formulation in first-century categories; the relation of Tradition to scripture and to the history of the church; and the criteria for interpreting both scripture and Tradition in the present cultural and religious situation. Here further work is needed in the field of hermeneutics — applied to both scripture and the church fathers — and the question of the authority of both scripture and Tradition.

Second, in the area of experience the questions identified were the criteria for evaluating present experience; how this experience relates to both scripture and Tradition; what constitutes the proper interpretation of scripture, and what in the teaching and history of the church is, in fact, Tradition; and how this is determined, and by whom. Here work is needed on both the criteria for evaluating experience and the inter-relation of this experience to scripture and Tradition.

Third, with respect to the area of community the issues are the nature and elements of Christian community; the criteria for determining this, and who decides; the limits of diversity within Christian community; and the relationship of particular Christian communities to the larger church. What is needed here is work on the elements of renewed community, and the relation of these to both the biblical witness and the Tradition of the church, including the many diverse forms which Christian community has taken over the centuries.

A fourth issue emerges from the three just discussed. It is striking that all of them include the question of authority, whether of scripture or the Tradition in themselves, or the prior questions of who decides — and who decides who decides — about the proper interpretation of scripture, or what elements from the teaching and history of the church are, in fact, Tradition. Issues of authority, particularly the search for forms of nurturing, empowering authority rather than authority experienced as domination and control, have been insistent themes throughout the Community Study and at Prague. Clearly further work is needed in this area, which touches so intimately the interior lives of the churches and the existential realities of power and decision-making.[88] Such a study should help to shape the proposed Faith and Order work on structures of common decision-making among the churches.

In the area of *method* we discovered a fifth point, that Faith and Order needs to reclaim important elements of its *own* "tradition": namely the extensive and substantial work done since its last world conference at Montreal (1963) in the areas of scripture, Tradition and traditions, hermeneutics and the authority of scripture; the commitment to contextual theology, and to including more elements of the experience of all the people of God in our work, along with more traditional approaches; and the beginnings of a search for elements of new and renewed community. At times we operated as if these discussions had never taken place; this impoverished our reflection and led us to miss chances to move the ecumenical discussion ahead. Here we cannot afford to commit the dreaded "loss of ecumenical memory"[89].

Another set of learnings at Prague relates to the *style* of Faith and Order work. As a sixth point it became clear that we must learn to handle psychological and human factors with something like the care and expertise we devote to technical theological discussion. To discern the theological and ecclesiological implications of our experience it is first necessary to learn to share it, to share both good and bad experiences, and to give and receive experience, as stated above, in "ways that uphold and do not deny the other".[90] We must learn to be realistic about the human implications and the cost of our words to others.

This includes becoming much more sensitive to factors of process, to the patterns of interaction within groups, to personal rhythms and to the rhythm of the meeting itself. This suggests as a seventh and final point that most ecumenical meetings — particularly when the subject matter has a personal, existential dimension — work with far too much material and allow too little time for reflection and discussion. We must learn to take sufficient time for all to share, for participants to absorb information and new points of view, time to reflect, time for speaking and listening to one another, for hearing properly what is said, time ultimately to worship and pray together.

This brings us back to the quotation with which we began. Words can divide or unite, hurt or heal. Prague was a search for words, for language which would enable us to move forward in difficult, complex and sensitive areas. We discovered with the poet T. S. Eliot that our words do "strain,/ crack and sometimes break", that they may "decay" and may be "assailed". But we learned equally the importance of a commitment to one another and to the wholeness of Christ's body, the church. Through this power and hope we sought to go on speaking, to continue speaking through and beyond our differences and so, ultimately, to move beyond unity-in-tension towards a vision of more complete community, where the gospel message of justice and reconciliation would be more fully realized among the women and men who are Christ's body.

28   *Beyond Unity-in-Tension*

NOTES

[1] "Burnt Norton V, Four Quartets", by T. S. Eliot, in T.S. Eliot, *The Complete Poems and Plays 1909-1950*, New York, Harcourt, Brace & Co., 1958, pp.121-122.

[2] Accounts of the consultation (25 September-2 October 1985) have been published as follows: Tom Best and Janet Crawford, "Towards Unity-in-Tension: the Ecclesiology of Community", *One World*, No. 113, March 1986, pp.17-19; Thomas F. Best, "Einheit und Erneuerung und die Gemeinschaft von Frauen und Männern", *Una Sancta*, 1/86, pp.72-75; Arlette Roy, "L'autorité des femmes dans l'Eglise? pas partout! pas demain!", *Le Protestant de l'ouest*, 101, janvier 1986, pp.16-17.

[3] Further documentation on the Programme is available from the Faith and Order Commission, World Council of Churches, 1211 Geneva 20, Switzerland. The principal texts so far include "Minutes of the Meeting of the Standing Commission 1984, Crete", *Faith and Order Paper No. 121*, Geneva, WCC, 1984 [hereafter "Crete Minutes"], pp.33-52: also in *The Ecumenical Review*, Vol. 36, No. 3, July 1984 [hereafter "Crete", ER], pp.323-329; "Faith and Renewal: Reports and Documents of the Commission on Faith and Order, Stavanger 1985, Norway", ed. Thomas F. Best, *Faith and Order Paper No. 131*, Geneva, WCC, 1986 [hereafter "Stavanger"], pp.166-221; "Minutes of the Meeting of the Standing Commission 1986, Potsdam, GDR", *Faith and Order Paper No. 134*, Geneva, WCC, 1986 [hereafter "Potsdam Minutes"], pp.28-30,45; "Minutes of the Meeting of the Standing Commission (Majadahonda, Madrid, Spain, 1987)", Geneva, Commission on Faith and Order, 1987 [hereafter Madrid Minutes], pp.6-12 (draft minutes; the final version will be published later in 1987); "Church, Kingdom, World: the Church as Mystery and Prophetic Sign", ed. Gennadios Limouris, *Faith and Order Paper No. 130*, Geneva, WCC, 1986 [hereafter "Church, Kingdom, World"], including "The Unity of the Church and the Renewal of Human Community: a Historical Survey", by Gennadios Limouris, [hereafter "Historical Survey"] pp.176-185; "The Unity of the Church and the Renewal of Human Community: the Church as Mystery and Prophetic Sign" (FO/85:4) [hereafter "Church as Mystery and Prophetic Sign"], available in its latest form for study and comment from the Faith and Order Commission, 150 route de Ferney, 1211 Geneva 20, Switzerland (the original (Chantilly) version is printed in "Church, Kingdom, World", Appendix 2, pp.163-175); "Unity and Renewal: the Ecclesiological Significance of the Churches' Involvement in Issues of Justice" (F/O 87:13), available from Faith and Order; "Faith and Renewal: a Study Guide for Local Groups", *Faith and Order Paper No. 136*, Geneva, WCC, 1987. For a popular account of some aspects of the programme see "What Kind of Community are we Looking for?", Marlin van Elderen, in *WCC 87*, special issue of *One World*, No. 122, January-February 1987, pp.18-19 [hereafter "What Kind of Community?"].

[4] See "Towards Unity in Tension", a "Statement of the Conference" in Accra 1974: "Uniting in Hope: Reports and Documents from the Meeting of the Faith and Order Commission", *Faith and Order Paper No. 72*, Geneva, WCC, 1975 [hereafter "Accra"], pp.90-94. This text was then submitted to the Fifth Assembly of the WCC at Nairobi under the heading "What Unity Requires"; see *Breaking Barriers: Nairobi 1975*, ed. David M. Paton, London, SPCK and Grand Rapids, Wm. B. Eerdmans, 1976 [hereafter "Nairobi"], pp.57-69. The term was then taken up in a new context in "The Unity of the Church and the Renewal of Human Community: an Assessment of the Relationship of Unity and Renewal", Mary Tanner, *Mid-Stream*, Vol.1, XXIII, No. 1, January 1984 [hereafter "Assessment"], p.42; also published in slightly altered form as "Unity and Renewal: the Church and the Human Community", in *The Ecumenical Review*, Vol. 36, No. 3, July 1984 [hereafter Tanner, ER], pp.252-262.

[5] "The Fourth World Conference on Faith and Order: the Report from Montreal 1963", eds P.C. Rodger and L. Vischer, *Faith and Order Paper No. 42*, London, SCM Press, Ltd, 1964 [hereafter "Montreal"], para. 47, p.52. Also printed in "The Bible: Its Authority and Interpretation in the Ecumenical Movement", ed. Ellen Flesseman-van Leer, *Faith and Order Paper No. 99*, Geneva, WCC, 1980 [hereafter "The Bible"], p.21.

[6] "Montreal", *op. cit.*, para. 50, p.53. Also in "The Bible", *op. cit.*, p.21.

[7] "New Directions in Faith and Order: Bristol 1967", *Faith and Order Paper No. 50*, Geneva, WCC, 1968 [hereafter "Bristol"], p.33. Also in "The Bible", *op. cit.*, p.31.

[8] On this see my discussion in "Baptism, Eucharist, Ministry and Us: the Challenge of BEM for Disciples", in *Mid-Stream*, Vol. XXV, No. 1, January 1986, p.23.

[9] "Bristol", *op. cit.*, pp.37-38. Also in "The Bible", *op. cit.*, p.36.

[10] "Bristol", *op. cit.*, pp.37-38. "The Bible", *op. cit.*, p.36.

[11] "Faith and Order, Louvain 1971: Study Reports and Documents", *Faith and Order Paper No. 59*, Geneva, WCC, 1971 [hereafter "Louvain"], para. 9, p.18. Also published in "The Bible", *op. cit.*, pp.51-52.

[12] "Church as Mystery and Prophetic Sign", *op. cit.*, para. 50, p.11. In the original (Chantilly) version of the text (see "Church, Kingdom, World", Appendix 2, pp.163-175) the citation is found in para. 40, p.171.

[13] "Bristol", *op. cit.*, p.37. Also in "The Bible", *op. cit.*, p.35.

[14] "Bristol", *op. cit.*, p.43. It is a pity that the material on hermeneutics with respect to the church fathers was not included in the volume "The Bible". This reflects (and subtly encourages?) a separation between scripture and Tradition — the overcoming of which was precisely the point of earlier Faith and Order work!

[15] *Ibid.* (emphasis original).

[16] *Ibid.*, p.46.

[17] *Ibid.*, pp.43-44.

[18] *Ibid.*, p.44.

[19] *Ibid.*, p.46.

[20] *Ibid.*, pp.46-47.

[21] "In the reality of present urban technological and pluralistic society, there is no separate role for women any more than there is for men. Changes in the life of urban women invite a reconsideration of traditional views." "From the Margin to the Forefront", Metropolitan Emilianos Timiadis, in *The Ecumenical Review*, Vol. XXVII, No. 4, October 1975, p.372.

[22] See for example this statement from an Orthodox local group involved in the Community of Women and Men in the Church Study process: "Whatever a woman's profession, however, all would agree that in the Orthodox view women having the same jobs and professions as men should have the same wages and benefits, and the same opportunities for promotion and advancement. This is simply a matter of justice." From *In God's Image: Reflections on Identity, Human Wholeness and the Authority of Scripture*, eds Janet Crawford and Michael Kinnamon, Geneva, WCC, 1983 [hereafter *In God's Image*], p.26.

[23] See, for example, this statement from the WCC Nairobi Assembly (1975): "As a result of rapid cultural, economic, and social change, women (and many men) reject the passive or restrictive roles formerly assigned to women, and search for fuller participation in the life of the Church and in society at large. The relations of women and men must be shaped by reciprocity and not by subordination." "Nairobi", *op. cit.*, p.62.

[24] See, for example, the communitarian Bible studies, often with penetrating insights, collected in *The Gospel of Solentiname*, 4 vols, ed. Ernesto Cardenal, trans. Donald D. Walsh, Maryknoll, NY, Orbis Books, 1982.

[25] *The Second Sex*, Simone de Beauvoir, trans. and ed. H.M. Parshley, New York, Alfred A. Knopf, 1953. She notes in a discussion of the writer D. H. Lawrence that "it is once more the ideal of the 'true woman' that Lawrence has to offer us — that is, the woman who unreservedly accepts being defined as the Other." P.224

[26] Adrienne Rich, *On Lies, Secrets, and Silence — Selected Prose 1966-1978*, New York, W.W. Norton & Co., 1979, p.78.

[27] "The Church as Mystery and Sign in Relation to the Holy Trinity — in Ecclesiological Perspectives", Gennadios Limouris, in "Church, Kingdom, World", *op. cit.*, pp.18-49; see p.24.

[28] This issue is developed in another context in "Tradition 'vs.' Experience in the Church Fathers", a paper presented by this writer at the Tenth International Conference on Patristic Studies (Oxford, August 1987).

[29] "Accra", *op. cit.*, p.87.

[30] "The Unity of the Church and Unity of Mankind: an Appraisal of the Study", John Deschner in "Accra", *op. cit.*, pp.85-86. The reference was to "Louvain", *op. cit.*, p.198.

[31] "Accra", *op. cit.*, p.89.

[32] "Concluding Comments", John Deschner, in "Unity in Today's World: the Faith and Order Studies on Unity of the Church Unity of Humankind", by Geiko Müller-Fahrenholz, et al, *Faith and Order Paper No. 88*, Geneva, WCC, 1978 [hereafter Deschner, "Unity in Today's World"], pp.206-210; see p.207.

[33] "Towards a Whole Theology", Nelle Morton, in *Sexism in the 1970s: Discrimination Against Women: a Report of a World Council of Churches Consultation, West Berlin 1974*, Geneva, WCC, 1975 [hereafter *Sexism*], pp.57.

[34] For a powerful statement of the new understanding of pluralism as a positive factor — as a gift of God to God's people — see "Reflections on Models of Christian Unity", Paul A. Crow, Jr, pp.2-3. This, the background paper to the fifth international consultation of united and uniting churches (Potsdam, GDR, July 1987), is presently available from the Faith and Order Commission. This text and other materials from the consultation are scheduled for publication in 1988.

[35] *Sexism, op. cit.*, p.64.

[36] "Accra", *op. cit.*, pp.110-112.

[37] "Minutes of the Commission on Faith and Order, Bangalore 1977", *Faith and Order Paper No. 93*, Geneva, WCC, 1979, pp.47-70.

[38] For a general review of the "Unity of the Church-Unity of Humankind" studies through the 1970s see "Unity in Today's World", *op. cit.*, esp. chapters I (pp.11-13) and II (pp.14-27), the latter a retrospect tracing the emergence of this theme from Oxford (1937) to Bristol (1967); and also "Historical Survey", *op. cit.*, pp.177-179.

[39] See "Racism in Theology and Theology Against Racism", the report of a consultation jointly organized by Faith and Order and the Programme to Combat Racism of the WCC, Geneva, WCC, 1975.

[40] See "Church and State: Opening a New Ecumenical Discussion", *Faith and Order Paper No. 85*, Geneva, WCC, 1978; includes the report of a colloquium on this issue held in August 1976, pp.151-178.

[41] See for example "Partners in Life: the Handicapped and the Church", ed. Geiko Müller-Fahrenholz, *Faith and Order Paper No. 89*, Geneva, WCC, 1979.

[42] "Assessment", *op. cit.*, pp.39-46, Tanner, *ER, op. cit.*, pp.253-258.

[43] Deschner, "Unity in Today's World", *op. cit.*, p.210.

[44] See *The Community of Women and Men in the Church: the Sheffield Report*, ed. Constance F. Parvey, Geneva, WCC, 1983 [hereafter Sheffield]. Summaries and analysis of some reports from local study groups, together with reports from two preparatory consultations on specific themes (anthropology and the authority of scripture), are included in *In God's Image, op. cit.* A survey of some responses with respect to language and imagery used of God is found in "Conversations on Language and Imagery of God: Occasioned by the Community of Women and Men in the Church Study", Melanie A. May, *Union Seminary Quarterly Review*, Vol. 40, No. 3, 1985, pp.11-20.

[45] "In particular it would seem important to convene regional and/or local groups as soon as possible..." "The Community of Women and Men in the Church: a proposal for study groups", pamphlet, Geneva, WCC, 1975 [hereafter "Proposal"], p.2. The text also appeared in *The Ecumenical Review*, Vol. XXVII, No. 4, October 1975, pp.386-393 [hereafter "Proposal", *ER*]; see p.387.

[46] "Proposal", *op. cit.*, p.3, and "Proposal", *ER*, p.388. See also the comment by Mary Tanner: "The Community Study was also based on the conviction that the experience and reflection had to be that of as wide a group of women and men as possible." In "The

Community Study and the Unity of the Church and Renewal of Human Community",
Mary Tanner, in "Towards Visible Unity: Commission on Faith and Order, Lima 1982",
Vol 2, ed. Michael Kinnamon, *Faith and Order Paper No. 113*, Geneva, WCC, 1982
[hereafter Tanner, "Community Study"], p.154.

[47] For example: "In 1923 feminist economist and philosopher Charlotte Perkins Gilman
published a book called *His Religion and Hers* in which she outlines two fundamentally
different orientations to life based on the crises of male and female experience. For man...
the pivotal experience is death...for woman, on the other hand, the pivotal experience is
birth and her basic concern is how to nurture ongoing life here on earth. Perkins believes
that religion needs to be transformed by focusing on the female birth experience rather
than on the male death experience." Rosemary Radford Ruether, *Sexism and God-Talk:
Towards a Feminist Theology*, London, SCM Press Ltd., 1983 [hereafter *Sexism and
God-Talk*], p.236.

[48] See from the Sheffield discussion the presentation by the American psychoanalyst Jean
Baker Miller: "...Women have been said to be 'more emotional' and here too have been
made to be the carriers of emotion, but there is no such thing as 'more emotional.' Every
thought and action is simultaneously emotional. What is probably true is that women have
been more attuned to the emotional aspects which are present in every event...there is a
long tradition of trying to dispense with, or at least control or neutralize, the emotions
rather than valuing, embracing, and cultivating the contributing strengths of emotion.
Being in touch with the emotions does not mean that one cannot be intelligent or analytical
if the situation calls for it. In fact, one can analyze better. One can grasp the totality of a
situation more fully." From "The Sense of Self in Women and Men: In Relation to Critical
World Questions", pp.52-60 in *Sheffield, op. cit.*, citation, pp.56-57.

[49] Central Committee of the World Council of Churches, Minutes of the Thirty-Third
Meeting, August 1981, Geneva, WCC, 1981 [hereafter Dresden Minutes], p.18
(emphasis mine).

[50] "Baptism, Eucharist and Ministry and the Community of Women and Men Study", Mary
Tanner, in *Mid-Stream*, Vol. XXIII, No. 3, July 1984, p.245.

[51] For a survey of the historical antecedents of the present programme, see also "Historical
Survey", *op. cit.*

[52] "By-Laws of the Faith and Order Commission", 2 [Aim and Functions] (a), (second
emphasis mine). The By-Laws are most recently available in "Stavanger", *op. cit.*,
pp.243-249. This issue of the "two wings" of the ecumenical movement was addressed
powerfully in John Deschner's presentation at Vancouver, published as "Advancing
Towards Unity", *The Ecumenical Review*, Vol. 36, No. 3, July 1984 [hereafter Deschner,
ER], pp.248-250.

[53] From "Unity and Renewal: Introductory Reflections", Paul A. Crow, Jr, in "Stavanger",
op. cit., p.166.

[54] "Assessment", *op. cit.*, p.42; Tanner, *ER, op. cit.*, p.255.

[55] The study material has recently been published as "Unity and Renewal: a Study Guide for
Local Groups", *Faith and Order Paper No. 136*, Geneva, WCC, 1987. For the mandate
for this aspect of the Unity and Renewal programme, see "Stavanger", *op. cit.*, pp.211-
212.

[56] "Crete Minutes", *op. cit.*, p.38; "Crete", *ER, op. cit.*, p.326.

[57] For the initial programme outline see "Crete Minutes", *op. cit.*, "Crete", *ER, op. cit.*;
programme revisions and developments are reflected in "Stavanger", *op. cit.*, pp.166-
221, "Potsdam Minutes", *op. cit.*, pp.42-45, and "Madrid Minutes", *op. cit.*, pp.6-12.

[58] From the report of the Amsterdam consultation (1980) on "The Authority of Scripture in
Light of the New Experiences of Women", published in *In God's Image, op. cit.*, pp.79-
108; see p.102.

[59] *Ibid.*

[60] "Crete Minutes", *op. cit.*, pp.38-41; "Crete", *ER, op. cit.*, pp.326-328.

[61] Tanner, "Community Study," *op. cit.*, pp.153-154.

[62] *Ibid.*, p.154.

[63] "Crete Minutes", *op. cit.*, p.39; "Crete", *ER, op. cit.*, p.326.

[64] *Ibid.*, p.39.

[65] "Louvain", *op. cit.*, p.18. Also in "The Bible", *op. cit.*, pp.51-52.

[66] "Louvain", *op. cit.*, p.22. Also in "The Bible", *op. cit.*, pp.56-57. Emphasis mine.

[67] "Louvain", *op. cit.*, p.22. Also in "The Bible", *op. cit.*, p.57.

[68] For example: "It has frequently been said that feminist theology draws on women's experience as a basic source of content as well as a criterion of truth. There has been a tendency to treat this principle of 'experience' as unique to feminist theology (or, perhaps, to liberation theologies) and to see it as distant from 'objective' sources of truth of classical theologies. This seems to be a misunderstanding of the experimental base of all theological reflection. What have been called the objective sources of theology; Scripture, and tradition, are themselves codified collective human experience... The uniqueness of feminist theology lies not in its use of the criterion of experience but rather in its use of women's experience, which has been almost entirely shut out of theological reflection in the past." Rosemary Radford Ruether, *Sexism and God-Talk, op. cit.*, pp.12-13.

[69] *The First Assembly of the World Council of Churches*, ed. W.A. Visser 't Hooft, London, SCM Press, Ltd, 1949, p.56.

[70] *Nairobi, op. cit.*, p.47.

[71] To take one example: "There is no doubt, however, that neither the practice nor the official declarations of the historical Orthodox churches, nor of those who have spoken in their name, have always honoured this vision. Cultural conditioning and the natural hardness of hearts have prevented its incarnation in an ethic of reciprocity and mutual respect, particularly with regard to man-woman relationships. We constantly need to convert ourselves to the celestial vision, and then to invent creative ways of incarnating that vision in our existence." From an "Orthodox Affirmation: the Mystery of Persons and Role of Typology", from the report of a consultation on "Towards a Theology of Human Wholeness" (Niederaltaich, 1980), published in *In God's Image, op. cit.*, p.77.

[72] See especially paras. 11-14, 34-43, 44-60, and 61 of "Church as Mystery and Prophetic Sign," *op. cit.*

[73] From "Historical Survey", *op. cit.*, p.184.

[74] *Nairobi, op. cit.*, p.62.

[75] "Third World Women and Men: Effects of Cultural Change on Interpretation of Scripture", Constance F. Parvey, in *The Church and Women in the Third World*, ed. John C.B. & Ellen Low Webster, Philadelphia, Westminster Press, 1985 [hereafter *Church and Women*], p.112.

[76] See for example the sections "Ministry and Worship in New Community" and "Authority and Church Structures in New Community", in *Sheffield, op. cit.*, pp.127-131 and 131-138; the discussions of elements of community in the papers of Martin Cressey and Janet Crawford in this volume; and the 13 "Marks of a Renewed Community" from Working Group 1 of the seminar "Models of Renewed Community" held May 1987 at the Ecumenical Institute, Bossey (to be published with the report of the seminar, 1988). The aspect of community in the Unity and Renewal programme is stressed in "What Kind of Community?", *op. cit.*, pp.18-19. It is noteworthy that such "community" themes as participation and renewal played an important role at the recent fifth international consultation of united and uniting churches (Potsdam, GDR, 1-8 July 1987); see the consultation report "Living Today Towards Visible Unity" (available from Faith and Order as FO/87:23, to be published with documentation of the consultation in 1988), para. 13-25, pp.6-8.

[77] Historians have noted that an increased use of "feminine" imagery within society does not necessarily mean increased sympathy towards women themselves, or an interest in improving the conditions of their lives and work. Thus Carolyn Walker Bynum, on the basis of an exhaustive study of medieval spirituality, concluded that: "There is little evidence that the popularity of feminine and maternal imagery in the high Middle Ages

reflects an increased respect for actual women by men." *Jesus as Mother: Studies in the Spirituality of the High Middle Ages*, Caroline Walker Bynum, Berkeley, University of California Press, 1982, p.143.

[78] "Women in Philippine Basic Christian Communities", Mark Jeffery Ratkus, F.S.C., in *Church and Women, op. cit.*, pp.123, 132 (emphasis mine).

[79] "Accra", *op. cit.*, pp.90-94. John Deschner aptly referred to this text as "a remarkable and too-little-known document". See Deschner, *ER, op. cit.*, p.250.

[80] *Ibid.*, p.90. The quotation from Uppsala is from *The Uppsala Report 1968*, Geneva, WCC, 1986, p.17.

[81] "By-Laws of the Faith and Order Commission", 2 [Aim and Functions] (g) (ii). See most recently "Stavanger", *op. cit.*, pp.243-249.

[82] "Accra", *op. cit.*, p.94.

[83] "Assessment", *op. cit.*, p.43; Tanner, *ER, op. cit.*, p.256.

[84] See the Sheffield recommendations, together with the preface by Mercy Oduyoye for presentation to the Dresden Central Committee meeting, in *Sheffield, op. cit.*, pp.81-90. The recommendations and discussion at Dresden are recorded in its minutes: Dresden Minutes, *op. cit.*, pp.16-30. Note in particular Recommendation E. 2. a. (p.25) that "50% of all membership elected to sub-units and committees of the WCC be women". As Mary Tanner commented: "So incredible did this appear to some that it was thought to be absurd" (Tanner, "Community Study", *op. cit.*, p.163). The force of the recommendation, of course, was neither statistical nor juridical but theological and ecclesiological.

[85] See the "Third World Statement — European Response" in *Sheffield, op. cit.*, pp.96-101.

[86] See for example the reality pointed to in this statement: "Official Christianity has tended, and tends, to see all experience of sex as aggressive and individualistic, utterly removed from the sacred, and therefore, from man's and woman's experience of the Holy. Sexuality has been treated as a power that is essentially material, dangerous, and evil." "Roles of Women within the Church", Sister Teresa A. Mount, S.P., *The Ecumenical Review*, Vol. XXVII, No. 4, October 1975, pp.332-342.

[87] *Sexism, op. cit.*, p. 28.

[88] For an example of a creative and fresh approach to the issue of authority — relating it to the traditional Christian theological category of the Trinity — see "Authority-In-Community", Madeline Boucher, *Mid-Stream*, Vol. XXI, No. 3, July 1982, pp.402-417. (The paper was originally prepared for the Commission on Faith and Order of the National Council of Churches in the United States as a contribution to the Community of Women and Men in the Church study.)

[89] *Is* there a "loss of ecumenical memory"? To be sure; but perhaps there is also, and more often than we care to admit, *an ecumenical avoidance of difficult issues*. See further the present writer's remarks in "The Community Study: Where Do We Go From Here?", to be published in *The Ecumenical Review*, 1988.

[90] See note 83.

The Continuing Significance of the Community of Women and Men in the Church Study: its Mixed Meanings for the Churches

CONSTANCE F. PARVEY

Jane, a doctoral student at Temple University in Philadelphia where I teach, is in the warm-up room near the swimming pool. She is doing stretch exercises in her swimming suit, preparing for a rigorous swim. A young man enters dressed in a T-shirt and shorts, wearing sneakers. He introduces himself as an instructor and proceeds to give her some pointers about stretching. Taking him at his word, she follows his instructions. He begins to touch her body, first on the arm, the leg, then parts of her torso. When he instructs her to lean forward, she notices that he is standing close behind her. He touches her abdomen. His hand sweeps her genitals. Suddenly she realizes what is happening. Without a word — because she is confused and afraid to confront him — she straightens her body and walks out.

Has she been sexually abused? What does she do about it? If she reports it to the campus police, what has the man done that could amount to a charge against him? She asks herself: "Why was I so stupid? Why did I fall in line and obey him? Again, it was a superior/subordinate relationship and I lost my sense of self to 'authority'." She felt weakened, ashamed and enraged.

I begin with this story because it is women's experience. When Jane called me, the first thing that came to mind were similar experiences I had had. Many women encounter something of this kind. Sometimes the

---

● Rev. Dr Constance F. Parvey (Lutheran) was director of the Community of Women and Men in the Church Study, and is now training as a Gestalt analyst.

aggression is more violent; sometimes it is careful and subtle, as was this. Whether or not any particular woman has had such experiences, the fact that some women have means that it is an issue for all.

As it turned out, the man was a member of the teaching staff. He knew exactly how far he could go. When she left, he did not try to hold her back. What was he thinking? Would he try it again on another woman?

Physical or mental violence against their bodily life is part of women's reality. Teachings in culture and religious tradition that ask women to submit to men — using both moral and theological justifications — lead to a false consciousness in both sexes. Why should a PhD student submit to a recreational instructor she doesn't even know, hasn't seen before? The answer: cultural conditioning of women to please men and to obey, their socialization and religious upbringing as inferior, always needing to be taught. Why should a male instructor — abusing the privilege of his male role and his university status — use a woman student as an object to play out his sexual fantasies? The answer: cultural conditioning and socialization to conquest, strength, superiority; and sometimes a religious upbringing including teachings of male domination, buttressed with a patriarchal ideology of man as sole provider, protector/aggressor.

Where does a woman who has had this experience go to get help in sorting out her feelings and deciding what to do? In trying to support her I discovered that she cannot go to the university, for there it is considered mainly as a legal issue; if there is no legal case, then it's seen as just another nuisance complaint of a neurotic, super-sensitive woman. She cannot go to the nearby church because, on the basis of what she has heard from the pulpit, she cannot trust that the pastor would understand her concern and mental anguish. She ends up finding a group called "Women Organized Against Rape". These are the people she can be sure will accept her, listen to her, share their stories and experiences with her, help her regain self-esteem and self-confidence so that she can decide what she is going to do about this encounter and how she might protect other women against similar assaults.

The relevance and method of the Community Study

How does the Community of Women and Men in the Church Study relate to this? What was discovered in the Community Study process, based on the many responses to it, was *the enormous need in the churches for women's stories to be heard as the basis for new levels of female/male dialogue*. In a religious sense, the Study was seen as an opportunity to speak to issues of ultimate meaning and human dignity for women. The Study tapped a long silence; through it words turned into sentences and paragraphs into essays. Today, five years later, reading the reports from local groups is still moving, fresh, painful and full of hope. At Sheffield Philip Potter shared his thoughts on reading the local reports. He said:

> ...I felt here through this enormous study which has gone on in so many parts of the world, the incredible pain and agony of it all — and with it the extraordinary love and patient endurance and perseverance which lie behind it.
>
> I perceived also the tremendous insights and wisdom — which have been lying there wasted for so many years and which are still emerging, thank God, for our enrichment — which have come out of this common effort largely by women. I have been aware, reading these reports, of the impotence of our male-dominated churches to see, hear, feel, decide and act. And incensed with this impotence, I wait for the potency which God's Spirit can bring to us. For me, this study is a veritable test of our faith and of the ecumenical movement which is concerned about the unity of the whole people of God, as a sign and sacrament of the unity of all the peoples of the world. [1]

That the Community Study method answered a need in the churches to approach women/men in an ordered way *by posing open questions, not suggesting answers*, was its most enduring contribution. The testimony to the importance of the method can be seen in the fact that the Study continues — in some cases even in its original form — in many places in the church. After the WCC Community Study desk was closed down, the Study itself continued, primarily on the initiative of women, and appeared in revised forms in Norway, the German Democratic Republic, Great Britain and several locations in Africa, Latin America and Asia. New versions were tailored to specific cultural/ church situations.

Towards the Community Study

The Community Study helped to bring issues raised in the women's movement into the churches — issues that should already have been raised within the churches themselves. It is important to remember that the churches had not been challenged by the questions of justice and equality for women being raised worldwide in the context of the UN Decade for Women. When I came to Geneva to direct the Community Study programme some people told me that so-called "feminist" issues were a North American problem and not relevant worldwide. Three years later, no one was saying this.

In fact it had *never* been true. Specific issues vary from culture to culture and church to church, but the basic framework of a history of injustice and exclusion appears worldwide in more-or-less tolerable degrees. One needs only to look back in the history of the WCC to the first attempt to do a study of "men-women relationships". Published in 1952, it was co-authored by Sarah Chakko of India and Kathleen Bliss of England. In speaking about the equality of women and men in non-Western countries, they stated:

> In Asia and Africa nationalism has been a factor in the emancipation of women. It has been felt by nationalist movements that the emancipation of women is one of the marks of a civilized and forward looking country.[2]

So already twenty-five years before the Community of Women and Men in the Church Study, the issue of changing roles of women and men and the movement for women's equality was recognized in the so-called "third world" as well as in Europe and North America. One might call the Chakko/Bliss study of 1952 "phase I" of the present Community Study, although I did not see a copy of the 1952 study until near the end of the Community Study process when I ran across a copy in a sale of second-hand books. Phase II then would be the study booklet that came from the (West) Berlin Conference on Sexism in 1974 and the Accra Faith and Order meeting of the same year. A major force behind this second effort was Brigalia Bam, a "third world" woman, then head of the WCC Sub-Unit on Women, along with Letty Russell, an American member of the Faith and Order Commission. The booklet, published in Geneva in 1975[3], became the Nairobi Fifth Assembly working paper out of which was formed the recommendation for a special WCC programme on the Community of Women and Men in the Church.[4]

This brief historical sketch should help us reflect on the significance of the Sheffield International Consultation on the Community of Women and Men in the Church in 1981. To begin with, it was the first time in the history of the ecumenical movement, and indeed of Christianity, that an international conference of its size and breadth was held in order to focus on the specific issue of *the quality of community life between women and men in the church*. There were 240 participants from almost a hundred member churches and about fifty countries. Though for the "secular" world the Sheffield conference may have seemed "behind the times", for the churches — as seen in the debate about the Sheffield recommendations at the Dresden WCC Central Committee Meeting, 1981 — it proved to be too far ahead.

Some issues from Sheffield

Sheffield is remembered for its vigorous and heated debate and its uncompromising positions. Out of its deep conflicts came many impulses for renewal. Among these are that:

a) If equality means 50/50 partnership, then responsibility on committees and commissions of the WCC should be shared. This was not an attempt to set quotas — the legal mind at work — but to be just and fair, the goal of the ethical/moral spirit. When this recommendation was presented before the Dresden Central Committee, it became completely distorted. A moral/ethical appeal exploded into a legal and theological battle over the term "equality". What was learned in that exchange is that there is no theological tradition for the word "equality", and certainly no consensus about its meaning and use.

b) Sexuality is not opposed to spirituality. Here the issue of Sheffield was wholeness, the anthropological question of the unity of the body, divine and human, over against the neo-Platonism of much Christian tradition since the fourth century. Within the eschatological framework of the early church, Sheffield gave witness to a Christian bodily existence that here and now is in an inescapable tension between the old and new aeon.

One consequence of a theology based on a spirit/body dualism is that woman are projected as belonging to the bottom half of the dualism: spirit/body, reason/emotion, culture/nature, superior/inferior. Men and God are given the top attributes, and women the bottom ones. I do not need to elaborate the psychological, social and theological consequences of this false anthropology.

c) A pastoral and supportive position was taken towards all women who struggle either to be ordained in churches that do not ordain them, or to be placed in positions of ministry, lay and ordained, where this is theoretically possible. Though the Sheffield conference recognized that some churches do not ordain women, it refused not to recognize the women within those churches for whom ordination is a call and a part of their Christian hope, whether ecclesiastically recognized or not. The affirmation was that of the wider Christian family; the church is larger than any institution claiming its name.

d) Race, sex and class form a "web of oppression". Sheffield moved the WCC forward at this point. Previously, issues of race and class were seen as part of political/economic justice but the category of gender was not seriously integrated. Instead it was left to the work of the Sub-Unit on Women as a separate task. Sheffield refused to see sexism as a single issue but recognized it, along with race and class injustices, as belonging to a patriarchal and hierarchical structure of authority, dominated by privileged men from rich Western countries. What was lifted up as a problem was not simply one of attitudes — the personal level — but of institutional arrangements in which power functions to keep women, people of colour and poor people in vulnerable dependent, subordinate situations, separated from each other and struggling against each other for the same marginal attention. The "web of oppression" also signalled that the values of white middle-class women and men could not be a priority for the Community of Women and Men in the Church.

e) Issues of family life recognized not only changing male/female roles in the family, due to adaptation of the family to post-technological culture, but also that transition in the family meant the seeking of new familial relationships and ways of covenanting and being in communities of responsibility. Recognizing that in many areas and social classes the family is not just in transition but being transformed, it acknowledged and supported the fostering of relationships of faithfulness between people across gender and generation lines. This works itself out differently where circumstances vary. For example, where the majority of the population is under 15 years of age it means fostering a wider network of family life for the larger numbers of children. Where a large minority — perhaps a third of the population — is over 60 it means exploring new ways of their living well and being connected within a larger community. Or in parts of the world where divorced and separated persons far outnumber widows/widowers, it means giving more attention to single-parent family households, many at poverty levels.

Issues of family violence and sexual assault were not "up front" at Sheffield. However, the related issue of traffic in prostitution emerged unexpectedly. The two places where the issues of sexuality were openly pursued in the Community Study were at the Niederalteich consultation on theological anthropology and at the African regional meeting in Ibadan. They were raised as well at the European consultation at Bad Segeberg, but they were such a source of deep unresolved conflict that little forward vision was given. As we have seen already under point (b), issues of sexuality are part of the socialized conspiracy of silence in the churches. It is the women's movement — worldwide — that is helping us in the churches face the reality of domestic violence, its religious rationalizations, and its impact on women, children and men.

There is the further question of the primary role of the family itself; in Christian language, we often call it "the little church". Among other questions, how do the patriarchal concepts, images, symbols and rituals of the churches reinforce male dominance in the home, and when the model of dominance fails (e.g. the man is not the chief breadwinner), what are the consequences for all persons involved? It is important to remember here that the Sheffield conference did not have a eucharistic service, because no matter what would have been done it would have offended someone. The planning committee chose instead an agape ritual, with a partaking in honey — as in early Christian ritual — in order that symbolically everyone could be included, everyone could participate, all gifts could be welcomed. It was a familial sharing, giving thanksgiving and praise, asking forgiveness and renewal in a community of equals, women with women, women with men.

f) Scripture and Tradition do not only belong to the past but to the present and the future. In fact, in so far as they would be engraved in stone, part of "playing yesterday", they could not be considered as giving witness to the dynamic activity of God. For Tradition, like scripture, is "derived from the activity of God in Christ through the Holy Spirit" and without the aid of the Holy Spirit, God's revelation becomes identified with custom, tradition and history. As a consequence, woman/man relationships are frozen in their past forms; there is no risk-taking for the radical vision of God's revelation heard and given meaning in the present, in the midst of our diversities and through those called to represent its apostolic ministries.

At many points the relationships of scripture to culture and tradition to culture were raised — pushing the boundaries of the Faith and Order Study on the authority and interpretation of scripture within the ecumenical movement.[5] See also my own work on the effects of culture and the interpretation of scripture.[6]

Yet far beyond any single impulse forward begun at Sheffield (and they are not exhausted by these few comments), it was the overwhelming experience of 240 women and men working together night and day, finding ways through profound and deep conflicts, that made the Sheffield conference itself *a foretaste of a new ecclesial reality.* No one who was present there can now be satisfied with a church that continues the exclusion of women at many levels and male dominance in images, rituals and symbols, as well as teachings. This "ecclesial reality" was characterized by a community of equals. In this setting it is surprising that conflict between women and men was not the central dynamic. Rather, what surfaced as much more formidable divisions were the political and economic issues that divide the world today. This was the essence of the third-world statement and the European response.[7] In 1981 as now, the over-riding issues were those of justice and peace. Underneath these issues are those of militarism and control of the world's resources. In both of these focii of mega-world power women have hardly any voice at all, except as victims; and most men are socialized to fall into line.

What *united* Sheffield was its struggle to name specific injustices, exclusions, points of violence and silence in both theology and cultural life. Through struggling to name what is of evil and of sin, it could emerge to acknowledge a common vision. Sheffield will be remembered as the largest, most representative gathering held in the history of the Christian church for the purpose of making a constructive critique of its own gender-, class- and race-linked power structures. And it should be remembered for the new stepping stones it created and the hope to which it gave voice as stated in its powerful "Letter to the Churches":

> Brothers, can you not hear the "sighs too deep for words" of women who suffer war, violence, poverty, exploitation and disparagement in a world so largely controlled by men? Sisters, can you not see how the lives of men have been trapped by the effects of their having their power and a supposed superiority?
>
> We speak as those who have been seeking to listen anew to scripture and to live the Tradition of the Church in its many forms. Thus we have heard a word of God for today about a vision for our human life, a renewed community of women and men.[8]

The impact of the Community Study

Having set forth these few aspects of the Community Study and the Sheffield conference we now ask, what meanings has this had for the churches? From my perspective it appears to be mainly ecumenical groups, and not churches, that have picked up and followed up the Community Study. It would be important to know, in a systematic way, what has really happened. For example, where have male theologians (and in particular Faith and Order constituents and members) used the Study as part of courses in ecclesiology, or in sacramental theology where baptism, eucharist and ministry are taught? What communions are they from? On the Lutheran seminary faculty where I also teach no one seems to have heard of the Community of Women and Men in the Church Study, or if they have heard the name they have no idea of its possible relevance for what they are doing. But "Baptism, Eucharist and Ministry" is widely known and discussed, and even materials from the Accra "Account of Hope" study are still used (1974), although the Community Study, drafted as part of that earlier work, remains unknown. With the exception of places where there are ecumenically informed women theologians teaching in seminaries, there appears to be little use of or knowledge of the Community Study. With the exception of a few women and men who have continued the discussion, it has been silenced — not forceably silenced by any one person, but simply ignored by those who set priorities in the churches' theology and seminary education.

What is needed is a committed effort to keep the issues before the churches so that studies such as BEM can be seen in a broader ecclesial context. In church bodies — with the exception of Francine Cardman's critique of BEM in light of the Community Study[9] and my own recent survey article[10] — I know of no published work that attempts to bring these areas together.

In the Faith and Order volume of essays on BEM none of the articles deal with the insights gained from the Community Study.[11]

Similarly, the Community Study has not been integral to the work on the unity of the church and the renewal of human community. The separate issues in this area suffer from lack of dialogue with each other, and attempts are needed to see a coherent whole rather than just maintaining the separate parts.

The basic problem is not that WCC or Faith and Order work does not get to the churches but that, in the case of the Community Study, the leadership itself was not committed to giving the Study support at local levels. Church leaders on judicatory levels have not heard of it. Many seminaries do not use it. Some church women's organizations have used it, but it was not written in a style for those groups but was intended more as a learning instrument for training women and men in the church who were entering parish and church leadership roles. The publications of the Sheffield report in German may have travelled another route. It is important to know more about that. Part of future work should include a research component on the Sheffield follow-up.

In every way the Community Study is a study in tension. Its success in raising and probing issues to the point of open debate is also the source of its failure to be promoted. Perhaps its failure will be the basis for its rebirth? In a new form, it will have to have a less idealistic and a more challenging title. "The community of women and men in the church" appears to be a non-issue in contrast to "women in the church", which suggests more forthrightly what the problem is about when women enter this sacred space of concepts and images shaped and dominated by men.

To underline the seriousness of the mixed meanings for the churches of the issues raised by the Community Study, I will close with a quote from Bishop James Malone, President of the National Conference of Catholic Bishops, USA. In the *New York Times* for 16 September 1985 he is quoted as saying:

> Cultural factors originating outside the Church and the Council account for many recent problems in Catholic life in the United States, as in many other countries. Among these factors are exaggerated individualism, the culturally conditioned disinclination of many persons to make permanent commitment, the breakdown of marriage and family life, the sexual revolution, and exaggerated secular feminism.

Rather than the church claiming some responsibility for these "factors", it is placing the *blame* outside itself. It will be hard to unscramble "mixed meanings" if such attitudes prevail.

NOTES

[1] Constance F. Parvey, ed., *The Community of Women and Men in the Church*, Geneva, WCC, 1983, p.25.

[2] *A Study of Man-Woman Relationship: a Study Outline*, London, SCM Press, 1952, p.10.

[3] *The Community of Women and Men in the Church: a Proposal for Study Groups*, Geneva, WCC, 1975. The text had first appeared in *The Ecumenical Review*, Vol. 27, No. 4, October 1975, pp.386-393.

[4] For the recommendations see David M. Paton, *Breaking Barriers: Nairobi 1975*, London, SPCK, and Grand Rapids, Wm. B. Eerdmans, 1975, pp.113-115.

[5] See Ellen Flesseman-van Leer, ed., "The Bible: its Authority and Interpretation in the Ecumenical Movement", *Faith and Order Paper No. 99*, Geneva, WCC, 1980.

[6] Constance F. Parvey, "Third World Women and Men: Effects of Cultural Change on Interpretation of Scripture", in *The Church and Women in the Third World*, eds John C.B. and Ellen Low Webster, Philadelphia, Westminster Press, 1985, pp.105-119.

[7] See *The Community...*, *op. cit.*, pp.96-101.

[8] *Ibid.*, p.91. For the Letter and Introduction see pp.90-91.

[9] "BEM and the Community of Women and Men", in *The Search for Visible Unity*, ed. Jeffrey Gros, New York, Pilgrim Press, 1984, pp.83-95.

[10] "Stir in the Ecumenical Movement: the Ordination of Women", an appendix (pp.139-174) to Brita Stendhal, *The Force of Tradition: a Case Study of Women Priests in Sweden*, Philadelphia, Fortress Press, 1985.

[11] Max Thurian, ed., "Ecumenical Perspectives on Baptism, Eucharist and Ministry", *Faith and Order Paper No. 116*, Geneva, WCC, 1983.

The Continuing Significance of the Community Study: Sheffield and Beyond

JANET CRAWFORD

The Community of Women and Men in the Church Study existed as a distinct World Council of Churches programme for only four years, from 1978 to the end of 1981. It is now part of our ecumenical history and the final conference at Sheffield has became another of those signposts which mark the churches' pilgrimage towards unity. My purpose today is to discuss the continuing importance of the Community Study but I intend to begin with a brief account of how the programme came into being, for its history is significant also.

The genesis of the Community Study

A major impulse towards the formation of the Community Study programme came from the Berlin conference on sexism in the 1970s organized by the WCC in 1974. At this meeting women defined sexism as "any kind of subordination or devaluation of a person or a group solely on the ground of sex",[1] declared sexism to be a sin, and pointed to the presence of this sin in the churches as well as in society. The following year participants at the 1975 Nairobi Assembly of the WCC recognized that "the church's unity includes women and men in a true mutuality... The unity of the church requires that women be free to live out the gifts which God has given to them and to respond to their calling to share fully

---

● Rev. Janet E. Crawford (Anglican) was on the staff of the Community of Women and Men in the Church Study, and is now lecturer in church history and Christian origins, College of St. John the Evangelist, Auckland, New Zealand.

in the life and witness of the church."[2] They recommended the Community of Women and Men in the Church Study as a major focus for study and theological reflection by the member churches.[3] Thus the impulse for the Community Study came from Berlin and the mandate from Nairobi.

Yet it is important to realize that the concerns of the Study had been part of the ecumenical agenda for many years. As long ago as 1927, at the first (Lausanne) meeting of Faith and Order, the few women present asserted that "the right place of women in the church is a question of grave moment and should be in the hearts and minds of all".[4] Some twenty years later, at the first Assembly of the World Council of Churches in Amsterdam, delegates affirmed that "the Church as the Body of Christ consists of men and women, created, as responsible persons, to glorify God and to do His will", and acknowledged that, "this truth, accepted in theory, is too often ignored in practice".[5] During the years since 1948 the WCC sought to overcome this division between theory and practice, particularly through the work of its Women's Department. However the Berlin conference in 1974 made it clear that after almost thirty years the division between theory and practice still existed, the conference report stating that the churches with their theological and ecclesiastical oppression have turned women into "second-rate Christians".

The Community Study was stimulated by, and drew inspiration from, the worldwide movement which flourished in the 70s as women struggled against oppression, discrimination, and sexism, and for rights, responsibilities, equality and full participation in society and in the churches. The Community Study was influenced by this struggle for justice for women and in turn contributed to this struggle.

However the fundamental purpose of the study was not to provide a feminist critique of Christianity or a programme against sexism in the church. Its fundamental purpose was rather to explore issues of *community*, in the belief that *the church's unity must include both women and men in true mutuality*. For this reason, although the programme was jointly sponsored by the Commission on Faith and Order and the Sub-unit on Women in Church and Society, it was lodged in Faith and Order. *The essential nature of the study was ecclesiological; its central focus was not on "women's issues" but on inclusive community — in the church — of women and men.* As such an ecclesiological study the Community Study was, in the words of Philip Potter, "a veritable test of our faith and of the ecumenical movement, a movement which is concerned about the unity of the whole people of God".[6]

The Community of Women and Men in the Church Study is now widely recognized as having involved more people and generated more interest than perhaps any other WCC study. It has now been several years since the Sheffield conference (July 1981) which was the culminating point of the programme. Since then the Community Study has received major attention at the Vancouver Assembly (1983)[7] and at the Faith and Order Plenary Commission meetings at Lima (1982)[8] and Stavanger (1985).[9] Thus it is an appropriate time to evaluate the continuing significance of the study, to look at what has happened in the post-Sheffield era, and to make some suggestions for the future — which will now be the "post-Prague" period! I do this from the perspective of a Community Study participant, for I was first a member of a local study group, then a consultant to the programme and a staff person at Sheffield, and my involvement with the Study has continued in various ways since then.

The methodology of the Community Study

I will begin my reflections on the continuing significance of the Community Study by commenting on its *methodology*. The Community Study was, and is, significant because it developed *a new kind of study process, one which took experience as its major starting point*. WCC studies have traditionally been done from "above" by bringing together experts in a certain field to seek a consensus which can then be presented to the churches for their discussion and response. The Community Study deliberately started from "below" by inviting women and men, "non-experts", to form local study groups in which to talk about and reflect upon their experience. The Study also used the traditional model of holding specialized consultations on specific topics (the ordination of women, Klingenthal 1979;[10] theological anthropology, Niederaltaich 1980;[11] the authority of scripture, Amsterdam 1980[12]) and a number of regional conferences also took place. But the major impetus, input and interest came from the local groups, 150 of which sent reports to Geneva.[13] It is estimated that over 2,000 people were represented in these responses and in addition many others were involved in groups which participated in the Study but did not, for various reasons, send reports to the WCC. This unprecedented response shows the success of the theological methodology of the study, which involved the continuous interplay between experience and Christian tradition, Christian tradition and experience.

The methodology of the Community Study was not perfect and the response was not as comprehensive as it could have been: Although reports did come from all over the world, the greatest number came from the North Atlantic region, and third-world countries were generally under-represented. Although the Study was designed for the whole church community — women and men — women participants outnumbered men by about two to one. Although Orthodox and Roman Catholic groups took part, the greatest participation came from the large Protestant denominations. However the process of the Community Study was itself a *learning process*. The experience of the study itself contributed new understandings about methodology, new insights into how to plan and organize such a study, how to avoid some of the difficulties, how to increase participation and how to communicate more effectively with the churches. In thus initiating and learning from a new methodology the Community Study made a significant contribution to the ongoing work of the WCC.

Developments since Sheffield

What has happened since Sheffield? What influence has the Community Study had on the WCC and its member churches? How have its impulses towards unity and renewal been frustrated or fulfilled? Detailed answers to these questions would require much time and diligent research. Here I can only outline briefly the most significant results of the Community Study since Sheffield.

Vancouver and the WCC

The Community Study undoubtedly influenced the Sixth Assembly of the World Council of Churches in a number of ways. The Assembly was notable for, amongst other things, the increased participation of women — from 22 percent of the delegates at Nairobi in 1975 to 30.4 percent at Vancouver in 1983. This increased participation can be largely attributed to the influence of the Community Study and to the determined efforts of the Sub-unit on Women to fulfill its recommendations on participation.

The Community Study concepts of partnership and inclusive community were highlighted in many of the Assembly issue groups, discussions and reports. Great applause greeted the general secretary when in his report he stated: "More insistently we have painfully tried to come to terms with the fact that the house of living stones is a community of women and men fulfilling a common ministry of witness and service to the world."[14] However his remarks on "hierarchical and institutional exclusiveness" and the disparity and concentration of power in the life of the churches[15] (remarks directly related to issues raised by the Community Study) drew a defensive response from many delegates, and focused the tension at the Assembly between commitment to the representation of the whole people of God and the established power structures in the churches.

One commentator has carefully analyzed this tension at Vancouver with particular reference to the nominations and elections for the Central Committee, and has concluded that "at Vancouver, in the nomination process, the power of the churches emerged more strongly than the power of women and youth. The power of constituted leadership in the churches exerted power at the expense of newly emerging groups. The ideals of people's participation and more inclusive representation suffered."[16] Thus although some progress was undoubtedly made, participation continued to be a difficult and painful issue at Vancouver.

However, the principle of full participation was affirmed as a priority for the WCC in the report of the Programme Guidelines Committee. This report is one of the most important products of the Assembly, for in it are formulated guidelines for the future work of the WCC, based on proposals emerging from the Assembly. The Community Study made a significant contribution to these guidelines. For example, the report names as one of eight priorities the need to integrate the concerns and perspectives of women into the work of *all* WCC Units and Sub-units and stated that the insights of the Community Study should be translated and appropriated by all WCC programmes, with specific reference to the establishment of a systematic and contextual study on sexism, using the Community Study methodology.[17] The section on the priority of ecumenical learning also affirmed the use of this methodology "in order that the needs, perspectives and contributions of Christians at the local level be kept at the forefront of the educational processes".[18]

The Programme Guidelines Committee named unity as the first priority area and noted the development of an important new dynamic calling for "more exchange of experiences and for a more inclusive approach".[19] This was in reponse to the report from the issue group on "Taking Steps Towards Unity" which stated: "Through the study on the Community of Women and Men in the Church, many have discovered that life in unity must carry with it the overcoming of division between the sexes and have begun to envision what profound changes must take place in the church and the world."[20] This issue group also called for the insights of the Community Study to be deepened and built upon in Faith and Order's work on unity and renewal.[21]

The implementation of the Vancouver priorities in specific programmes and policies of the WCC will take time and cannot yet be evaluated. But it is clear that the Community Study has made, and will continue to make, a lasting and significant contribution to the whole work of the WCC. Already results are obvious in the increased participation of women, commitment to contextual methodology, and heightened awareness of sexism. *Above all, the WCC has recognized and acknowledged that the unity of the church, which is its aim and purpose, requires an inclusive community of women and men.*

Faith and Order

No one can doubt that the Community Study has made a significant contribution to the work of Faith and Order, for our very presence at this meeting in Prague is proof of that! The Commission has chosen "movements towards or away from fuller community of women and men" as one of the two foci for its study on "The Unity of the Church and the Renewal of Human Community",[22] a study which has itself been affirmed as "of strategic significance for the orientation of the whole work of the WCC" (WCC Executive Committee, February 1984).[23] This is a study of the church in its need to overcome human sinfulness and division among its members, and of places in the world where creative renewal has happened and challenges the church. The Community Study has already contributed much to unity and renewal; this consultation will contribute more, especially perhaps towards the understanding of the church as "mystery and prophetic sign". It is also planned to develop the ecclesiological insights of the Community Study by broadening the process through the creation of a new study guide and the involvement of more local groups, particularly in third-world areas. First steps have been taken in this direction and it is hoped that process will be underway soon.[24] The results will undoubtedly contribute significantly to the report on Unity and Renewal which will form a major part of the agenda at the next world conference on Faith and Order.

WCC member churches

The contribution of the Community Study to the life of the member churches is less easy to judge, for there was no provision for any follow-up of the Study once the programme ended in 1981. Consequently there is little information on which to base an evaluation. We do know that the CWMC study guide continues to be used, that the Sheffield report and other publications from the Study are widely read, and that some churches and councils of churches have made serious efforts to grapple with issues raised by the Study and to put some of its recommendations into practice. I think we may claim with some confidence that the Community Study has been a significant factor contributing to specific changes in a number of aspects of church life, at least in some churches, e.g. increased participation of women; policies on inclusive language; developments in theological education; debate on the ordination of women; development of women's ministries. In some situations there has also been, of course, a growing opposition to change. In general the Community Study has contributed to a heightened awareness of sexism, to a greater commitment to partnership between women and men, and to a *widening of the classical debate on church unity to include issues of community.*

The ecclesiological implications of the Community Study

We meet in Prague as part of the Faith and Order Study on "The Unity of the Church and the Renewal of Human Community", and in this context the ecclesiological implications of the Community Study are particularly important. Through its methodology the Community Study gave a voice to those who in the past were voiceless, or whose voices had not been heard; it involved new participants in the quest for unity.

Through the articulated experience of these new participants, the Community Study has made a significant contribution to our understanding of *ecclesiology*, by telling us *what sort of community women and men actually experience in the churches and by giving us a vision of the renewed community for which they long.* I would suggest that the following aspects of the Community Study are important for their ecclesiological implications:

1. *The Community Study drew attention to the diversity of cultural and ecclesial contexts in which women and men live.* Participants in the Community Study came from first-, second- and third-world countries, from developed technological societies and from developing societies, from capitalist and socialist nations. And the ecclesial diversity was as great as the cultural diversity. Reports came from Protestant, Roman Catholic and Orthodox Christians, from state churches, mission churches and minority churches, from congregational, independent and hierarchical churches and from "grassroots" Christian communities; from churches with centuries of history and tradition, and from "new" churches. Despite this broad involvement, of course, the Study was still not fully comprehensive.

From this diversity the Community Study taught us that although Christians believe in a universal church, an invisible community which exists outside time and space, they always (and inevitably) experience the church in and through its local manifestations, in visible communities which exist in a particular time and place. For most, this visible, limited community is the local congregation. Responses to the Community Study also illustrated the diversity of historical and cultural factors which influence these particular local expressions of the church. They emphasized the interaction between ecclesial community and cultural context, the interdependence of church and the wider human community. An adequate ecclesiology must give due consideration to this distinction between local churches and the universal church, and to the ways in which culture influences church communities.

2. The Community Study emphasized the understanding that all communities are made up of human beings, women and men, and that the nature of a community depends on the quality of the relationships which they experience. As is now well-known, the Community Study began with *an exposé of the broken relationships and broken community experiences by women and men* at the present time. In the words of Philip Potter at Sheffield, the group reports are "a sort of algebraic sign of a very great depth of well-buried meaning" and what is most significant is "the incredible pain and agony of it all".[25] Women and men described their experience of sexism in the churches and in society and named it as sin — a distortion and perversion of human relationships, a form of oppression contrary to God's will, a denial of the fullness of life desired by the Lord of the church for all people. Women described their identity as that of "second class citizens and second class Christians". For many, theology itself was part of the problem. No discussion of ecclesiology or unity should ignore the reality of sexism and the fact that, as William Lazareth (then director of Faith and Order) remarked at Sheffield, the myth of female inferiority distorts the church's faith and corrupts the church's order.

3. The Community Study did not understand sexism as an isolated phenomenon, the sole cause of broken community. On the contrary, a significant result of the Sheffield conference was *the naming of the "web of oppression"*, an understanding that sexism, racism, classism, economic exploitation and other forms of oppression are all closely interwoven. Participants at Sheffield emphasized that all forms of domination, rejection and marginalization are linked together in the "web" or "demonic symphony" of oppression and that the struggle for justice and freedom must be against all forms of oppression, wherever they exist.[26]

More work needs to be done to develop our understanding of the "web of oppression" and its implications for the renewal of the whole human community. Certainly this concept shatters all complacency and challenges both individuals and churches to recognize their own complicity in oppressive structures, and to commit themselves to the struggle for freedom and justice in a global context.

4. The Community Study moved from an exposé of broken relationships and broken community to an *envisioning of renewed community*. This vision of renewed community was described in many ways but there was a clear consensus on its most significant elements. A renewed community would be:

— an inclusive community in which no individual or group would be excluded, oppressed, subjugated or exploited;
— a community in which relationships would be characterized by love and mutuality;
— a community of equals without domination and subordination, superiority and inferiority;
— a community embracing and celebrating diversity and difference;
— a community encouraging the full participation of all its members and the development of the gifts of each individual;
— a community of women and men, living together as equal partners.

This vision is essentially holistic, all-embracing. It speaks of a dynamic, living, loving and joyful community, a community which would be a creative force for further renewal.

5. The Community Study's vision of renewed community was a theological vision. It was essentially *biblical, Christological and Trinitarian*. Thus it was not merely a reflection of certain contemporary cultural values or issues, but was deeply and quite consciously rooted in the Christian traditions. This *theological basis to the vision* offers rich material for further study and development.

It is biblical because it is based on faith in the biblical God who has made humanity, male and female, in God's own image, who loves all people, and whose will is for justice and freedom for all; the God who is victorious over sin and evil and who makes all things new. It is Christological because it is based on faith in Christ who is the expression of God's self-giving love for humankind and on the belief that Christ promises fullness of life for all, that in Christ new creation is possible, that women and men are called to be partners in Christ with God. The Community Study vision is rooted in faith in Christ in whom "there is neither Jew nor Greek, slave nor free, male nor female" (Gal. 3:28), and who is the servant Lord. It is also a Trinitarian vision, understanding the Holy Trinity as the expression of ideal community, a model for interdependent, loving and mutual relationships, a paradigm of authority-in-community.

The Community Study emphasized that renewed community is essential not only for the unity of the church but also for the sake of the church's mission, witness and service to the world. Thus we may also describe it as a *missiological vision*, based on a belief that the church exists not just for its own members but for others, that the ecclesial community is set in the midst of human community for the service of that community, and that it is called upon to witness to the gospel by its own life-style, to be both "light" and "salt". The Community Study challenges us with its vision of the church as a renewed, redeemed and redeeming community which is called to be a sign for the renewal of the whole human community living in the global context of desperate struggle against exploitation, poverty, oppression, hopelessness and despair.

A further significant point which could be developed in more detail is the realization expressed by a number of Community Study groups, that the transformation from broken to renewed community is essentially a matter of *spiritual transformation*. Renewal calls for repentance and conversion, on the part of individuals and groups; and churches, too, may need to repent.

6. The Community Study articulated the experience of broken community and set against it a vision of new community, making it clear that the realization of this vision would require changes in many aspects of church life. In the sections (working groups) at Sheffield, participants focused on the most significant issues which had emerged during the course of the study and made suggestions and recommendations for change. The section on *authority and church structures in new community* was especially important because it raised ecclesiological questions directly.[27] In particular it emphasized that participation and the ordering of authority should not be seen as two separate issues but as part of one movement towards the unity of the church as a sign for the renewal of the whole human community.

Sheffield recognized that living in community always involves the structuring of the common life and the exercise of authority, and claimed that the life, ministry and teachings of Christ, and the demands of the kingdom of God, give Christians a particular understanding of power and authority. In the words of the section report: "We know that the historical expression of the life of the church often runs counter to this understanding"[28] and "in many church laws and structures the full participation of women in leadership and power-sharing with men is not possible".[29] However Sheffield did not merely want women admitted to equal power-sharing and authority; rather, it insisted on *the need for different models of authority, and renewed structures which would create new and inclusive community.* Based on the experience of women, who have historically been without power, Sheffield offered both a critique of traditional hierarchical structures of authority, and an emerging new understanding of authority rooted in service, and of power which, like love, is limitless and to be shared with others for the enrichment of all. Sheffield asked: "What if the model for authority and community no longer were the pyramid of hierarchy but the circle, or perhaps the rainbow of colours, symbol of hope?"[30]

7. As was frequently stated during the Community Study, the real community of women and men is yet to be. We do not yet know exactly what forms and structures it might have, for our vision itself expands as we experience a renewed community. For many, participation in the process of the Community Study and at Sheffield was a foretaste of new community, an experience, even if brief and partial, of living together as women and men in a new relationship of wholeness. This may in fact be the most significant contribution of the whole Community Study, that through it some women and men were able to experience what new community could be. Such experiences are both life-giving and life-changing.

So far I have highlighted seven aspects of the Community Study as making a significant contribution to ecclesiology. In summary, they are:
— diversity of cultural and ecclesial contexts;
— exposé of broken community;
— the web of oppression;
— vision of renewed community;
— theological basis of the vision;
— authority and church structures;
— foretaste of new community.

8. Finally I would like to mention some probing questions about the nature of the church which were raised, directly and indirectly, by the Community Study, especially in some of the group reports. Theologians will recognize that these questions are not new. But in the context of the study they become more poignant because they are so

clearly born from the experience of women and men in the churches. For example:

— Apartheid has been declared a heresy by many churches. Should we try to work towards a *status confessionis* on sexism? Is it ever possible to say that because of its practice and/or teaching of discrimination based on gender a particular church is no longer part of the church?

— Some women reject the church (and churches) on the grounds that because of sexism it is no longer faithful to the gospel. How do we relate to Christians who are alienated from the church?

— Some people argue that the Holy Spirit is working to lead the church from outside, especially through prophetic voices raised in the human community. How do we respond to such arguments?

— The Community Study sought changes in many church practices and teachings. How much change is possible if the church is to remain faithful to Christian tradition?

— Some of the issues in the Community Study are controversial and it is not yet possible for churches to agree on some matters (e.g. the ordination of women). How can community be sustained where there are deep differences in understanding and practice? How do individuals and churches handle conflict? Can we develop our understanding of unity-in-diversity to include unity-in-tension?

Conclusions and the way ahead

Clearly the case studies presented at this consultation will give us valuable insights into the significance of the Community Study in a few specific situations. However what we really need is some sort of systematic follow-up process which would enable us to analyze and monitor the results of the Study. It would be particularly interesting to contact the original local groups and participants at the various consultations and at Sheffield to find out what their experience has been in the last few years, to ask if their visions of new community are any nearer realization, if they see signs of renewal.

In the meantime, I think we must accept that although a number of siginificant steps have been taken along the rocky road to new community, the tension between experience and vision still remains and challenges us and our churches. In view of the brokenness of the human community, the oppression, injustice and suffering in the world, the threat of nuclear destruction, renewal is a matter of some urgency and we cannot afford to be complacent.

The Community Study has given us a vision of new community and foretastes of just what that community might be. It is a prophetic vision, rooted in the same faith which stimulated the very creation of the WCC. In the words of Willem Visser 't Hooft, the ecumenical movement is based on the faith that "it belongs in the very nature of the people of God, to live as one reconciled and therefore united family, and that it belongs to its witness to present to the world the image of a new humanity which knows no walls of separation within its own life".[31] The Community Study has made a lasting and important contribution to our understanding of that new humanity, a humanity based on the community of women and men.

NOTES

[1] *Sexism in the 1970s: Discrimination Against Women*, a report of a WCC consultation, West Berlin 1974, Geneva, WCC, 1975, p.10.

[2] *Breaking Barriers: Nairobi 1975*, report of the Fifth Assembly of the WCC, Nairobi 1975, ed. David M. Paton, London, SPCK, and Grand Rapids, Wm. B. Eerdmans, 1975, p.62.

[3] *Ibid.*, p.113.

[4] *Faith and Order: Proceedings of the World Conference, Lausanne, August 3-21 1927*, ed. H.N. Bate, London, SCM, 1927. The quotation (p.372) is from the "Memorial by the Women Delegates to the Conference", pp.372-373. There were, in fact, 7 women delegates out of a total of nearly 400.

[5] *The First Assembly of the World Council of Churches,* ed. W.A. Visser 't Hooft, London, SCM Press, 1949, p.146.

[6] *The Community of Women and Men in the Church: the Sheffield Report*, ed. Constance F. Parvey, Geneva, WCC, 1983, p.25.

[7] *Gathered for Life*, official report of the Sixth Assembly of the WCC, ed. David Gill, Geneva, WCC, and Grand Rapids, Wm. B. Eerdmans, 1983. See pp.49-50,88; also 68, 70.

[8] "Towards Visible Unity: Commission on Faith and Order, Lima 1982", 2 vols, ed. Michael Kinnamon. Vol. I: pp.126-130; Vol. II: pp.47-50, 153-165. *Faith and Order Papers Nos 112 and 113,* Geneva, WCC, 1982.

[9] "Faith and Renewal: Commission on Faith and Order, Stavanger 1985", ed. Thomas F. Best, *Faith and Order Paper No. 131,* Geneva, WCC, 1986, pp.144-145,208-214.

[10] See "Ordination of Women in Ecumenical Perspective", ed. Constance F. Parvey, *Faith and Order Paper No. 105*, Geneva, WCC, 1980.

[11] See "Theological Anthropology: Towards a Theology of Human Wholeness", in *In God's Image*, eds Janet Crawford and Michael Kinnamon, Geneva, WCC, 1983, pp.47-78.

[12] See "The Authority of Scripture in Light of New Experiences of Women", in *In God's Image, op. cit.*, pp.79-108.

[13] Several themes from the local group reports are analyzed in *In God's Image, op. cit*, pp.1-46.

[14] *Gathered for Life, op. cit.,* p.202.

[15] *Ibid.*, p.201.

[16] Robert J. Marshall, "Power and Politics in the WCC Nominations Process", *Mid-Stream*, XXIII, No. 1, 1984, p.113.

[17] *Gathered for Life, op. cit.,* p.256.

[18] *Ibid.*

[19] *Ibid.,* pp.252-253.

[20] *Ibid.,* p.49.

[21] *Ibid.,* p.50.

[22] "Minutes of the Meeting of the Standing Commission, 1984, Crete", *Faith and Order Paper No. 121,* Geneva, WCC, 1984, p.38.

[23] *Ibid.,* p.34.

[24] See "Faith and Renewal", *op. cit.,* pp.211-212.

[25] *The Community of Women and Men in the Church, op. cit.,* p.25.

[26] *Ibid.,* pp.145-154.

[27] *Ibid.,* pp.131-138.

[28] *Ibid.,* p.131.

[29] *Ibid.,* p.132.

[30] Betty Thompson, *A Chance to Change: Women and Men in the Church,* Geneva, WCC, Risk Book Series No. 15, 1982, p.41.

[31] Quoted in "Service of Thanksgiving for the Life of W.A. Visser 't Hooft", 9 July 1985, p.6.

Liberation, Unity and Equality in Community: a New Testament Case Study

ELISABETH SCHÜSSLER FIORENZA

Introduction: an incarnational approach

The method suggested for this consultation is not platonic or docetic but incarnational. Case studies about the relations of women and men in society and church are theological reflections on very concrete experiences and ecclesial situations. Such a theological method is incarnational insofar as it does not begin with timeless ideas, principles or doctrines but seeks to discover divine presence and salvation in and through the communal, social-political life-praxis of the church, and to name it theologically. This method rests on an understanding of theology "as emerging from the interaction between what we make of the Christian story and tradition and what we make of contemporary life. It is at these points of interaction that God is to be encountered and discovered."[1] In preparing these Bible studies, then, I sought consciously to follow this approach by analyzing four New Testament texts — Luke 13:10-17, Galatians 3:28, 1 Timothy and Mark — in terms of their actual historical-social-ecclesial settings. Rather than elaborating theoretically my own theological hermeneutics of liberation, I decided to actualize it in the process of interpretation. The following is a summary account of these NT case studies in terms of a critical feminist theology of liberation.[2]

● Prof. Dr Elisabeth Schüssler Fiorenza (Roman Catholic) is Talbot Professor of New Testament at Episcopal Divinity School, Cambridge, USA.

Luke 13:10-17: the woman bent double and the bondage of women

Only Luke's Gospel has the story of the woman who was bent over and could not stand upright (Luke 13:10-17).[3] She came to praise God in the synagogue where Jesus was teaching. In distinction to other miracle stories the woman makes no request for healing; it is Jesus who calls her, and lays hands upon her. The woman straightens (literally "was straightened up", using the so-called divine passive construction), lifts up her head, stands upright and continues to praise God. The story is simple: the woman was bent double, she has suffered from a "spirit of infirmity" for eighteen long years. She hears the call, feels the touch of Jesus, and experiences wholeness and freedom. As a liberated woman she stands upright and praises God, who has freed her from her bondage.

This story is connected with a controversy dialogue.[4] The leader of the synagogue objects that it was not necessary to break the Sabbath Torah. Jesus' response does not argue that he broke the Sabbath Torah in order to save life, since the illness was not fatal. Rather he did so in order to make her healthy and to free her from her infirmity. The point of comparison is: just as it is permitted to care for household animals on the sabbath, so one can act for the welfare of a daughter of Israel. What is puzzling is that Jesus seems not to have heard the objection of the "ruler of the synagogue", whose precise point was that there are six days on which one could be healed. If the woman was bent double for eighteen years why could Jesus not wait a day longer?

The dialogue startles, and leads us to ask: Why *did* Israel observe the Sabbath? Since the Babylonian Exile, Sabbath observation was the ritual celebration of God's creation and Israel's election. While the head of the synagogue insists on a complete rest from work, Jesus heals the woman so that she is able to fulfill the purpose of the Sabbath — to praise God the creator of the world and the liberator of Israel. This means that a final aspect of this healing controversy is significant. This daughter of Israel was in the power of Satan, in a bondage that deformed her whole bodily being for eighteen long years. In freeing her from her bondage, God's power of salvation becomes manifest.[5]

The salvation of God's *basileia* (kingdom)[6] becomes available experientally whenever Jesus casts out demons, heals the sick and ritually unclean, or tells stories about the lost who are found, about the uninvited who are invited, or about the least who will be first. The power of God's new creation is realized in Jesus' table community with the poor, the sinners, the tax collectors, the prostitutes — with all those who do not "belong" because they are cultically deficient in the eyes of the pious and righteous. For Jesus and his movement the *basileia* does not spell cultic holiness but human wholeness. It is like the dough that has been leavened but not yet transformed into bread, like the fetus in the womb not yet transformed in birth to a child.

Although the future of God's new world can be experienced already in Jesus' healings, parables, and inclusive discipleship community, Jesus and his first followers, women and men, nevertheless still hope and expect the future inbreaking of God's *basileia* when death, suffering and injustice will finally be overcome. The Jesus movement's praxis and vision of the *basileia* is the mediation of God's future into the structures and life-experiences of its own time and people. But this future is available to *all* members of the people of God; everyone is invited. Not the holiness of the elect but the wholeness and happiness of all is the central vision of the Jesus movement. The healing of the woman bent double reveals, and makes experientially available, the caring presence and power of the *basileia* at work in the words and praxis of the Jesus movement. Despite opposition from the religious leadership the common people recognize the wonderful things that have happened in their midst.[7]

I have chosen this text to begin our biblical reflections because this story has become one of the key texts of the women's movement in the churches. The woman bent double has become a paradigm for the situation of women, not only in society but also in the churches. We usually read biblical texts either as a confirmation of, or as a challenge to, our own Christian self-understanding.[8] If Christian theologians and preachers identify with Jesus they will read the passage anti-semitically, get angry with the leader of the synagogue and feel religiously and morally superior to Judaism. Should churchmen identify with the leader of the synagogue, however, then they would find his statement to the crowd ("There are six days when one has to work; come on one of these to be cured") to be reasonable church policy — biblical or ecclesiastical law and tradition, after all, cannot be changed just because a woman is in bondage and is not able to stand upright. Reading the story in this way should give pause to ecclesiastical officials who use the Bible, tradition, ecumenical theology and church unity to exclude women from ecclesial and liturgical leadership, and thereby make it impossible for more and more women to praise God today.

Patriarchy: culture bent double and the bondage of women

A feminist theological reading of this story must translate it into the language and structures of our own time. The miracle story understands the illness of the woman as bondage that was caused by Satan. Early Christian theology sees the world and human beings as caught up in the struggle between the life-destroying powers of evil and the life-giving power of God.[9] While in the last analysis these evil powers cannot frustrate the life-giving purpose of God, their power is still real and has its effects in the present world. Their hostility against life and human wholeness is expressed in their attempt to enslave human beings and ultimately in their crucifixion of Christ. Apocalyptic New Testament theology explains the execution of Jesus as caused by these cosmic and political powers, but not as willed by God.

Much Western New Testament scholarship, under the influence of Rudolf Bultmann, has sought to "demythologize" this apocalyptic language of mythic powers. In the process it is translated into the categories of existentialist philosophy; it is individualized, and de-politicized.[10] A critical feminist theology of liberation, however, does not seek to demythologize this apocalyptic language but to translate it into socio-political language.

It has named patriarchy, as a complex system of structural dependencies and individual oppressions, as the life-destroying power of Western society and religion. Patriarchy must not be understood solely in terms of male supremacy and misogynist sexism[11] but must be seen in terms of the systemic interaction of racism, classism and sexism in Western militarist societies.[12] This Western understanding of patriarchy was first articulated in Aristotelian political philosophy.[13] Aristotle did not define patriarchy simply as the rule of all men over all women, but as a gradated male status system of domination and subordination, authority and obedience, rulers and subjects in household and state. Wives, children, slaves and property were owned and at the disposal of the freeborn Greek male head of the household. He was the full citizen who determined public life.[14] Since the democratic ideal invites the participation of all citizens, Aristotle has to legitimate the exclusion of freeborn women and Greek-born slaves from democratic government.[15] Therefore he defines their "nature" in terms of their subordinate status and social function, in order to argue that their "nature" does not make them fit to rule.

This basic contradiction between the democratic claim to the full equality of all human beings and their subordinate position in the patriarchal structures of household and state has also defined Western Euro-American notions of democracy.[16] Although patriarchy has been modified in the course of history it has not been replaced by private or state capitalism. In feudalistic and slave societies freeborn women as well as women serfs and slaves were legally, economically and sexually subject to the lord of the castle or the master of the house; in capitalist patriarchy all women become dependent on the male heads of households.[17] Women's social status is defined by the class, race, and nationality of the men to whom we belong. Capitalist patriarchy has generated a separate system of economics for women: on the one hand, child-rearing and household maintenance are considered as women's "natural vocation" (and therefore are not remunerated); on the other hand, women's work outside the home is paid less because it is assumed that men are the breadwinners of the family. Moreover, women's economic dependence is reinforced through "feminine" education and sexual violence in and outside the home.[18]

Insofar as the Aristotelian pattern of patriarchal submission has been incorporated in the NT in form of the household-code texts,[19] it has influenced Christian self-understanding and community throughout the centuries. Theologians such as Augustine[20] or Thomas of Aquinas[21] have woven this Aristotelian construct of the inferior human "natures" of slaves and freeborn women into the basic fabric of Christian theology. Just as societal patriarchy, so also religious Christian patriarchy has defined not only women but also subjugated peoples and races as "the other", as "nature" to be exploited and dominated by powerful men. It has defined women and colonialized peoples not just as "the other" of white men, but also as subordinated and subjected to them. Obedience, economic dependence, and sexual control are the sustaining force of societal and ecclesiastical patriarchy. Such patriarchal Christian theology has provided religious legitimizations of racism, colonialism, classism and hetero/sexism in society and church. It has not only encouraged the sacrifice of people to authoritarian systems but also the exploitation of the earth and its resources. Its posture of divine domination and absolute power over the "other" has legitimated an imperialism and militarism that have brought us to the brink of nuclear annihilation.[22]

In short, a critical feminist theology of liberation names theologically the patriarchal bondage of women in Western society and church.[23] Patriarchy inculcates and perpetrates not only sexism but also racism and property-class relationships as basic structures of women's oppression. In a patriarchal society or religion all women are bound into a system of male privilege and domination, but impoverished third-world women constitute the bottom of the oppressive patriarchal pyramid. Patriarchy cannot be toppled except when the basis or bottom of the patriarchal pyramid — which consists of the exploitation of triply oppressed women — becomes liberated.[24]

The black feminist poet June Jordan articulates this goal of feminist liberation not so much as freedom *from* men, but as a movement *into* self-love, self-respect, and self-determination. Such a self-love and self-respect, she argues, has the strength to love and respect women who are "not like me" and to love and respect men "who are willing and able, without fear, to love and respect me". [25] Just as Jesus, who was born with the privileges of a Jewish male, focused attention on the woman bent double and insisted that she must be healed, so Christian men must recognize the patriarchal exploitation and oppression of women in society and church. They must not only reject all theologies of subordination or of "women's special nature and place" as patriarchal ideologies, but must also relinquish their patriarchal privileges and join women in our struggle to end patriarchal exploitation and bondage. [26]

Recognizing ourselves in the story of the woman bent double, we women must identify ourselves *as women* deformed and exploited by societal and ecclesiastical patriarchy. Those of us who are privileged in terms of race, class, culture and education must realize that as long as a single woman is not free, no woman is able to overcome patriarchal infirmity and bondage. Just as the woman bent double did not ask for healing from the man Jesus, but came to the synagogue to praise God, so Christian women must realize that our liberation will not come from the men in the churches. As long as we who are privileged in terms of race, class, culture or education identify with men who hold positions of power in society and church — rather than with our sisters living on the bottom of the patriarchal pyramid — we will not be able to realize that we suffer from the same patriarchal bondage. Only when we see ourselves and our daughters in the women who are today bent double in our midst, will we be able to articulate theologically a vision of God's salvation and community which enables all women to become free from patriarchal dehumanization. Mutuality between women and women, women and men is only possible when, in a feminist conversion, we reject the structural evil of patriarchy and our personal collaboration in it. [27] The "preferential option for the poor" must be spelled out as a commitment to the liberation struggle of women, since the majority of the poor are women and children dependent on women.

Equality in the Spirit: the basis of Christian community

Western patriarchy was not invented by Christianity and the struggle against patriarchal dehumanization was not initiated by Christians. [28] However, I would argue that the struggle with patriarchal structures is constitutive for Christian faith and community from its very beginnings. Some exegetes have maintained to the contrary that the early Christian missionary movement outside Palestine was not in conflict with its society, but was well integrated into it. The radicalism of the Jesus movement was supposedly assimilated by the urban Hellenistic communities into a family-style love patriarchalism, which perpetuated the hierarchical relationships of the patriarchal Greco-Roman household in a softer, milder form.[29]

However the textual basis for such a contention is not derived from the early Pauline literature but only from Acts, which was written at the end of the first century when Christian writers (for apologetic reasons) began to advocate the Aristotelian patriarchal pattern of submission. It is not the patriarchal household, but the more egalitarian community structures of private *collegia* or cultic assocations, which provide the organizational models for the early Christian missionary movement in the Greco-Roman cities.[30] This movement was suspect to Greco-Roman authorities not only because it accorded women and slaves equal standing, but also because it was a religious cult from the Orient. Because it admitted *individuals* irrespective of their status in the patriarchal household, it stood in conflict with Greco-Roman patriarchal society.

The theological self-understanding of this movement is rooted in the experiences of the Spirit. While the experience of God's gracious goodness in the ministry and life of Jesus is fundamental for the Jesus movement and its vision, the experience of the power of the Spirit is basic for the Christian missionary movement and its vision.[31] God did not leave Jesus in the power of death but raised him "in power" so that he becomes "a life-giving Spirit" (1 Cor. 15:45). Christ is preached to Jews and Greeks as the "power of God" and the "sophia of God" (1 Cor. 1:24). The *basileia* of God does not consist in "mere talk" but in "power" (1 Cor. 4:20). Those who are "in Christ" are "filled with the Holy Spirit". Those who have been baptized into Christ, live by the Spirit (Gal. 5:25) — they are "pneumatics", Spirit-filled people (Gal. 6:1). Both women and men have received spiritual gifts for the upbuilding of the body of Christ, the church. In the second century Justin still can assert that among the Christians *all* — women and men — have received charisms from the Holy Spirit. This "equality" in the Spirit is summed up by the early Christian movement in the words of Galatians 3:28, which is today generally understood as a pre-Pauline baptismal confession.[32]

Galatians 3:28: an incarnational approach

Traditional ecclesiology has often overlooked or explained away the ecclesial character of Galatians 3:28. Some theologians still maintain that women have a different role from men in the order of creation and redemption: in creation or in the natural order of society women are assigned a position of subordination by God, while in the order of redemption all have equal standing. With respect to baptism and the gifts of the Spirit all are equal before God. But the sociological implications of this equal standing before God cannot be applied either to society or the ministry of the church; this is given only in heaven, or postponed until the eschatological future. While traditional theology insisted on the subordination and inferiority of women, slaves and Jews in society and church, the more recent "theology of women" proceeds from the assumption of "equal but different" that postulates the complementarity of roles of women and men. It is striking, however, that this theology does not insist on a "symbolic" difference of race or class, but only on the symbolic difference of sex, which still must be lived out by women in "subordination".[33]

Over and against such an interpretation of Galatians 3:28, which restricts equality and oneness to the soul or to one's standing before God, an incarnational theology insists that what happens in Christ through baptism manifests itself in the social dimensions of the church. In his recent commentary on Galatians Hans Dieter Betz observes that commentators "have consistently denied that Paul's statements have political implications". According to Betz they are prepared to state the opposite of what Paul actually says in order to preserve a "purely religious" interpretation. In doing so they can strongly emphasize the reality of equality before God sacramentally, and at the same time "deny that any conclusions can be drawn from this in regard to the ecclesiastical offices (!) and the political order".[34] The exegetical discussion linking Galatians 3:28 and the household code tradition,[35] however, points to a historical-political dynamic that does not come to the fore when it is forced into the traditional oppositions between "order of creation" and "order of redemption" on the one hand, and between "enthusiastic excess or gnostic heresy" and "Pauline theology or NT orthodoxy" on the other.

Understood as a baptismal confession, Galatians 3:28 expresses the ecclesial self-understanding of the early Christian missionary movement. In baptism Christians entered into a kinship relationship with people coming from very different racial, cultural and national backgrounds. These patriarchal status differences, however, do not determine the social structures of the community. Therefore both Jewish and gentile women's status and role were drastically changed, since patriarchal household structures did not determine the social structures of the Christian community.

This seems to be stated explicitly in the final pairing of the baptismal confession: "there is no male and female". This last pair differs in formulation from the preceding two, insofar as it does not speak of opposites but of male *and* female. Exegetes have speculated a good deal about the fact that "male and female" are used here, rather than "man and woman". It is sometimes argued that not only "the *social* differences (roles) between men and women are involved but the *biological* distinctions" as well. Therefore, it is conjectured that Galatians 3:28 is gnostic and advocates androgyny.[36]

This argument, however, overlooks the fact that designations of the sexes in the neuter can simply be used in place of "woman and man".[37] Such designations do not imply a denial of biological sex differences. Galatians 3:28 probably alludes here to Genesis 1:27, where humanity created in the image of God is qualified as "male and female" in order to introduce the theme of procreation and fertility. Jewish exegetes understood "male and female", therefore, primarily in terms of marriage and family. Galatians 3:28c then does not assert that there are no longer men and women in Christ, but that patriarchal marriage relationships between male and female are no longer constitutive of the new community in Christ. Irrespective of their patriarchal status in the household, persons will be full members of the Christian movement in and through baptism. Women and men in the Christian community are not defined by their sexual procreative capacities or by their religious, cultural or social gender-roles, but by their empowerment by the Spirit.

Not only sex or gender roles were considered in antiquity to be grounded in biological nature but also cultural, racial and social differences. Although most would concede today that racial or class differences are not natural or biological (but rather cultural and social), gender differences are still proclaimed as given by nature or ordained by God. However, feminist studies have amply documented that most perceived gender differences are cultural-social.[38] We are socialized into gender roles as soon as we are born. Every culture gives different symbolic significance and derives different social roles from the human biological capacities of sexual intercourse, childbearing, and lactation. Sexual dimorphism and strictly defined gender roles are products of a patriarchal culture, which maintain and legitimize structures of control and domination, i.e. the exploitation of women by men.

Galatians 3:28 does not only proclaim the abolition of religious-cultural divisions, and the exploitation wrought by institutional slavery, but also domination based on patriarchal gender divisions. It asserts that within the Christian community no structures of dominance can be tolerated. Galatians 3:28 is therefore best understood as a communal Christian self-definition rather than as a statement about the soul of the individual. It proclaims that in the Christian community all distinctions of religion, race, class, nationality and gender are insignificant. All the baptized are equal; they are one in Christ. Being baptized into Christ means entering the sphere of the resurrected One, the life-giving Spirit whose reality and power are manifested in the Christian community. It is not anthropological oneness but ecclesiological oneness or unity in Christ Jesus which is the goal of Christian baptism. The unity of the church comes to the fore in the ecclesial equality of all those baptized. Such equality is not restricted to baptism, but determines the organizational structures of the church.

The household-code texts and Galatians 3:28: subordination vs equality in the Spirit

Insofar as the Christian community did not withdraw from society the early Christian missionary movement provided the experience, for those who came in contact with it, of alternative community in the midst of the Greco-Roman city. As an alternative association which accorded freeborn women and slave initiates equal status and access to leadership roles, the Christian missionary movement was a "conflict movement" standing in tension with the patriarchal institutions of slavery and family. Since Christians admitted to their membership freeborn women as well as slaves who continued to live in pagan households, tensions could arise not only within the community but even more so with respect to the larger society. The prescriptive post-Pauline exhortations of the household-code texts testify to these tensions. They seek to lessen these tensions in the face of accusations and harassment which Christians had to endure in Asia Minor.[39]

These household-code injunctions, which demand the subordination of slaves, women and young people, may also express the interests of the "owner and patron class", as some exegetes have suggested.[40] They could reflect the interests of Christian husbands and masters, heads of households, who felt that their prerogatives were being undermined. Of course it is difficult for us to decide whether or not such motivations played a role in these modifications of the Christian baptismal self-understanding. It is hard to know which admonitions to subordination were due to a genuine concern for the Christian group's embattled situation, and which arose from a defence of patriarchal dominance couched in theological terms. We hear only one side of the story; the theological counter-arguments by slaves or women have not survived in history.[41]

To assume that such patriarchal interests were at work is historically plausible, to the extent that the baptismal declaration of Galatians 3:28 runs counter to the general acceptance of male religious privilege among Greeks, Romans, Persians, and also Jews of the first century C.E. It was a rhetorical commonplace that Hellenistic man was grateful to the gods because he was fortunate enough to be born a human being and not a beast, a Greek and not a Barbarian, a freeman and not a slave, a man and not a woman. Conversion and baptism into Christ, therefore, implied for privileged men a much more radical break with their former social status and religious self-understandings than it did for freeborn women and slaves.

While the baptismal declaration cited in Galatians 3:28 offered a liberating religious vision to freeborn and slave women, it denied, within the Christian community, all male religious prerogatives based on patriarchal status. Just as Jewish men had to abandon the notion that they alone were the chosen of God, so masters had to relinquish their power over slaves, and husbands that over wives and children. And for men conversion to the Christian movement also meant relinquishing their religious prerogatives, since their social-political patriarchal privileges were, at the same time, religious privileges.

It is often argued that it was impossible for the tiny Christian group to abolish the institution of slavery and other social hierarchies. That might have been the case or it might not. However, what is often overlooked is that relinquishment of religious male prerogatives within the Christian community *was* possible, and that such a relinquishment included the abolition of social privileges as well. Legal-societal and cultural-religious patriarchal status privileges were no longer valid for Christians.[42] Insofar as this egalitarian Christian self-understanding did away with all patriarchal privileges of religion, class, and caste, it allowed not only gentiles and slaves but also women to exercise leadership functions within the missionary movement.

It is also true that the pre-Pauline baptismal formula of Galatians 3:28 does not reflect the same notion of anthropological unification, and the same androcentric perspective, that has determined the understanding of equality found in later gnostic and patristic writings. According to various gnostic and patristic texts, becoming a disciple means for a woman becoming "male", "like man", and relinquishing her sexual powers of procreation, because the male principle stands for the heavenly, angelic, divine realm; whereas the female principle represents either human weakness or evil.[43] While patristic and gnostic writers could express the equality of Christian women with men only as "manliness" or as abandonment of women's sexuality, Galatians 3:28 does not extol maleness but the oneness of the body of Christ, the church, where all patriarchal social, cultural, religious, national and gender divisions, as well as all structures of domination, are rejected. Not the love-patriarchalism of the post-Pauline school but the ecclesial self-understanding of "equality in Christ" expresses the vision and praxis of the early Christian movement in the Greco-Roman world.

The vision of Mark's Gospel: equality in the Spirit, discipleship and suffering

That this vision and praxis is still alive at the beginning of the second century is apparent not only from the pre-scriptive household-code texts, which advocate patriarchal submission over and against an egalitarian ecclesial praxis, but also from the gospels. Independent of each other, the evangelists called Mark and John have gathered traditional materials and stories about Jesus and his first followers and moulded them into the Gospel form. They did so not because of antiquarian interest in the life of Jesus — now past — but because they believed that the resurrected One was, at that very moment, speaking to their communities through the words and deeds of Jesus of Nazareth.

Both Mark and John[44] emphasize service and love as the core of Jesus' ministry and as the central demand of discipleship. The Gospel of Mark was written at approximately the same time as Colossians, which marks the beginnings of the patriarchal household-code trajectory, or line of development. The final redaction of the Gospel of John emerges at about the same time as the Pastorals and the letters of Ignatius, and might address the same communities in Asia Minor. It is, therefore, significant that the first writers of gospels articulate a very different vision of Christian discipleship and community than that presented by the writers of the injunctions to patriarchal submission, although both address Christian communities in the last third of the first century.

Discipleship in Mark is understood as a literal following of Jesus and of his example. Mark's Christological emphasis, however, is on the necessity of Jesus' suffering, execution, and death. Suffering is not an end in itself, but it is the outcome of Jesus' life-praxis of solidarity with the social and religious outcasts of his society. The threefold announcement of Jesus' suffering in Mark 8:22-10:52 is followed each time by the disciples' misunderstanding, and by Jesus' call to discipleship as a following on the way to the cross. Just as rejection, suffering and execution as a criminal are the outcome of the preaching and life-praxis of Jesus, so will they be the fate of the true disciple. In Mark's view this is the crucial Christological insight that determines both Jesus' ministry and Christian discipleship. [45]

This theology of suffering is developed for Christians who are persecuted, handed over to sanhedrins, beaten in synagogues, and standing trial before kings and governors "for Jesus' sake" (Mark 13:9). Such persecutions are instigated by their closest relatives and friends: "Brother will betray brother to death, and the father his child; children will rise against their parents and have them put to death" (Mark 13:12). Thus the Markan Gospel situates the persecutions and sufferings of its community in the context of tensions within their own households. While the writers of 1 Peter or the Pastorals seek to lessen these tensions by advocating adaptation to the dominant patriarchal Greco-Roman society, the Markan Jesus clearly states that giving offence and experiencing suffering must not be shunned. A true disciple of Jesus must expect suffering, hatred and persecution.

In conclusion: I have read Mark's theology in light of early Christian developments at the end of the first century not by construing hypothetical "heretical opponents", but by placing this Gospel in the context of other New Testament writings. The Markan community gathers in house-churches. It struggles to avoid the patriarchal pattern of dominance and submission that characterizes its socio-political environment. Those who are the farthest from the centre of religious and political power — slaves, children, poor, gentiles, women — become the paradigms of true discipleship.

Most of our New Testament literature was written to Christian communities in the last third of the first century or at the beginning of the second. These communities seem to have experienced tensions with (and even persecutions by) their patriarchal Greco-Roman society. These tensions were not only religious but also social-political. In order to lessen the threat of persecution, the post-Pauline writers sought to lessen these tensions between the Christian community and Greco-Roman society, by adapting the alternative Christian missionary movement to the patriarchal structures and values of their Greco-Roman environment and Asian culture.

The writers of the primary gospels, Mark and John, choose a different approach. Written around the same time as Colossians and Ephesians, Mark's gospel insists that suffering and persecutions engendered by an alternative form of community and life-style must not be avoided.

Whereas the advocates of the household-code texts appeal to Paul or Peter to legitimize their injunctions for submission and adaptation to Greco-Roman patriarchal structures, the writers of Mark's and John's Gospels appeal to Jesus himself to support their stress on love and service, a love and service which is demanded not from the slaves and the lowliest in the community but from masters and would-be leaders, not from women but from men.

While for apologetic reasons the post-Pauline writers seek to limit women's leadership in the community to roles that are culturally and religiously acceptable, the evangelist known as Mark insists on "equality from below" in the familial community of disciples and therefore highlights the paradigmatic discipleship of the apostolic women followers of Jesus. In historical retrospective, the post-Pauline writers' theological stress on the submission of the subordinate members in patriarchal household and church has won out over the early Christian vision and praxis of the discipleship community of equals.

However, this historical success of the Greco-Roman societal pattern of patriarchal submission must not be justified theologically today just because it can claim a longer tradition. Rather it must be assessed theologically in terms of the early Christian vision of the discipleship of equals. By insisting on it the writer of Mark's Gospel, like other New Testament writers, has kept this vision alive in the church. The inclusion of this vision into the canon has spawned reform movements throughout the centuries. It has made it impossible for Christian churches to forget Jesus' invitation to realize the discipleship of equals. Church unity and community must not be bought at the expense of this vision. Only when the church rejects all patriarchal structures of domination and exploitation will we be able to offer a vision of community for a human future that is not sustained by domination and exploitation.

NOTES

[1] Mary Tanner, "Unity and Renewal: the Church and the Human Community", *The Ecumenical Review*, Vol. 36, 1984, p.254.

[2] See my articles "Feminist Theology as a Critical Theology of Liberation", *Theological Studies*, Vol. 36, 1975, pp.606-626; "Claiming the Center: a Critical Feminist Theology of Liberation", in M. Buckley and J. Kalven, *Women's Spirit Bonding*, New York, Pilgrim Press, 1984, pp.293-309; I. Carter Heyward, "An Unfinished Symphony of Liberation", *The Journal of Feminist Studies in Religion*, 1/1, 1985, pp.99-118; Renate Rieger, "Inhaltliche und methodische Voraussetzungen einer Feministischen Theologie als Befreiungstheologie", *Schlangenbrut* 13, 1985, pp.26-30.

72   Beyond Unity-in-Tension

[3] Cf. J. Wilkinson, "The Case of the Bent Woman in Luke 13:10-17", *Evangelical Quarterly*, 49, 1977, pp.195-205; J. Fitzmyer, *The Gospel According to Luke X-XXIV*, Anchor Bible 28A, Garden City, Doubleday, 1985, pp.1009-1014.

[4] For a review of the sabbath-healing controversies, see C. Dietzfelbinger, "Vom Sinn der Sabbatheilungen Jesu", *Evangelische Theologie*, 38, 1978, pp.281-297; A. Hultgren, *Jesus and his Adversaries*, Minneapolis, Augsburg, 1979, pp.111-115; L. Schottroff and W. Stegemann, *Jesus von Nazareth. Hoffnung der Armen*, Stuttgart, Kohlhammer, 1978, pp.15-28.

[5] The structural analysis of Antoinette C. Wire ("The Structure of the Gospel Miracle Stories and Their Tellers", *Semeia*, 11, 1978, pp.83-113) shows that the structure of the NT miracle story consists in a juxtaposition of an oppressive situation and the breaking open of it.

[6] For a review of the literature on the *basileia* (kingdom) message of Jesus and its interpretation in Christian literature see N. Perrin, *Jesus and the Language of the Kingdom: Symbol and Metaphor in New Testament Interpretation*, Philadelphia, Fortress, 1976, pp.15-88; see also his earlier book *The Kingdom of God in the Teaching of Jesus*, Philadelphia, Westminster, 1963, and W.G. Kümmel, *The Theology of the New Testament*, Nashville, Abingdon, 1973, pp.32-39.

[7] For such an interpretation and bibliographical documentation see my book *In Memory of Her: a Feminist Theological Reconstruction of Christian Origins*, New York, Crossroads, 1983, pp.105-159.

[8] For an elaboration of this hermeneutical perspective cf. J. Sanders, "Hermeneutics", *The Interpreters Dictionary of the Bible: Supplementary Volume*, Nashville, Abingdon, 1976, pp.402-407.

[9] For a review of the NT materials but with a somewhat different approach see W. Wink, *Naming the Powers: the Language of Power in the New Testament,* Vol. I, Philadelphia, Fortress, 1984. See also my book *The Book of Revelation: Justice and Judgment*, Philadelphia, Fortress, 1985, for an apocalyptic theology of power.

[10] For an excellent critique of R. Bultmann's programme see D. Sölle, *Political Theology*, Philadelphia, Fortress, 1974.

[11] See e.g. E. Wendel Moltmann, *Das Land wo Milch und Honig fliesst. Perspectiven einer feministischen Theologie*, STB Seibenstern 486, Gütersloh, Mohn, 1985, pp.37-50.

[12] Feminist literature often uses the term *patriarchy* as synonymous with "sexism" or "androcentric dualism". However such understanding of patriarchy in terms of male-female dualism or masculine privilege cannot explain the interaction of racism, classism, sexism, and imperialist militarism in modern industrialized societies. For a discussion of the different meanings of patriarchy in feminist literature see V. Beechy, "On Patriarchy", *Feminist Review*, 1, 1979, pp.66-82.

[13] E. Baker ed., *The Politics of Aristotle*, New York, Oxford University Press, 1962; L. Lange, "Woman is Not a Rational Animal: on Aristotle's Biology of Reproduction"; E. V. Spellman, "Aristotle and the Politization of the Soul"; and J. Hicks, "The Unit of Political Analysis: our Aristotelian Hangover"; all three articles in S. Harding and M.B. Hintikka eds, *Discovering Reality: Feminist Perspectives on Epistemology, Metaphysics, Methodology, and Philosophy of Science*, Boston, D. Reidel, 1983, pp.1-43.

[14] E.C. Keuls, *The Reign of the Phallus: Sexual Politics in Ancient Athens*, New York, Harper & Row, 1985.

[15] The contradiction between the patriarchal social structures and the democratic ideals of the Athenian city-state has been pointed out especially by M.B. Arthur, "Women in the Ancient World", in *Conceptual Frameworks of Studying Women's History*, New York, Sarah Lawrence College, 1975, pp.1-15; *id.*, "Liberated Women: the Classical Era", in R. Bridenthal & C. Koonz eds, *Becoming Visible: Women in European History*, Boston, Mifflin, 1977, pp.60-89.

[16] See especially the study of Susan Moller Okin, *Women in Western Political Thought*, Princeton, University Press, 1979; and H. Schröder, "Feministische Gesellschaftstheo-

rie", and "Das Recht der Väter", in L.F. Pusch ed., *Feminismus. Inspektion der Herrenkultur*, Frankfurt, Suhrkamp, 1983, pp.449-506.

[17] See Z.L. Eisenstein, *The Radical Future of Liberal Feminism*, New York, Longman, 1981; H. Hartmann, "Capitalism, Patriarchy, and Job Segregation by Sex," in Abel & Abel eds, *The Signs Reader: Women, Gender, and Scholarship*, Chicago, University Press, 1983, pp.193-225; and D.K. Lewis, "A Response to Inequality: Black Women, Racism, and Sexism", *ibid.*, pp.169-199 on the double and triple jeopardy of poor and minority women.

[18] The literature on sexual violence against women and children is too extensive to be listed here. See e.g. K. Barry, *Female Sexual Slavery*, New York, Avon, 1979; F. Rush, *The Best Kept Secret: Sexual Abuse of Children*, New York, McGraw Hill, 1980, and the review of the literature by W. Brines and L. Gordon, "The New Scholarship on Family Violence", *Signs*, 8, 1983, pp.490-531.

[19] Such texts of patriarchal submission are: [Romans 13:1-7]; Colossians 3:18-4:1; Ephesians 5:22-6:9; 1 Peter 2:18-3:7; 1 Timothy 2:11-15; 5:3-8; 6:1-2; Titus 2:2-10; 3:1-2, 1 Clement 21:6-8; Polycarp 4:2-6:1; Didache 4:9-11; Barnabas 19:5-7. See my discussion of these texts and their interpretation in *Bread Not Stone: the Challenge of Feminist Biblical Interpretation*, Boston, Beacon, 1984, pp.65-92.

[20] See K. Thraede, "Augustin — Texte aus dem Themenkreis 'Frau', 'Gesellschaft' und 'Gleichheit'," *Jahrbuch für Antike und Christentum*, 22, 1979, pp.70-97.

[21] See K.E. Børresen, *Subordination and Equivalence: the Nature and Role of Women in Augustine and Thomas of Aquinas*, Washington, University of America Press, 1981.

[22] See the trenchant criticism of life-destroying structures in Christianity by M. Daly, *Beyond God the Father: Toward a Philosophy of Women's Liberation*, Boston, Beacon, 1973, and *Gyn/Ecology: the Metaethics of Radical Feminism*, Boston, Beacon, 1978; R. Radford Ruether, *New Woman, New Earth: Sexist Ideologies and Human Liberation*, New York, Crossroads, 1975; B. Wildung Harrison, *Making the Connections: Essays in Feminist Social Ethics*, Boston, Beacon, 1985; E. Sorge, "Feministische Theologie mit oder ohne Göttin?", *Schlangenbrut*, 12, 1986, pp.14-21; and the contributions of Ynestra King, "Making the World Live: Feminism and the Domination of Nature", and M. Condren, "Patriarchy and Death", in Buckley & Kalven eds, *Women's Spirit Bonding*, pp.56-64 and pp.172-189.

[23] See my "Breaking the Silence — Becoming Visible," in E. Schüssler Fiorenza and M. Collins eds, *Women Invisible in Church and Theology*, Concilium 181, Edinburgh, T&T Clark, 1975, pp.3-16.

[24] See Bell Hooks, *Feminist Theory: From Margin to Center*, Boston, South End Press, 1984, and the articles on "Racism, Pluralism, Bonding", in Buckley & Kalven, *op. cit.*, pp.67-136.

[25] June Jordan, *Civil Wars*, Boston, Beacon Press, 1981, p.143.

[26] K.G. Cannon, "The Emergence of Black Feminist Consciousness", in L. Russell ed., *Feminist Interpretation of the Bible*, Philadelphia, Westminster, 1985, pp.30-40; D. Williams, "Women's Oppression and Life-Line Politics in Black Women's Religious Narratives", *Journal of Feminist Studies in Religion*, 1/2, 1985, pp.59-72.

[27] See my "Sexism and Conversion", *Network*, 9, 1981, pp.15-22 and P. Cooey, "The Power of Transformation and the Transformation of Power", *Journal of Feminist Studies in Religion*, 1/1, 1985, pp.23-26.

[28] Neither should Jesus be understood over against Jewish "patriarchy", an interpretation also found in feminist literature, cf. most recently E. Sorge, *Religion und Frau. Weibliche Spiritualität im Christentum*, Stuttgart, Kohlhammer, 1985, and her articles in *Schlangenbrut*. J. Plaskow, a Jewish feminist, has consistently deplored the Anti-Judaism in Christian feminist writings, see e.g. "Christian Feminism and Anti-Judaism", *Cross Currents*, 28, 1978, pp.306-315; "Blaming Jews for Patriarchy", *Lilith*, 7, 1980, pp.11-17; for the leadership of Jewish women in the synagogue see B. Brooten, *Women Leaders in the Ancient Synagogue*, Brown Judaic Studies 36, Chico, Scholars Press, 1982.

[29] See e.g. G. Theissen, *Sociology of Early Palestinian Christianity*, Philadelphia, Fortress, 1978; *The Social Setting of Pauline Christianity: Essays on Corinth*, Philadelphia, Fortress, 1982. What Theissen calls "love patriarchalism", B. Malina (in *Christian Origins and Cultural Anthropology: Practical Models for Biblical Interpretation*, Atlanta, John Knox Press, 1986) terms "maternal- uncle- archy" or "emarchy" within dominantly patriarchal or patrilineal societies. Yet neither Theissen nor Malina questions critically the sociological or anthropological models which are assumed by their own model for the reconstruction of early Christian history.

[30] For a discussion of the different organizational forms which were available see A.J. Malherbe, *Social Aspects of Early Christianity*, Philadelphia, Fortress, 1983; W.A. Meeks, *The First Urban Christians: the Social World of the Apostle Paul*, Yale, University Press, 1983; J.E. Stambaugh and D.L. Balch, *The New Testament in its Social Environment*, Philadelphia, Westminster, 1986.

[31] For a fuller elaboration and bibliography see *In Memory of Her*, pp.160-204; see also G. Lohfink, *Jesus and Community: the Social Dimension of Christian Faith*, Philadelphia, Fortress, 1984.

[32] For a discussion of the literature see H.D. Betz, *Galatians*, Hermeneia, Philadelphia, Fortress, 1979; H. Paulsen, "Einheit und Freiheit der Söhne (Sic!) Gottes—Gal. 3:26-29", *ZNW*, 71, 1980, pp.74-95 and *In Memory of Her*, pp.205-241.

[33] For a critique of such interpretations which were developed especially in the controversy around women's ordination see already K. Stendahl, *The Bible and the Role of Women*, Philadelphia, Fortress, 1966.

[34] *Op. cit.*, p.189, No. 68.

[35] E.g. J.E. Crouch, *The Origin and Intention of the Colossian Haustafel*, FRLANT 109, Göttingen, 1972, speaks of "enthusiastic excesses" of slaves and women inspired by Gal. 3:28. Different is D. Lührmann, "Wo man nicht mehr Sklave und Freier ist. Überlegungen zur Struktur frühchristlicher Gemeinden", *Wort und Dienst*, 13, 1975, pp.53-83.

[36] See e.g. W.A. Meeks, "The Image of the Androgyne: Some Use of a Symbol in Earliest Christianity", *History of Religions*, 13, 1974, pp.165-208.

[37] For textual material see M. de Merode, "Une théologie primitive de la femme?", *Revue théologique de Louvain*, 9, 1978, pp.176-184.

[38] The literature on the topic is vast although biblical scholars are for the most part unaware of it. For a review of the discussion see A. Oakely, *Subject Women*, New York, Pantheon Books, 1981; A.M. Jaggar, *Feminist Politics and Human Nature*, Totowa, Rowman & Allanheld, 1983; Lewontin/Rose/Kamin, eds, *Not in Our Genes: Biology, Ideology, and Human Nature*, New York, Pantheon Books, 1984; C. Burton, *Subordination: Feminism and Social Theory*, Winchester, Allen & Unwin, 1985.

[39] C.F. K. Thraede, "Zum historischen Hintergrund der Haustafeln des Neuen Testaments", *JAC Ergänzungsband*, 8, 1981, pp.359-368; D. Lührmann, "Neutestamentliche Haustafeln und Antike Ökonomie", *NTS*, 27, 1981, pp.83-91; D.L. Balch, *Let Wives be Submissive: the Domestic Code in 1 Peter*, SBLM 26; Chico, Scholar's Press, 1981.

[40] See e.g. E.A. Judge, *The Social Pattern of Christian Groups*, London, Tyndale Press, 1969, pp.60-71.

[41] However, S.L. Davies, *The Revolt of the Widows: the Social World of the Apocryphal Acts* (Carbondale, S. Illinois, University Press, 1980) and D.R. MacDonald, *The Legend and the Apostle: the Battle for Paul in Story and Canon* (Philadelphia, Westminster Press, 1983) argue that such counter-arguments are still found in the Apocryphal Acts.

[42] See e.g. D.C. Verner, *The Household of God: the Social World of the Pastoral Epistles*, SBLDiss 71, Chico, Scholars Press, 1983, for the literature.

[43] Cf. E.H. Pagels, *The Gnostic Gospels*, New York, Random House, 1979; G.H. Tavard, *Woman in Christian Tradition*, Notre Dame, University Press, 1973.

[44] For discussion of the literature and interpretation see *In Memory of Her*, pp.316-342.

[45] For literature and discussion of Mark see the introductions to the NT, e.g. H. Koester, *Introduction to the New Testament. Volume II: History and Literature of Early Christianity*, Philadelphia, Fortress, 1982, pp.164-171.

Renewal in Unity:
a Case Study from South India

PADMASANI GALLUP

In Ibsen's play "A Doll's House" the heroine Nora's husband admonishes her, stating that before all else she is a wife and mother. She replies: "I no longer think so. I think that before all else I am a human being just as you are, or at least I have to try to become one."

"I no longer think so" was the starting point in my own theological growth. I was wife and mother for several years. After my youngest child started school I went back to school myself. My first degree was in zoology, and with that science background I undertook theological studies. When I finished the first level theology degree I was encouraged to undertake doctoral studies. In all the years that I taught I would watch my students going up automatically for ordination in the church. In the beginning I did not think much about the fact that no one — but no one — ever mentioned the word "ordination" to me. All my teaching colleagues (all theologically-trained men) were ordained ministers. They could conduct services and preach in the seminary chapel on a rota system. My desire for personal theological formation, an attempt to "become human" as Ibsen's Nora says, looked as if it might end with my obtaining theological degrees, but without validation for ministry in Christ's name or in his church.

● Rev. Dr Padmasani Gallup is a pastor in the Church of South India, and now director of Women's Concerns, Diocese of Madras.

Unity, renewal and the ministry of women in the Church of South India

But change is happening and there is hope. Some months ago there was a momentous event — it was not accompanied by the appearance of a comet, and it was perhaps only a dim and hazy recapitulation of the vision of the prophet Joel: "I will pour out my spirit on all flesh" (2:28). It was sharing anew God's life as God had gifted it to me in Christ. It was an impetus towards new creation; a new lease on a chosen vocation of service in Christ's name. It was a new understanding of the gospel as God's present reign in Christ; of the world as the arena of God's unfolding purpose; of the church as a sign of God's mystery and of God's people as a symbol of God's rule in the life of the nations.

It was renewal for me, personally. It was a choice to be the medium for the revelation of God's nature, God's will and purpose, and God's love and grace outpoured towards God's world.

It was renewal within the church as well. It was a challenge to evolve and adapt its life, to make full and creative use of new opportunities, to become a new community that could respond to the rapid intellectual and spiritual changes taking place all around it. It was an undeniable reminder that the church is primarily God's instrument rather than a privileged minority community existing for its own glory and conforming to society's norms and goals. For the church it was also a reaffirmation of the central biblical theme of God's choice of persons and peoples to bear God's mission to the world — a mission that is continuous with that of the chosen people of Israel and of Jesus himself.

It was a further sign of the unity that has been bestowed on the Church of South India — a unity that was granted when individuals in the different churches struggled to be obedient to God's will in response to the prayer of Jesus "that all may be one".

What was this sign, this reaffirmation of God's choice, this personal and corporate renewal? It was the ordination of women to full participation in the full ministry of the Church of South India.

Three of the twenty dioceses of the Church of South India have ordained women since early 1984. The CSI approved and voted the ordination of women at its Fifteenth Synod meeting in 1976, after only about four years of debate and discussion both at the synod and pastorate levels. The ordination of women was not so much a response to a felt-need within the total ministry of the church, as a witness to the unity within the CSI. As you all know, the CSI is a wondrous living witness of the presence and work of the Holy Spirit among individuals and groups who had been open to God's will in deep penitence and supplication. "The most important event in church history since Pentecost" was a remark made at the inauguration of the Church of South India in 1947 — an event that was the fruition of nearly forty-five years of negotiations between the uniting churches.

The theological and psychological basis for union

Within the context of church union as experienced in the CSI and women's ordination as further evidence of the unity within the church, I would like to make two general observations. First, there is the experience of release from the bondage of the past. It is not that history and tradition are not important; rather, it is that they need not dominate. Many churches and institutions have a tendency to look backwards and, appealing to precedents (or the absence of them), attempt to avoid answering radically new questions. In our negotiations for church union both Indian and Eastern Christians had the courage to ask themselves whether the time had not come for them to do what they had never done before, *in order that God's Spirit might begin to heal the divisions among humankind.* Here one might recall Peter's words as recounted in Acts 10:14; "No Lord, for I have never..." Tradition has value insofar as it is preparation for the future and points to it. Neither individuals nor institutions can successfully continue to live in the past, resisting change. Any attempt to do so, on the assumption that old answers are the given and final ones, degenerates into a timid or truculent avoidance of issues considered dangerous. It also becomes a refusal to trust and be open to the Holy Spirit in prayer and penitence.

Secondly, unity was not pursued as a mere human ideal, but as the will and purpose of God as affirmed in the scriptures. With this conviction it becomes clear that Jesus' prayer "that they may all be one" (John 17:21) is attainable in reality. One cannot know the power of the Holy Spirit to guide and bestow until one has sought to do the will of God with conviction, commitment and a sense of urgency. Unity was sought as an immediate goal, not as some almost eschatological, future fulfilment. Unity was recognized as *essential for the mission and ministry of the church in the Indian context.*

With this pragmatic approach, certain points were acknowledged. The first was acknowledgment that unity would not mean absorption by one church of all the others, but that all the churches would be changed. The negotiators recalled that "dying to live" is as true of separate denominations as it is of the individual Christian. Each would give up something of its claim to uniqueness in order that the whole might be viable and strong. Secondly, there was the recognition that the church exists because God wants it to exist for the sake of the world: with a deep concern for mission, for making known the gospel of the reconciliation of the world initiated by God in Christ. "God so loved the world, that He sent His.. Son..." (John 3:16). Thirdly, there was recognized the need for an ordered ministry. All the uniting churches agreed eventually on the threefold ordained ministry of bishop, presbyter and deacon, and accepted the principles of "the historical episcopacy" rather than apostolic succession.

At the Lambeth Conference of 1930, Anglicans had disliked the participation of presbyters in the consecration of bishops and said: "If (this practice) is adopted, it should be fully explained that the presbyters did not take part as consecrators." In the discussions leading to the formation of the CSI this position was unacceptable to many, if not to all, of the non-Anglican negotiators, and discussion over two days produced no solution. After this long debate, all members became silent and bowed their heads in prayer. After several minutes Bishop Loyd rose and quietly asked: "Would this reading do? 'It should be understood and taught that the real consecrator is God.'" Immediately all agreed. Thus, nine ministers of the CSI, three from each tradition, laid hands on the first new bishops.)[1] Consequently, as one of the most important insights given to the CSI, the preface to its Ordinal states:

> An ordination service is the rite by which one of these ministries (deacon, presbyter, bishop) is conferred. It is an act of God in His Church. The Church of South India believes that in all ordinations and consecrations, the true Ordainer and Consecrator is God, who, in response to the prayers of His Church, and through the words and acts of its representatives, commissions and empowers for the office and work to which they are called the persons whom it has selected.[2]

There was no attempt to impose uniformity of worship or use of the ancient creeds and confessions. Nor was there a requirement to draw up a detailed new statement of belief. The right answers, it was acknowledged, could be found after the act of union.

> The realization of the inescapable Westernness of all our inherited documents, as seen from Asia, and of the almost complete unintelligibility of the confessions apart from Western historical events, has helped to bring this about. The movement of thought which found expression in the CSI Basis of Union has attained a much wider recognition, as was shown in the resolution

of the First British Faith and Order Conference at Nottingham in 1964: "While we affirm standards of belief to be an essential element of the life of the Church, our remaining differences concerning the use of these standards, and concerning the relation between Scripture and Tradition, though important, are not sufficient to stand as barriers to unity. They do not separate us at the point of the central affirmation of our faith, and they can be better explored within a united Church.[3]

Above all, it was vital for all the churches concerned to make a commitment to unity without looking back to the past, or leaving a way open for retreat. The CSI came into existence on these firm foundational principles, supported by prayer and inspired, guided and constrained by the Holy Spirit and the grace of God.

In ordaining women the CSI followed its early pattern of openness and firmness, conviction and commitment, prayer and supplication on behalf of this new venture in faith. As had been the case with almost all the secular, socio-economic reforms pertaining to the status of women in Indian society, it was the handful of enlightened, concerned men who initiated discussion, introduced resolutions and worked for grassroots support for the ordination of women. Thus Indian women have not had to fight for these rights, or get caught up in a male/female polarization.

Now *in witness to its spirit of unity* the church has begun to ordain women to enable them fully to participate in all its ministries. This, of course, has not been arrived at easily. But it is not necessary here to spell out the points of controversy. The pain and hurt of litigations, the misunderstandings, and the final, quiet implementation of the vote of the Synod at the diocesan level are all parts of the story. Now four of our young ordained women have been assigned regular pastorates. One has managed to have a baby in the midst of her pastoral duties, and the heavens did not fall! (One of the objections which had been raised was about the "image" of a full-term pregnant pastor. I was wicked enough to suggest that the objectors take a good hard look at some of our middle-aged presbyters and bishops in full profile!)

New opportunities for ministry

From its very inception the CSI has been serious about and supportive of its Women's Fellowship, which has continued to be active and to grow. In 1951, the Order of Sisterhood was inaugurated; more than sixty women have been initiated into this order. The tradition of "Bible women" has continued, but on a smaller scale. Bible women work in their own neighbourhoods among Christian women and women of other faiths.

Theirs is an unsung mission of evangelism which has touched the lives of countless "secret Christians" who have not been allowed by their Hindu husbands to receive baptism. My maternal grandmother was a Bible woman until the end of her life. These were the traditional avenues for women to be in ministry within the church.

But now the church has realized that there is no true unity and renewal without *equality*, including equal access to the full ministry of the church. There is no denying that this has been brought home to the church hierarchy as a result of the feminist ferment in the West regarding structural inequalities in both the secular and ecclesial world. The challenge and charge to the church is to see the renewal resulting from this new venture as a recommitment to mission. One of the ideas that has been sparked by the ordination of women is a new category called "special ministries", to which both ordained women and ordained men will be called. In a small way some ordained men are already involved in this type of special ministry as agricultural experts, non-formal education leaders, and as counsellors in development projects. As ordained women, with their theological training and commitment to Christ, become available they may be invited to serve the desperately needy rural congregations as pastors, in addition to being experts in agriculture, preventive health work, cooperatives, and enablers for women's organizations. Theirs may be a theology and philosophy of service similar to that of our Roman Catholic sisters who, instead of being ordained, have taken vows of poverty and chastity. In Indian culture there are many things which a woman can do that a man cannot.

This is but a small example of a *visioning for mission* that is possible for ordained women in the church. The visioning is not all starry-eyed. There are 17 other dioceses in the CSI, some of which have said they would never ordain women as presbyters. (Remember that one very wise step that the uniting churches took was to eliminate the term "priest" for pastor, substituting "presbyter" to recall and honour that rich tradition of ministry). Other dioceses have voiced all manner of excuses, both cultural and pseudo-theological.

New visions of ministry and mission in the Indian context

There is another vision that I have for women ordained to the full ministry. It is based on upside-downness! It is related to Hindu culture, which is of course the overwhelming context for our churches. As all of you are aware, Hindu society is hierarchically organized into rigid castes. That hierarchy is traditionally explained by saying that Brahma, the

Creator, made the different castes from different parts of his body: the head gave rise to the Brahmins, the priestly caste; the chest to the Kahatriyas, the warriors; the mid-section to the Vaisyas, the merchants; and the legs to the Sudras, the labourers. The outcastes, or the harijans, arose from Brahma's feet, and women — beyond the pale — from the soles of the feet!

The contrasting image of the church as the body of Christ is startlingly liberating! This traditional rationale of Hindu society has no use for the concepts of mutuality, inter-relatedness and inter-dependence. But St Paul, with a rare sense of humour, asks: "Can the eye say to the hand, 'I do not need you'?" (1 Cor. 12:21) St Paul goes further. He depicts Christ as the head of the church; but Christ is also the paradigm of kenotic incarnation: the head comes down... emptying himself, taking the form of a servant, being born in the likeness of men (Phil. 2:7).

One of the *asanas* or postures for the discipline of yoga is called the *sirasaasana* (standing on one's head). It is said to be one of the most health-giving *asanas*, and Jawaharlal Nehru is reported to have practised it daily. We may use this *asana* to talk about ministry of women in our context. In terms of the social hierarchy, most Indian women have experienced the status of being next to the dust on the ground. They, of all persons, are able to relate to others similarly dehumanized. Indian women, ordained to mission in ministry, are called to be the agents to turn the Brahma image upside down, to bring about the topsy-turvyness portrayed in the Song of Mary (Luke 1:46-55) to realize the healthfulness and healing of the *sirasaasana*. Acts 17:6 need not be confined to "These men...!" but could well read "these women who are turning the world upside down". This is a vision for radical change. This is a vision for disciples and followers of Jesus, the radical son of God. Perhaps some may see this as too radical, too violent a change.

Perhaps another Indian image may make for peace and reconciliation as a result of true equality. I refer to the image of Vishnu in repose, or the image of the reclining Buddha. Perhaps these images imply a less radical change, a less violent striving: the head and feet are at the same level when one is reclining. There is an equality inherent in the horizontal, as opposed to the vertical. Indian women have the reputation of being able to adapt and respond in non-violent ways to situations of stress. Although the violence done to human beings calls out a response of violence in kind, the Christian, Christ-like response would be non-violence, and women may best be able to show how violence could be overcome by non-violence.

I would like to superimpose St Paul's imagery of the body of Christ on the image of the reposing Vishnu or the reclining Buddha. I would like to challenge all Christians, not only women, to be involved in that type of mission through incarnational and kenotic struggle in non-violence that would make real the justice of equality, the interdependence of mutuality, and the dynamic peace which is of a God in repose.

This is the vision I have for the ministry and mission of ordained women within the Indian context as ministers, as presbyters of the Church of South India. As was said so well in the biblical study by Elisabeth Schüssler Fiorenza, it is an invitation to identify with all the bent-over humanity — both women and men — and bring them into uprightness, through turning our present hierarchical orientations "upside-down" .

NOTES

[1] Adapted from Michael Hollis, *The Significance of South India*, Ecumenical Studies in History, London, Lutterworth Press, 1966, p.75.

[2] Constitution II, 10, *Book of Common Worship*, London, CUP, 1963, p.160.

[3] Hollis, *op. cit.*, p.23, quoting *Unity Begins at Home*, report of the First British Faith and Order Conference at Nottingham, 1964, ed. Davies and Edwards, London, SCM Press, p.75.

Towards the Community
of Women and Men in the Church

The Story of St John's Presbyterian Church,
Berkeley, California

PRESENTED BY REV. SANDRA WINTER PARK

I come with greetings from the people of St John's Presbyterian Church, Berkeley, California; from the Presbytery of San Francisco; and from the Center for Women and Religion, Berkeley, California. I bring their prayers that the love, peace, justice, forgiveness and joy of God in Christ will be with us as we work together this week in Prague.

I have been asked to present a case study of a specific congregation in a "progressive" setting, as a complement to case studies from a traditional context and from an Orthodox situation. By "progressive context" I understand one where a congregation is confronted with rapid social change and seeks, in the midst of this, to be faithful to the gospel; a congregation forced to re-examine its traditional forms of Christian life and witness; and especially, for this Prague consultation, a congregation which has struggled with issues of the community of women and men in their relation to the unity and renewal of the church.

St John's Presbyterian Church, Berkeley, California, is certainly such a congregation. While it represents one specific denomination in the United States and one cultural setting, it is a very diverse congregation and I believe its experience will be relevant to many other situations. And

---

● Rev. Sandra Park (Presbyterian) is now associate pastor at St John's Presbyterian Church, Berkeley. This report has been compiled by the editor from notes, information and records provided by Rev. Sandra Park. The presentation was illustrated by numerous photographs of which only a sample could be included here.

although neither the congregation nor I was involved in the World Council of Churches' Community of Women and Men in the Church Study, or the Sheffield consultation, you will see that we were in fact deeply involved in the themes and issues raised in the Community Study.

Our self-study process

My presentation is the result of a long process within the life of our congregation, embracing both its official structures and many individual members, both clergy and lay. Formally it has been endorsed by our Session (the main governing body of a local church in our Presbyterian system of polity), the Peace Committee, and the Church in the World Commission. As our process went on it gained support from the San Francisco Presbytery, as well as at the national Presbyterian level.

St John's Presbyterian Church, Berkeley, California, USA

We understood from the beginning that our self-study would involve all aspects of the life of our church, including theological issues (the "identity" of women and men before God, and their role within the life of the church, including service as ministers, elders, and deacons, preaching, general participation in worship, ushering, serving communion); issues of the structure of the church and its administration (the status and leadership of men and women on session, as trustees, clerk of session, fund-raising and administration of funds and property); other jobs in the life of the church (teaching, visiting new members or the sick, cooking, preparing communion); and broader concerns (family roles and relationships, positions on or advocacy for women's issues).

It was very important that we understood these as not just "women's issues", of interest only to a particular group, but as reflecting and affecting our whole understanding of ourself as church and of what kind of life we should experience as Christians together within the body of Christ, the church. By looking at our own experience we sought to understand how our church could be faithful *both* to the Christian mandate of the *unity* of the body of Christ *and* the mandate of *renewal* — i.e. mutuality and justice for all members of that body.

We settled on the following elements for our self-study:
— statistical research on membership and participation from annual reports and records of session;
— interviews with individuals and couples representative of the congregation;
— study and discussion in church school classes;
— general discussion of the issues in small groups, in the context of a church meal;
— a retreat for more intensive review of the results, and to look ahead to the future;
— a worship service to celebrate our work together, and to embody some of the insights we had gained;
— a "trial presentation" of the material to be given at this consultation, so that the congregation would have a chance to see our results.

This process occurred within a formal framework:
— an initial presentation and approval of the self-study by appropriate church committees, and by the session;
— at the end, a formal commissioning service, in which the congregation formally sent the report (and the reporter!) on the way;
— there was, finally, a commissioning service by the Presbytery of San Francisco.

I will review the basic elements of our study process, and then indicate the main results of our experience and reflections.

Some historical background

We knew that understanding our own past was essential to our self-understanding in the present. The story of St John's unfolds against the background of the dramatic changes in American society and culture through the 1960s and 1970s. At the beginning of the 1960s, buoyed by high membership and an extremely active programme, we launched an ambitious plan of constructing new church buildings and facilities. We expanded into new areas of ministry, developing work with pre-school children, the elderly, and in many other areas of need.

But soon we were caught in the changes in membership patterns in many American churches at this time, driven by factors such as increasing secularism and the movement of traditional church members away from "inner city" areas to the suburbs. In a fourteen-year period (1961-1975) St John's membership dropped 67 percent, from its peak of 1267 members to only 418, with the most severe drop occurring in the decade 1964 to 1974 (from 1,119 to 451). When the buildings were in the planning stages we had a thriving and growing programme for all ages and activities; when they were completed we could hardly begin to fill them and to use the space.

This dramatic decline in membership is such an important part of our experience that it deserves a closer look. There are several possible explanations; I will mention some of the most likely factors. First there was a general decline in church membership in the 1960s in American "main-line" Protestant churches. Secondly, we developed a more "active" (and, we felt, honest) definition of church membership, leading to a clearing of our membership rolls of long-time inactive "members".

A third factor was certainly the events in Berkeley during the 1960s and later — years of the civil rights movement, the assassination of Dr Martin Luther King, Jr, the "free speech" movement at the university, protests against the war in Vietnam, social activists such as Saul Alinsky, and also rapid social change such as an increasing divorce rate. Unlike many congregations, St John's did not try to escape this reality; it struggled to witness to the gospel within this dynamic, sometimes chaotic situation. This led many churches, including St John's, to become more involved in social and political issues. As one member said: "The world impinged on the church. We were unprepared to deal with it." Some persons left the church over these issues (although others were attracted to our church because of its stands).

A fourth element was that our church leadership took a stronger stand on justice issues, including women's issues such as women serving on the session, women clergy, women preaching, and the language used in worship. Some persons were afraid that this would cause us to lose church members; it would be difficult, they felt, for many to make the transition to working with women in leadership roles. Indeed some were opposed to the very idea of this. A previous minister believes that several people did leave the congregation because of such developments; however some new members said that they were drawn to St John's because of the presence of strong women in leadership positions, and to our commitment, following from our Christian faith, to justice for women.

We have continued to experience dramatic change up to the present time. In the past two years before mid-1985 we have seen a complete turnover of staff, including the pastor, associate minister and the music director. This has also brought new possibilities. Our new pastor is married to a minister; the two have worked as co-pastors in earlier ministries but have not chosen to do that at St John's as their third child has recently been born. The couple baptized the child together with the husband (our present minister) taking the role of parent and his wife serving as minister. For me this was a new experience of both unity and renewal; I saw it as a sign of our hope for a greater community of women and men in our church.

(Incidentally, the pastor wrote to the congregation on "The Sacrament of Baptism", preparing us for the worship, and his text included lengthy quotations from a "World Council [of Churches] draft statement on baptism" — much of which material is now in paragraphs 1 and 9 of the Baptism section of BEM.)

Now our situation is more stable, both in terms of membership and of use of buildings and facilities. As we try to understand the present and plan for the future it is very important to remember the past, but also not to dwell on it or despair because of it.

The interviews

For some this was the "heart" of our self-study process. It was here that persons who had been through these years at St John's reflected most deeply on the changing roles and relationship of women and men in the congregation and in society, and on what this meant for our life as a community and our witness to the gospel. Each person at some point in the interview reached a deep level of insight and truth-telling from his or her experience of community at St John's. It was here that the "voice" of the congregation was heard most directly.

We were looking for a group which would reflect the congregation in its diversity, those who could best remember the past, understand the present, and envision the future, who brought varying views as to whether we had gone too far or not far enough, those who could *reflect theologically* on the theme of the community of women and men in the church.

After consultation with the session, the deacons, and the sponsoring committees within the congregation as well as individuals, some 52 persons were suggested for possible interviews. Further selection led to a final list of sixteen, all of whom readily agreed to be interviewed. This included both women and men, and three married couples who were interviewed as couples.

The questions to be asked were developed with equal care. It was important not to predetermine the issues and answers beforehand, but:
— to get persons to tell the story they needed to tell;
— to get them to speak the truth they knew and felt;
— to enable them to connect fact with feeling, past with future, theology with the everyday world, spontaneity with thoughtful reflection.

A set of draft questions was revised and amended by two groups within the congregation (the Peace Committee and the Church in the World

Among those interviewed were long-time members
of the congregation, Betty and Stewart Kimball

Commission). To allow time for reflection, the questions were sent to each person before the interview, and each was given the option of confidentiality in making their responses. In addition to getting basic information and reflections, I tried to enable persons to connect their personal stories with that of the church, to get at the process of change we had experienced as a congregation, to enable them to connect thoughts with feelings, to look towards future developments, and to lift their vision beyond the present and our own congregation, towards the future and our world as a whole.

The questions asked in the interviews included these:
— What is your connection with St John's, and what leadership roles have you had?

— What kind of community of women and men have you experienced at St John's in the past, and how has this changed?
— Think about one specific area of this change. What was the theological, and the practical, meaning of this?
— How did it come about?
— How did you feel about this? How do you think others felt?
— What happened in the church because of this change? What other changes are most needed now?
— What is important for you about the global and ecumenical context where the story of St John's will be presented?
— Finally, what would you like to talk about that I have left out?

An enormous amount of material came from the interviews — twelve hours of taped conversation, which converted to 350 pages of typed transcript.

The "table talk"

To broaden our consideration of the issues within the life of our congregation we held a session of "table talk". The purpose was not only to include more voices in our study, but to give persons a chance to experience a community of women and men reflecting together about these issues in a small group. This happened in the context of a meal, with each table having men and women, old and young, sharing and reflecting together on issues of women and men within the life of our congregation.

Women and men, young and old together...

The first element of the session was a sharing of what persons had done within the congregation — the various jobs or roles which they had had. These were listed by men and by women, who then indicated which they had found to be most satisfying and least satisfying, and most important and least important.

Each table could choose one of these questions (or if time allowed, more than one):

— Do you think St John's has *gone too far* or *not far enough* in changes to assure full inclusion of women and men in all areas of our life and work? What one change is most needed now — in *either* direction?

— What are the theological or biblical and spiritual reasons for seeking full inclusion and a fuller community of women and men in the church?

— What is the most important thing our congregation can say in this area for a *global* meeting, to a diversity of religious and cultural traditions?

Each table was asked to discuss also these questions:

— Recall and discuss times when you have, or have not, experienced a true community among women and men at St John's. What did this look like, and why did it happen?

— What do you see as the relationship between having a true community of women and men in the the church, and the *unity and renewal* of the church?

The retreat

At this stage it was time for a smaller, representative group to focus on our work so far and to begin thinking about what it might mean for our congregation. Thus we conducted a retreat for some 12 to 15 persons, with the following goals:

— to share the results of the study so far and to reflect together upon their meaning;

— to begin a shift in emphasis from the past to the present and future;

— as a part of this, to look at specific problems, conflicts, and possibilities which we now recognize as a result of our self-study;

— to experience for ourselves a deeper community of women and men;

— to visualize new images of unity and renewal for the people of St John's in the future: these new images included:

  — Sheffield as a model of community;
  — the family as a model for community;
  — the dance as a model of harmony and grace;
  — the quilt as a model of diversity in harmony.

I will not describe the discussions in detail because these will be covered in my conclusions later on. It is significant that we sought consciously to experience deeper community — we had a sense by this time that we had to try to model the theme we had committed ourselves to, that our own meetings and process had to reflect community. You will note also how a historical/programme model (Sheffield), a traditional model (the family), and two artistic/material models (the dance, the quilt) were serving as stimulus and inspiration to our work.

I do want to mention one aspect of our community-building because it became such an integral part of our project, and because it is such a beautiful concept in itself. This was the beginning of work on our "Fabric

"The fabric of the church": a quilt and quilter (Peggy Kitchen)

of the Church" quilt, which later became a central symbol of our connectedness, diversity, beauty, and usefulness in the church, and of our participation in the self-study leading to Prague. Such a quilt is made from squares of cloth, each with its special story and unique significance, brought by different persons. We felt it is a good symbol for God's people because it tells a story, and helps us remember it; it is built of things connected together, and shows our connectedness to each other and to God; it becomes a beautiful treasure; it is useful, practical; it helps people by keeping them warm, and symbolizes nurturing. Colours may clash, but there is a pattern big enough to include them, because God's design is big enough to have room for all. Finally, it's hard to put together, but even harder to take apart!

The worship

One high point of the project was a worship service lifting up the themes of our study, and giving them a liturgical shape and expression. The service united the concern for deeper and fuller community of women and men in the church with concerns for the unity of the church and its mission. Prayers from former World Council of Churches consultations (including Sheffield) and Assemblies were used, as an expression of our commitment to the unity of the church. A communion cloth previously used at St John's was used again, as a symbol of remembering and honouring our own history as a congregation. A man and a woman together removed the cloth from the table, as a statement of dedication to partnership, and mutuality of leadership. Special attention was given to our language in this service, to be sure that it was inclusive of all persons, and as a statement of our commitment to continuing renewal. The elders serving communion were persons who had been interviewed during the study process; and I preached on the theme of unity and wholeness, with the title "Nothing can separate us". People had been asked to bring squares of fabric to be included in the quilt which had been begun on the retreat, and the quilt itself was a central theme in my sermon.

In my journal notes not too long before this I had quoted the following passage from *In Search of Our Mother's Gardens* by Alice Walker:[1]

> In the Smithsonian Institution in Washington D.C. there hangs a quilt unlike any other in the world. In fanciful, inspired, and yet simple and identifiable figures, it portrays the story of the *crucifixion*. It is considered rare beyond price. Though it follows no known pattern of quilt-making, and though it is made of bits and pieces of worthless rags, it is obviously the work of a person of powerful imagination and deep spiritual feeling. Below this quilt I saw a note that says it was made by "an anonymous Black woman in Alabama a hundred years ago".

In a way our quilt was like a "sequel" to that one, and I pointed out that remembering and recalling the crucifixion as that one did — and as we were going to do in our communion service that morning — calls us to remember how we are Christ's body in the world, that community should lead to service.

The commissioning

I would finally like to mention the commissioning service held at St John's, through which its people (along with representatives of the Graduate Theological Union and of the Center for Women and Religion) formally sent me to Prague. The blessing given by Mary Cross, director of the Center for Women and Religion, included these words: "May you be protected in your travel, inspired in your message, loved in your associations, and joyous in your return." The statement of faith and mission by the congregation was taken from a proposed life and mission statement being recommended to the general assembly of our denomination. It echoed the themes we had been struggling with:

> We are one part of the body of Christ: a community of mutual interdependence in which diversity contributes to wholeness.
> We are called to live according to the model of the suffering servant: poured out on behalf of all people.
> We are becoming a new creation by the power of God's grace: to proclaim the good news of Christ and to manifest the justice of God.

There was also a later commissioning by the Presbytery of San Francisco in the context of worship. So you will see that I came to Prague with a strong sense of representing the church at different levels, of bringing with me the experience and hopes of many.

Our experiences and reflections

Our results are not easily summarized, but I want to indicate the most important insights which came through our self-study process. I will begin with some remarks on the meaning of the process itself for us. Throughout the past years, and in the staff changes which our church underwent there were, as you can well imagine, some difficult and painful elements which left our people sad, angry, and confused (and sometimes relieved!). But often no outlets were available for them to express and deal with these feelings, either as individuals or as a congregation.

This self-study has been our chance as a congregation to reflect systematically on this experience. Both our new pastor and I feel that St John's participation in the "case study" has given us an opportunity to deal with it on the level of the issues involved, rather than that of personalities. Contrary to what some might have expected, raising and discussing these matters openly has not "divided" the church; it was the situation which threatened to be divisive, and the study gave us the chance to begin dealing with it. It has helped us recognize, acknowledge and face openly the frustration and pain which has been a part of our life together over the past years of change in the world about us and in our congregation. Thus it has been a helpful and healing process for us.

This succeeded partly because we tried to make the study itself as inclusive as possible, a kind of model of community itself. This was crucial in making sure that the study united rather than divided us. We discovered the need for women and men to teach each other; the value and need in both men and women experiencing the freedom of knowing their own individual gifts; the need to talk about the issues rather than avoiding them; the need to talk about our history, to share our church tradition, to help, as someone put it, 30 year-olds learn from 80 year-olds.

Although we focused on issues of women and men, we recognized that there are many other aspects in our experience. And having addressed discrimination by sex, we recognize that there are many other differences between people based on their interests, styles, personalities, etc. which can be overcome only by knowing each other at a deep level as persons.

We learned that while we had diverse opinions about whether we had gone "too far" or not far enough, we agreed that the main criteria should not be gaining or losing membership but whether we acted as we "had to" from the gospel. In other words we recognized a common value — our Christian faith — even while we differed about its interpretation on specific issues. It was this sense of belonging to the same community, imperfect as it was, that enabled us to remain together even when we differed and struggled over issues.

This was symbolized by one especially hopeful sign. This is the fact that throughout all our changes, the percentage of women and men in St John's has remained virtually the same. Although the membership as a whole has declined, there is no indication of a "mass exodus" of either women or of men. Women as a group did not flee the congregation because they felt under-represented in leadership; nor did men as a group leave when women began to assume increased leadership roles. In fact a higher percentage of men now attends St John's than did 10 years ago, as the percentage of women has declined from 66 percent in 1974 to 60 percent in 1984. Through our changes we have been moving towards a community that was *more* balanced, not less.

Now I want to indicate the two central themes which emerged from the interviews and were reflected, in other ways, throughout our study as a whole. The first was the theme of *family*. This was raised by many persons, eager to reflect in a Christian context on such social issues as changing roles within the family, new possibilities of family relationships, and the loss of some traditional understandings of the family. They raised profound questions about the value of the family, the meaning of "home", and the importance of traditional family roles. They asked what is a Christian response to the growing numbers of single persons, single parents, divorce, women heads of households (now a major population group in the United States), and other issues which our tradition of the "nuclear family" has not prepared the church to deal with. They asked: "What really is a family? In light of all this, what is the meaning of the traditional understanding of the church as a 'family'? How does the church minister to *all* its members in the midst of these new social realities?"

We did not settle on answers to these questions, but obviously the symbol of family was deeply important to our congregation. This raises the question of how single persons can be brought within this symbol rather than feeling excluded by it.

A second and closely related issue was that of roles of women and men. This was a broad discussion, and some men spoke very honestly about their embarrassment with assuming "feminine" roles (e.g. helping wash up after church suppers) — while they would do it if necessary, they resented this being presented as a "principle or necessity". But we returned again and again to the issue of *leadership roles of women* at all levels in the life of the church, on church boards and commissions, the session, as deacons; as clergy; of leadership in women's organizations; and the unique role of the pastor's wife.

For some, traditional patterns remained normative. Some women and men felt that male leadership was a "given" for family life, and that male leadership in churches might be necessary to keep men involved in the church.

Community expressed through shared ministry: the Rev. Sandra W. Park and the Rev. Thomas McKnight, associate pastor and pastor of St John's

Others struggled to accept new possibilities and options in their lives. We experienced again and again how difficult it is to change, and how much pain can be involved. A striking example was one of the first women to be elected elder, who had participated in functions of church government, but still hesitated to offer the elements in communion. It was a very moving moment when, as a result of reflection and involvement in the study, she felt able to assume this additional role; she experienced this as a liberation and the acceptance of new possibilities in her life.

In our reflections we began to identify distinctive priorities and leadership patterns as typical of women and of men, and we saw how these differences had been reflected in congregational discussion and decisions about the use of money, buildings and facilities, about mission priorities, language in worship, and the role of women ministers.

It is important to remember that we were not speaking generally or in the abstract, but on the basis of our experience with changing leadership patterns in our congregation, and with women in leadership roles. For fifteen years now the session has been about 50 percent men and 50 percent women; the Board of Deaconesses was dissolved in 1966, in favour of using the term "deacon" for either men or women (and since then men and women have served as deacons in about equal numbers). For fifteen years we have had women on the professional ministerial staff (though never as the senior staff or sole pastor, or even in full-time service). For years we have as a congregation encouraged women seminary students and supported many women who are now pastors elsewhere. Women have been most active in developing the new ministries of our congregation, such as day care centres and programmes for the elderly. And of course they have been extremely active in education, groups and activities, and providing "support" for all areas of our life.

This makes it all the more striking that although both session and the deacons now have both men and women, the functional committees still tend to be more one or the other, men continue to predominate (as chair*men*) on commissions, and the central structures of programmatic and financial power in our congregation have continued to be "male bastions": only one or two women have ever been clerk of Session; only one or two women have been chair of the Budget Commission; the Trustees have had only token representation of women; and the Resources and Management Committee has been heavily dominated by men.

We realized that in a sense St John's was actually "two churches", claiming a common life, sharing one name, building and worship, but distinct in the kind and *level* of participation, on one side "culture bearers" and on the other "money and power keepers", with the women providing support services, fund-raising, educational and caring programmes, and emotional nurture in a whole range of activities and groups, and the men exercising authority over basic programme priorities, spending of funds, and buildings and facilities. We experienced this division between the "men's church" and the "women's church" as painful, and damaging to our life as a congregation. As I will mention later on, overcoming this division is our greatest challenge at the present time.

This led us to reflect on the nature of community, and on what promotes (or hinders) the growth of community. We were clear about what community was *not*. We had noted from our own experience that a breakdown of community often occurred when problems needed to be solved — that the men in the group often tended to "take over" with a particular style of problem-solving, anxious to get "results" quickly and efficiently. Others noted that community was lost when others simply told them what to do, leaving no room for movement, for one's own style. It was abundantly clear that there would be no unity *or* renewal when one person, or a few, were "calling the shots".

We had learned that God delivers and frees us in order to connect us — to God, to ourselves, to each other, and to the earth on which we live. We saw that if this "connectedness" negates or denies the freedom or wholeness of any part of it, then it is *not* the community that God in Christ offers and enables, and that if we are connected to God's love through Christ, then nothing can undo or separate us from it.

We recognized then that looking at the community of women and men is an issue of justice, and an issue of compassion. If any one group in the church retains or attains power and the cost is disempowerment, exclusion, or the demeaning of another, we are not being faithful to the gospel. If theology "looks the other way" on issues of justice or compassion, or chooses one to the exclusion of the other, then we are not being faithful.

Thus adequate and genuine participation is a key to community. In fact in our experience participation is *crucial*. Church events where lay persons were not included in the planning tended to isolate them, and reinforce an idea of the church as "belonging" to the clergy. When lay-persons were involved in planning, it was equally important to avoid "cliques" forming among them; these could also assume control, isolating those who are "outsiders" and making them feel cut off from the whole church. On the other hand, community appeared to develop when there was give and take between persons, when they allowed themselves to be vulnerable, when they were sensitive to recognize what skills others have, and what abilities they want to share with the congregation.

We found that the concern for community did not lead us to be self-centred as a congregation. The last question I asked in each interview was: "What do you have to say to the global and ecumenical context where this study will be presented?" One answer was particularly striking. It was a laywoman who said: "I believe there isn't any issue on the face of this earth that will be solved until people have an individual feeling and sense of God, and you cannot have that, and a personal knowledge of God, if you are cut out of the church. And if sexism is continually practised around the world in the churches, then there will be a lot of issues not solved because 50 percent of the population will not have that feeling and will not be able to participate." Thus deeper community does not exist for itself, but is a way to more extensive mission and service.

Conclusion

Such is the story of St John's. As we look to the future, what are our needs, hopes and dreams as a congregation? Our deep hope was that in the process of developing this study, God's people at St John's would be enabled to hear and to talk to each other in new ways, ways that enable us to envision a future where our sense of community with each other would be deeper and stronger and we would all be empowered to work for God's justice and wholeness in the church and in the world.

We are still a diverse congregation, and there are still different feelings among us about the right way to use our space, how to maintain it, and how to raise the money to employ the staff who can use the buildings and facilities as an instrument of our mission and ministry. But although these differences remain they do not seem as threatening or destructive as before.

The greatest challenge we face now is to incorporate what we have experienced and learned in our self-study into our life as a congregation. I spoke earlier about our sense of being "two churches". We have identified divisions within our common life, and begun to face the pain which they cause. Now we seek to heal the divisions, and integrate these "two churches" into the one body of Christ at St John's. We ask your prayers as we continue on our journey.

NOTE

[1] *In Search of our Mothers' Gardens: Womanist Prose*, New York, Harcourt, Brace, Jovanovich, 1983.

● I would like to express thanks to Faith and Order (World Council of Churches), the staff of St John's, the Session, the Church in the World Committee, Peace Committee, Membership Committee, and Women's Association of St John's; thanks for financial support from various St John's committees, from Faith and Order (WCC), from the San Francisco Presbytery, and from the Vocations Agency of the Presbyterian Church; thanks to the Center for Women and Religion, Graduate Theological Union, Berkeley; thanks to those who were involved as researchers, typists, photographers, retreat coordinators, dictating machine operators, computer operators, and a quilter; thanks to all those who were interviewed, to many individuals for their suggestions, support, encouragement, confidence and prayers; and finally thanks to all the people of St John's for being willing "to have the whole world watching".

"Men and Women: Equal Partners in the Christian Community": an Orthodox Point of View

GENNADIOS LIMOURIS

The following paper is not a philosophical essay but a theological reflection on the foundations of an authentic attitude to the role and place of women and men in the ecclesial community from an Orthodox standpoint, in an ecclesiological perspective and, above all, in the light of their fundamental being. It is not just a question of achieving a certain objectivity here, i.e., going beyond the usual myths, stereotypes and prejudices, but above all of remaining within an Orthodox tradition which has so much to teach us about this theme; in other words treating women and men, partners "divinized" by the Creator, as subjects and not merely as objects.

What we have to do, therefore, is to identify certain profoundly spiritual theological truths which can provide the basis for concrete attitudes enabling us to reunite certain fundamental values which are the living source of our analysis. In the last analysis the standpoint we must adopt here is not that of mythology or desires but that of an ecclesiological vision illuminated by the unity of the Church, within the present need for the renewal of the human community.

It seems that generations of ecclesiastical writers, celibate by vocation or psychological conditioning, have ignored or rejected the encounter of the first man and the first woman in a plenitude and an innocence — a nostalgia which can still be discerned even in the desperate search for

● This paper originally appeared in *Church and Theology*, Vol. VI, 1985.

● Rev. Dr Gennadios Limouris (Ecumenical Patriarchate) is on the staff of the Commission on Faith and Order, World Council of Churches.

eroticism; this "great mystery" restored by Christ. The *eros* of the beginning has simply been equated with genitality and closely linked with the Fall of humanity. Is it not the case, for certain church fathers, that God created woman in anticipation of the Fall and in order to ensure the continuance of the species, the only justification for marriage being, adds the great Russian theologian Paul Evdokimov ironically, to produce a monk from time to time?[1]

It was in terms of the metaphor of *eros*, moreover, that the miracle of Cana was performed. It was Christ's first miracle and the account of it is read in the Orthodox marriage service. It was the vision of it which confirmed the vocation of Alyosha in *The Brothers Karamazov*. Human love ceases then to be "the loss of virginity" but is its highest fulfilment in the divine. At this ignition point, says Berdyaev, the transfiguration, the renewal of the world, begins.[2]

I. Men and women in the vision of God

The difference between men and women is a radical and profound one which reaches into the depths of consciousness and affects every form of human behaviour. It is at the very origin of life. It is stated in Genesis (1:27): "God created man in his own image, in the image of God He created him; male and female He created them." His will was that they should be one, that they should be "one flesh" (Gen. 2:24). Physically and psychologically men and women are complementary.

Primarily, of course, they are defined in relation to God their creator; they are each in the image of God; they are each called to be "divinized". This is their fundamental and ultimate role in the universe. But they are in the image of God *also* in their union and the unity of their love: the one is *with* and *for* the other. Each is defined in relation to the other. Yet it is also clear from Genesis that when men and women turn away from God, when God is no longer present in their union, they lose their original innocence. They then become conscious of a void within themselves; they experience anguish; they become conscious of their nudity. It is then that the man accuses the woman and seeks to dominate her. Their "agapic" unity is wounded, broken, divided, they become rivals. They are no longer one flesh.

They are then in danger of turning inwards in themselves and shutting themselves up in a closed world. They at once seek power and possession in the hope of filling the void in their own souls. But the really important thing for a human being is to be open towards others and towards one another, to create links with them, to enter into a world of love, of communion (koinonia) and giving, of sharing and welcome. We cannot do this fully, however, unless we are reconciled with God our Creator and have rediscovered God's presence within ourselves.

The attraction of men and women for one another also tends towards transcendence of another isolation, that of death. Beyond and above individual attraction and choice, at the inmost centre of their being, there is a summons to communicate life to a new human being.

The Christian vision of the human being is very different from the vision which is extolled in industrialized societies. In being made flesh, the Word comes to reveal the supreme dignity of *each person*, and above all, of the poorest, and to summon them to life in a community united as one body, an ecclesial community. The last are the first. The values are not power or social influence, wealth or human glory, or even individual liberty as an end in itself. The values are those of the love which is practised in this "body".

II. The charisms of women and men

According to St Paul's luminous image, the Church is the "whole body, joined and knit together by every joint with which it is supplied, when each part is working properly" which "makes bodily growth and upbuilds itself in love" (Eph. 4:16). The context of this verse clearly refers to charisms received by each for the service of the whole Church where they complement each other. The charismatic reality of the human being is therefore essential for our theme.

The disturbance of the balance in history makes it easy to ask the wrong questions. "The question of woman" is one example. When men ask themselves this question without asking the question about themselves, they isolate themselves, cut themselves off from the limpid springs of life, set a question mark against their intelligence and show themselves to be out of date.

In a thoroughly masculine world where patriarchy prevails, men use their minds to rationalize human nature and life, lose their cosmic connections with heaven and nature as well as with women as the complementary mystery of their own being.

Woman has her way of being, her own mode of existence, the gift of weaving her being with her distinctive relation to God, to others, to herself. Despite the distortions from which woman sometimes suffers in history, at the deepest level of her being she preserves the mystery of her nature and her charisms: all designated by St Paul in the amazingly rich symbol of "the veil" (1 Cor. 11), an evident sign of the sacred. The great whore of Babylon (Rev. 17), on the contrary, profanes and degrades her womanhood *qua* religious essence of her femininity. She tears her "veil", strips, shrugs off her feminine mystery, the *fiat* decreeing her eternal motherhood. And this is the mystery which every woman must unravel if she is to read in it her own destiny, her own vocation, her own charisms.

What is set forth in the biblical account of the first pair — Adam-Eve — is the original archetype of the consubstantiality of complementary principles. These complementary principles are polarized by the Fall and henceforth the choice is between the struggle of opposites, on the one hand, and on the other, the mutual acceptance and complementarity of differences with the object of making of them one "new creature" in Christ.

Moreover, men pass beyond their own being, are more external to themselves: their charism, their gift for expansion, directs their gaze beyond themselves. They fill the world with their creative energies, and assert themselves as master and conqueror, engineer and builder.

Alongside himself man receives woman, his helper. At one and the same time she is his betrothed, his wife, his mother. A woman, more interiorized, is quite comfortable within the limits of her being, whereby she fills the world with her radiant presence. As "the glory of the man" (1 Cor. 11:7), in her luminous purity, woman is as it were a mirror reflecting the face of man, revealing him to himself and correcting him in the process. She thus helps man to understand himself and to realize the meaning of his own being; she completes him by revealing his destiny, for it is *via* the woman that man becomes more easily what he is. The words of St Peter (1 Pet. 3:4) are addressed to every woman and epitomize a gospel of womanhood concerning every woman's spiritual motherhood. This passage gives a very precise definition of the fundamental charism of women: the bringing to birth of the human being hidden within her heart, *homo cordis absconditus*.

Men tend more to be interested only in their own cause; the woman's maternal instinct, on the contrary, as at the wedding in Cana (John 2:1-10),[3] at once reveals the thirst even of men for the spirit and finds the eucharistic spring wherewith to quench that thirst. It is this ontological relationship of mother-child which makes woman, Eve = "source of life", watch over all life and being, protect life and the world. In virtue of her interiorized and universal charism of "maternity", every woman is drawn towards the hungry and needy, and this charism wonderfully epitomizes the essence of the feminine: whether virgin or wife, every woman is mother *in aeternum*; this is the "sacramental character" imprinted in her very deepest being.

If masculine love can be defined by saying that "to love is to have need of", for the woman "to love is to fill that need", to precede and anticipate it. "When Jesus saw his mother, and the disciple whom he loved standing near, he said to his mother, 'Woman, behold, your son'" (John 19:26). This is a fundamental dominical saying which makes the Virgin Mary, the Theotokos, a figure of the Church-Mother, and every woman an ecclesial being. The eternal virgin, the eternal feminine and the eternal maternal are rooted in the *Magna Mater*.

The Bible enables us to see woman as the predestined meeting point between God and man.

Whereas the male participates in the Incarnation by his silence in the person of St Joseph, it is the woman who utters the *fiat* for us all. Corresponding to the creative *fiat* of the Father is the humble *fiat* of the "handmaid of the Lord". It would have been impossible for Christ to have taken flesh and blood if these had not been given freely, as gift, pure offering, by humanity in the person of Mary. The Virgin is the meeting point, the crossroads and the gathering place for the two *fiats*.

Figure of the Church, the Virgin is a personal embodiment of its principle of motherly protection; the praying woman is the prayer of the Church, the one who intercedes.

Chastity, in Greek, signifies wholeness and integrity, the essence of the power to unite. An ancient liturgical prayer addresses to the *most pure Theotokos* the words: "By thy love, bind my soul!": make unity, the soul, spring forth from the totality of physical conditions.

Men, moreover, extend themselves into the world by means of the tools they create; women do so by the gift of themselves. They are linked to the rhythms of nature in the depths of their being. If the characteristic of men is to *act*, the characteristic of women is to *be*, and this is the religious state *par excellence*. Ecstatic man exists in the extension of himself, in the projection of his genius outside himself with the object of mastering the world; *enstatic* woman is turned in the direction of her being, in the direction of being. The feminine is practised at the level of the ontological structure; it is not the word but *being*, the womb of creation. It is the manifestation of Holiness, this holiness of being which the demons find intolerable.

III. Symbols in history

In the *Didascalia*, the feminine is connected ontologically with the mystery of the Holy Spirit: "The deacon has the place of Christ and you are to love him; you are to honour the deaconesses in the place of the Holy Spirit." This is why the woman is called the "altar" and represents prayer in the symbolism of the eucharistic assembly. She is the image of the adoring soul, humankind transformed into prayer.

In the famous fresco of St Calixtus in Rome, the man raises his hand above the bread of the offertory and it is the sacrificer, the bishop, the one who acts, who celebrates. Behind him is the praying woman, the *orante*, pure offering and total gift. Exercising her charism of protection, she lifts up life, the world, human beings, towards God. She, then, the woman under the sign of the Spirit who "broods" (using the Hebrew word from the creation narrative), is a sign of the paraclete, the Advocate, and the Comforter.

The ordained priesthood, the episcopate, the priests and deacons, is a masculine role of witness. The bishop attests the saving validity of the sacraments and has the power to celebrate them; he has the charism of supervising the purity of the deposit of faith and he exercises pastoral authority. The ministry of women appertains to the feminine royal priesthood; this does not consist in the functions attributed to it but in its very *nature*. The ordained ministry (the priest-hood) is not found among her charisms and would be a betrayal of her being. The personalized vocation in the Virgin Mary, however, is not inferior but quite simply different, and here we come very close to the heart of our subject.

Monastic spirituality is extremely revealing here. Whereas at all other levels women seem sometimes to be inferior beings to men, at the charismatic level, on the contrary, there is complete equality between men and women. Clement of Alexandria notes: "The virtue of man and of woman is one and the same, a conduct of the same nature."[4] Theodoret of Cyr notes that women "have struggled not less but even more than men... with a feebler nature they have shown the same determination as men"[5]. Their strong point is the "divine charity" and a special gift of attachment to Christ. No one regards them as inferiors; they are deemed capable of providing monastics (men and women) with spiritual guidance on equal terms with men. A charismatic woman, *theophotistos*, illuminated by God, is given the title of *ammas* or spiritual mother.[6] More often than not they are the "mothers" of their monastery just as St Pachomius was the "father" of his. So it is that in the monastic tradition we find an Abbé Isaiah compiling a collection of sayings of "mothers", the *Materikon*, similar to the *Paterikon* of spiritual sayings of the Desert Fathers.

IV. Differences and likenesses

Men and women are, above all, persons created in the image of the personal and trinitarian God in whom unity and difference coexist ineffably in the equal dignity of persons. The definition of "person" — a term introduced into philosophical language *via* trinitarian theology — implies its transcendence in respect of biological, social and cultural dimensions. Like the ineffable personal God, "the human being is a mystery" according to Gregory of Nyssa. Persons fulfill their potential, however, in different ways. The inexpressible and non-objectifiable personal difference is compatible with a sexually differentiated nature. According to Genesis, this is the will of the Creator: "So God created man (ἄνθρωπος) in his own image; male (ἀνήρ) and female he created them" (Gen. 1:27).[7]

In the present stage of empirical psychology, the differences between men and woman are difficult to determine. Certain stereotypes may be mentioned: strength as opposed to weakness, gentleness as opposed to violence, intuition and spontaneity as opposed to rationality and self-mastery — none of these are an exclusive feature of one or the other sex. In large measure, the ideal man and the ideal woman are the products of historical cultures. The Orthodox Christian will insist that in Christ and the Theotokos he finds the revelation of the eternal archetypes. Is this to say that, beyond biology and social psychology, there is no deeper universal archetypal profile corresponding to them in the human ψυχή (soul)? There is one question arising, however: Is Mary not the expression of humanity as a whole, men and women? The one who receives, the one in whom the God-man is to come?

In contrast to abstract idealism, Orthodox anthropology attaches great importance to the body. Following the direction of biblical anthropology and language, it emphasizes the structure and symbolic significance of human bodiliness; by means of the images and metaphors made possible by this symbolism, we are able to envisage the Wholly Other God. Such is the dignity of the human body, female as well as male; the basis of the virtual transfiguration of all its activities in the radiant light of Christ, beyond the Fall and sin. This awareness of a symbolism of the body and of the possibility of transfiguration would appear to be characteristic of Orthodoxy. In biblical anthropology, moreover, the human being, a person sexually differentiated, is understood as a simultaneously psychosomatic and spiritual whole which is called to become the temple of the Holy Spirit. Without destroying them, respecting in both men and women their distinctive mode of "being in the world" and of being "in the image of God", the one Spirit incorporates them into the Church, the Body of Christ (σῶμα Χριστοῦ). From an angle particularly evident in the prophet Hosea and later on in St Paul, masculinity points to Him like whom humankind is not and never will be, namely the transcendent God, the Creator, the Giver. Femininity, on the contrary, announces the mystery of the immanent God, the God who in His grace spreads out over the whole of His creation with the purpose of saving and purifying it and making it fruitful. The vocation of woman is to announce what will be, and is already in process of being born in her: the new humanity deified in Christ by the grace of the Holy Spirit.

At the same time, however, the Church teaches not only the infinite distance between humanity and God but also their infinite closeness. In virtue of the creation "in God's likeness", in virtue of the Incarnation, the cross of salvation and the resurrection, humanity in its spiritual and psychosomatic wholeness can become translucent to the Divine Light. This is the significance of the veneration of ikons; ikons of Christ and of his saints, ikons of the Theotokos "more venerable than the cherubim and incomparably more glorious than the seraphim". In the Church's consciousness, Mary is at one and the same time the figure of the Church-Humanity and, as Tatiana Goritcheva writes, the figure of a "femaleness which has been purified even in its bodily and unconscious aspects".[8]

V. Partners in communion with God

To collaborate with God is to participate in the work of the Triune God; in other words, to become a human being in communion. Just as there is one God in three persons who continue in an eternal movement of mutual love and these three persons reflect absolute diversity and each reflect a no less absolute unity — so too in Christ, in the expansion of this divine unity-diversity, we are all members one of another; in the most realistic sense, there is one single human being. Becoming a collaborator with God is to know that we are no longer separate, that we are not only alike but even identical, one sole being, one sole reality, one sole body, across time and space. To understand this, to do so with our whole being, is precisely to become ourselves without even setting out to do so.

The Body of Christ (σῶμα Χριστοῦ) is the scene of a permanent Pentecost; the Spirit's tongues of flame divide, each illuminating from within a freedom, a vocation, the unique distinctiveness of a face. The more rooted a human being is in the Body of Christ, the more he or she is animated by this flame; ultimately, in complete sanctity, the limits of personality or rather *their* personalities are abolished and the whole of humanity is in the individual man or woman; his or her face becomes an ikon. St Macarius the Great said: "It happens to those who have been worthy to become children of God and to be born from above of the Holy Spirit that they weep and are afflicted for the whole human race, shed tears as they pray for the total Adam... Sometimes, too, such love and joy kindle their hearts that, if it were possible, they would embrace all human beings, the evil and the good alike, in their hearts. Sometimes, taken with the humility of the Spirit, they so prostrate themselves before each human being as to consider themselves as the very last and least of all."[9]

Being a human being in communion today, whether a man or a woman, means hastening the advent of a universal consciousness and a justice embracing the whole of humanity. It is to join with all men and women of goodwill in the struggle to build and renew a worldwide civilization in which all human beings, all nations, all races, all cultures can find a place in a diverse unity, towards which the reunited Church, a free communion of local churches, should be humbly working as leaven.

For a Christian, the personal and the spiritual, the freedom of individual consciousness in the Holy Spirit, is the infrastructure of history. This is why we should try to "finalize" the coming civilization by a total vision of humankind in the divinized-humanity, of human beings who not only need bread but also meaning, since, as Dostoevsky used to say, "beauty will save the world". The material underdevelopment of some undoubtedly reflects only the spiritual underdevelopment of others. In these global developments, therefore, there can be no conflict between contemplation and an active love which thirsts for justice, but only the demonstration of their indispensable interconnection.

All these things, then, belong together, cross-fertilize one another and are interconnected: the contemplative's prayer, the shining example of model communities, veritable "workshops" of creative love, humble daily service, "structural" reforms or revolutions, the prophetic and aesthetic inventiveness of culture. These all belong together, and for us Christians, it all begins in the transformation of the stony heart into a heart of flesh, in the transformation of our basic elementary relationships, so that every eucharistic community of women and men may be something of an attempt to create communion.

VI. Ekklesia: place of rebirth and renewal

The *Ekklesia* or Church is neither primarily nor fundamentally a matter of sociology. The institution is simply the empirical vestige or trace of the "mystery". Above all, the Church is the power of resurrection, the sacrament of the Risen One who communicates to us his own resurrection. The New Eve is born from the open side of Christ, as Eve was born from Adam's side. From the open side. From the pierced side of Christ issued forth water and blood (John 19:34), the water of baptism and the blood of eucharist. In this connection Origen says: "Christ bathed the universe in divine and sanctifying torrents. He caused a spring of living water to flow for the thirsty from the wound opened up by the lance in his side." "From the wound in Christ's side sprang forth the Church which he made his bride."[10]

Deep down, the Church is simply the world in process of transfiguration, the world which in Christ is becoming transparent to the paradisiacal plenitude. The paradise of the presence is in fact Christ himself who was able to tell the believing thief crucified beside him: "This day thou shalt be with me in paradise" (Luke 23:43). The world-in-Christ, the new heaven and the new earth, in other words, the renewed heaven and earth, come to us in the sacraments (or "mysteries"), moreover, are only aspects of the global sacramental nature of the Church whose heart, whose sun, is the "mystery of mysteries", the eucharist.

This eucharist, however, constitutes the dynamic "heart" of the ecclesial community in which men and women each find their diaconal and active role.

Moreover, in the ecclesiastical community, which is so deeply divided in our world by race, nationality, language, class, labour, education, position and wealth, men and women are recreated in the Church by the Holy Spirit. On all of them alike, the Church imprints a divine form. From the Church, all receive a unique indestructible nature, one which forbids us in future to take any account of the many deep differences which affect them. All are thereby united in a truly catholic way. In the Church, no one is in any sense separated from community; all are founded, so to speak, in each other by the simple and indivisible strength of the faith. Christ is thus all in all, Christ who takes everything into himself in accord with the infinite and wholly wise power of his goodness, as a centre on which all lines converge in order that the creatures of the one God may not remain strangers or enemies in the absence of a common ground where they can show forth their friendship and peace.

As "image of the eucharist" therefore, the community becomes, as Cyril of Jerusalem says, a eucharistic community *par excellence* and is integrated with others into the unity of the universal Church, since, across time and space, there is one single eucharist celebrated by Christ our

Great High Priest. This multiple unity is expressed in a whole series of trinitarian analogies. It takes shape around centres of communion whose "concern" it is, i.e. whose responsibility it is, to ensure the circulation of information, witness, life and love among the local communities. For a local community manifests the one Church only as it is in communion (κοινωνία) with all other local communities, just as the divine Persons only exist in each other.

These trinitarian analogies are found in the so-called *Apostolic Constitutions*, paragraph 34: analogous to the role of the Father within the Trinity, the ministry of the first bishop is a "kenosis" which is to ensure a loving "coinherence" (περιχώρησις) between the local churches.[11]

The eucharist within the community defines not only the life of the Church and the communion between Christians but also their manner of life in the world, which is to be a life of sharing, service, a constant striving for the *koinonia* of men and women and the transfiguration of the earth. For each human being (man and woman) is called to "give thanks (eucharist) in all things" (1 Thess. 5:18), i.e. to become a "eucharistic human being".[12] The inward appropriation of the eucharist, in particular by the invocation of the name of Jesus, is one of the fundamental themes of Christian spirituality. Eucharistic collaboration, moreover, as a means of learning new relationships between men and women, and between humankind and the material world, must necessarily have a prophetic dimension.[13]

VII. Dialogue with Christ in the Church

The Church is "theandric" (Θεανδρική)[14] in *nature* (or constitution), the union of all that exists, or rather destined to embrace all that exists: God and the creation. It is the Body of Christ and therefore both one with him and distinct from him. The Church is immanent and has within it the transcendent community of the persons of the Trinity, which is filled with a boundless love for the world. Basically, the Church participates in the same movement which inspires the eternal act of the Persons of the Holy Trinity. The Church is not the salvation of men and women but is more closely bound up with it than time is to God's timelessness or space to God's spacelessness. It is holy because it is the expression on earth of the eternal love, life and omnipotence of the Trinity. It is the scene of the twofold movement of the incarnation in which divine and human energies are called to become the theandric energies of the believer and of God.

The Church's place in the world also rests on Christ, who unites God and the creation. "Christ", affirms Father Staniloae, "is the Pantocrator of the creation. He conducts a dialogue with the whole Church, understood as a symbolic partner, and thus dwells in a living manner in this house, which is his own house and in which every believer is a distinctive personal stone."[15]

Humanity itself, therefore, has been created partly as a body, partly as destined fully to become a body. Before being brought together in Christ, it is already a body in dialogue (σῶμα ἐν διαλόγῳ); once gathered together in him, it is a body in dialogue in an even more symbolic way.

In Orthodox Byzantine iconography, there is one ikon which depicts splendidly this unity of the Church in which each member is respected. This ikon shows human beings arriving in Paradise, gathered together in Abraham's bosom. The figure of the Patriarch is above the others, larger than all, yet not diminishing the distinct reality of each of the elect. Even though Abraham did not live in the historical time of the Incarnation, he is rightly called the "father of believers" because he was the first to know God as a Person, the first to have believed in Him and in His promise of the salvation to come in Christ.

VIII. The challenge of learning in a renewed community

No reading of the present situation in the world would be in any sense Christian if it aroused in us feelings of either fear or despair, and the foregoing presentation of the facts would be misleading if no reference were made to the Christian hope. The hope of the Christian has its anchor in what lies above and beyond the conflict. For those who believe in God, the last word is not spoken in this life.

No temporal circumstances, however dark and menacing, can touch the foundations of our faith. The ground of our confidence is the Word of God spoken in Christ. In the light of that revelation the forces of darkness have been robbed of their power. This doom is already writ. Our efforts may fail, but the triumph of God is sure. We neither made the world nor have we to bear the responsibility for directing its course — that is in stronger and safer hands. Our sole responsibility is in creaturely dependence to live each day in the circumstances in which we are given the task assigned to us, and to entrust the rest to God.

In that confidence our hearts and minds may remain untroubled under threatening skies and in the face of apparently insurmountable difficulties, guarded by the peace of God which passes human understanding.

Reasons for hope may be found also in the situation itself. If the Gospel contains the word which is needed to redeem humankind from its present errors and lack of the great periods in the history of the Christian Church.

We have the opportunity today to bear an effective Christian witness, "martyria", to the present world as a whole at a critical moment in history when humankind stands at the parting of the ways. The very strength of the opposition may be the means of opening the eyes of the Church to the depth and richness of the truth regarding human life and destiny which has been committed to its charge. Out of the strain of the conflict may be born a new assurance, a new certainty, a new heroism, a new creation. As Nietzsche taught, it is the greatness of the danger that reveals the knight or rather that creates him. Or, as Christians would rather say, God uses such occasions as a means of educating His children and making them worthy to be called His sons and daughters. Thus hope impels action.

By its central affirmations the Church is committed to the belief that the life of humankind finds its meaning and fulfilment in a community of persons.

God has spoken to us in His Son. He has revealed Himself through His cosmos. The word — used in the widest sense to include every form of self-expression — is the means by which persons communicate with persons. In addressing us, God invites a response from us. He asks for trust, loyalty and obedience. Through our response to the word addressed to us we become responsible persons, and only through such a response to the Father of our spirits can we become truly persons. God adopts us as sons and daughters and admits us to a life of communion (κοινωνία) and personal fellowship with Himself. His word to us is a word which binds us to our fellow human beings and unites us with them in a community where love rules. God bids us serve Him as His free sons and daughters in the only way we can serve Him by "ministering" (διακονεῖν) to the needs of our fellow human beings. What we do to them, He accepts as done to Himself. The love of God and the love of our neighbour are inseparable. For Christians the worship and service of a personal God, whom we have learned to recognize as our Father, and the relation of responsibility and love towards our fellow human beings — relations which can exist only between persons — are the supreme and ultimate goal. The Church is the community of those who have been redeemed from a self-centred existence, which is death, into the objectivity and freedom of a life of personal response to the demands of persons, a life of trust and loyalty of faith and love.

The reasons for emphasizing this central element in Christianity is that it is precisely this understanding of human life that is denied by all doctrines that are in the ascendant today. It is denied by those who maintain that the final and decisive factor in life is blood or race.

Humankind according to this view derives its being from below, from some blind, irrational power, and not from the word of the living God, which comes to it from above. The priority and supremacy of the personal is rejected by those who contend that people's ultimate loyalty is owed to a nation or a state. It is repudiated by those who hold that people's primary need is bread and that their life is wholly determined by material realities. The Christian doctrine that persons can be persons only in community is equally opposed to the view which regards human beings as individuals existing in their own right, concerned primarily with developing their own "personality", free to pursue their self-centred aims, unfettered by bonds which unite them inseparably with their fellow human beings. Against this self-seeking individualism the modern collectivist systems are a justifiable reaction. But notwithstanding the profound differences between them, they all have their origin in the same secular mind from which individualism sprang and in the same mistaken confidence in the self-sufficiency of humankind, and consequently they are in danger of setting up forms of collectivism which, as much as the individualism they replace, are a denial of the true nature and meaning of community which is love and trust between persons, in fellowship and mutual service.

The Christian belief in the supremacy of the personal is the antithesis of the individualism of the humanistic cult of personality. It is the recognition of the bounds set to the infinite expansion of the individual self by the obligations owed to other selves. There is no way in which one can be a person except through the give and take, the claim and response, of personal relationships. Persons can be persons only in mutuality. Persons and community are correlative terms. Neither can exist without the other. The habit of thinking of personality as something that belongs to the individual in isolation and then asking how this isolated individual can enter into community with other persons is fundamentally mistaken. Personal life is in its essence the acceptance of the responsibilities of community. The false view of personality as something existing apart from community is so deeply engrained that there may be an advantage in expressing the same truth in different phraseology. To assert the supremacy of the personal is the same as to say that the true and deepest meaning of life is found in encounter. Life is most real when we find ourselves confronted by another self in its separate, independent existence; when a word is addressed to us from without to which we must answer, when a claim is made on us to which we must respond. To subordinate the other to our own view, or will, is to destroy fellowship or community. For community implies the continued presence of the others in their otherness. There can be no community without the unrelieved tension of contrasting points of view each of which renounces any claim to absoluteness. Community with the other may be realized not only between individual persons but also between groups, between class and class, nation and nation. It is the attitude of reverence and responsibility towards other selves. If the foregoing statements — with whatever amendments and improvements of so bold a presentation may be necessary — are true, Christianity has something to say which is directly relevant to the present situation. The Church has the word to speak which more than any other might recall humankind to the true path and the renewal of the world to sanity. Accepted in all its implications, it is a condemnation and corrective of the errors and perversions of the new collectivist philosophies and no less of the selfish individualism against which they are in revolt. If the Church were able to speak this word with understanding, conviction and authority, the divorce which is widely felt to exist between the current preaching, teaching and acting of Christianity and the realities of actual life would be overcome. No one who reads attentively the literature of our time can fail to be aware that Christianity has ceased in large measure to be an integrative and directive force in human thinking and feeling; that because it lacks relevance to the actual problems of human life, it can no longer command a total act of the whole moral being. But our analysis of the present situation suggests that if the Church were able, with a full, deep and pastoral understanding of that situation and its demands, to declare the truth which lies at the heart of its own faith, it would step straight into the heart of the battle. Its witness would be a clearly recognized challenge to the prevailing understanding of the meaning of human life and to customary ways of living and unity. The Church would find itself at the very centre of a conflict in which all that is highest and most precious in the life of humankind is at stake.

The mission to which the Church is called is a high one. But it would be foolish to disguise from ourselves that its fulfilment must be costly.

It belongs to the essence of personal life that it is not concerned with thought alone but demands a response of the whole being. It is necessary, therefore, to recognize from the beginning that no merely intellectual affirmation of the supremacy of the personal can be effective. The truth that human life finds its meaning and fulfilment in the relations between people will not prevail by being formulated as a doctrine in contrast to other doctrines and philosophies. It is real only to the extent that it is lived. The only way in which we can respond to the claims of other persons is by the giving of ourselves. What a person asks for is unconditional trust, complete surrender. In the personal sphere the unity of thought and action is complete. It is the region of dedication in which life has to be integrally and wholly lived to the point of the surrender of life itself. In our relation to persons the attitude of the spectator, of the disinterested investigator, which is proper to science and the endeavour to understand the world, is no longer appropriate. One can enter into the personal sphere only through participation, through response. It is a domain in which we leave behind us the endeavour to master the world of thought and begin to learn life's deepest lessons through the acknowledgment of responsibility, through patience, endurance and suffering.

Hence to proclaim the supremacy of the personal merely in words, however eloquent, is, as St Paul perceived, to become sounding brass and a tinkling cymbal. The only cogent and dynamic assertion of the truth that the meaning of human life is found in friendship, love and ministering to the needs of our fellow human beings is a deeper entrance into a life of personal responsibility in our relations with those around us. It is of deep significance that one of the fields in which fresh discoveries are being made today of the meaning of the personal is the endeavour to bring relief to the unemployed and to find a means of overcoming the social curse of unemployment.

The attention of the world will be arrested not by a new doctrine, but by a community of persons resolutely set on realizing their faith in action and courageously challenging every denial of it in the system and practice of modern society.

NOTES

[1] P. Evdokimov, *La femme et le salut du monde*, Paris-Tournai, 1958, p.25.
[2] "Le devenir du féminin selon Nicolas Berdiaev", in *Contacts*, 100, 1977, p.270; see also O. Clément, "Orient-Occident deux passeurs", in *Perspective Orthodoxe*, No. 6, Geneva, Labor et Fides, 1985, p.165.
[3] The Church Fathers saw in the miracle of Cana the transformation of water and wine as a symbol of the eucharist.
[4] *P.G.* 8, 260C.
[5] *P.G.* 82, 1489L.
[6] *Vitae Patrum*, V, 18,19.
[7] Nemesius analyzing Gen. 1:27 affirms that "man" (ἀνήρ) should function as a "world in miniature", and this reason was created as a reflecting image of the whole cosmos; see Nemesius, *De Natura Hominis* 1, in *P.G.* 40, 529B.
[8] T. Gorichéva, "Délivrée des larmes d'Eve", in *Femmes et Russie, 1980*, Paris, 1980, p.101.

[9] St Macarius the Great, *Hom.* 18, 7 in *P.G.* 34, 640B.

[10] Origen, *Commentary on the Psalms* 77, 31, in *P.G.* 17, 141: see also *Commentary on the Proverbs* 31, 16, in *P.G.* 17,252.

[11] Maximus the Confessor, *P.G.* 91, 665-668.

[12] *34th Canon Apostolic Constitutions 8,47* (Ed. F.X. Funk, *Didasculia et Constitutiones Apostolorum, Paderborn*, 1905, Vol. I, pp.572-574).

[13] O. Clément, *Sources*, Paris, 1982, p.83.

[14] The terms "theandric" needs further clarification. "Theandric" designates the entirely unique and new relationship that is established in Jesus Christ as being both fully human and fully divine; God and man as cooperating for the benefit of the whole creation, not separated and yet not mixed, not confused and yet in full harmony. One might also say that the full implications of the term "theandric" could only become apparent after the definitions of the council of Chalcedon, where what is *theandric* in Christ is also defined as *personal*. See also Lars Thunberg, *Man and the Cosmos (The Vision of St Maximus the Confessor*, New York, St Vladimir's Seminary Press, 1985, pp.71ff.

[15] D. Staniloae, "Dieu est Amour", in *Perspective Orthodox*, No. 1, Geneva, Labor et Fides, 1980, p.116.

Some General Reactions and Comments from an Orthodox Point of View

GEORGE D. DRAGAS

1. Two contradictory perspectives

Two basic thoughts were in my mind as I sat down to write this paper. First of all I knew that the topic is huge and complicated, and secondly, that my time or space here is limited. Therefore I decided to be both modest and brief.

There are two basic tasks that I set out to tackle here. One is to give some kind of Orthodox response to or assessment of what has been done so far on this topic on the basis of the background material that has been circulated for our study and consideration.[1] The other is to give some initial theoretical account of the Orthodox understanding of the community of women and men in Church and society. I would have liked to deal with the topic under examination from a practical point of view as well, but time considerations have prevented me from doing so on this occasion.

In reading through the programme outline and also through the other documents included in the background material I cannot help noticing a certain inconsistency between the original Lima programme and what it has become. The original formulation of the topic speaks about "the unity of the Church and the renewal of the human community". But the emphasis has now shifted to something that sounds and, indeed, is quite

● This paper originally appeared in *Texts and Studies*, Vol. IV, London, Foundation for Hellenism in Great Britain, 1985.
● Very Rev. Dr George Dragas (Ecumenical Patriarchate) is professor of Patristics, University of Durham, UK.

different, "unity and renewal in Church and society"! An effort is, indeed, made in all the background material to explain and even justify this shift — for instance, it is clearly stated in both document No. 1 and No. 3 that unity and renewal are not two poles, referring to the Church and the human community respectively, because the two must go together. But the fact remains that the original formulation of the topic and the new one that has been advanced suggest two quite different perspectives. I am pointing this out because it matters very much to an Orthodox, if he has to move from the one perspective to the other. The Orthodox experience firmly asserts that the unity of the Church is the God-given and therefore unfailing basis for the renewal of the human community and the entire universe of created things. The concept, however, of the "renewal of the Church" sounds contradictory, if not completely unacceptable, to Orthodox ears.

In the first instance the Church is identified with the reality of Jesus Christ, the Incarnate Son and Logos of God, in whose humanity a "new creation" (καινή κτίσις) in a new man (εἰς καινὸς ἄνθρωπος) has been established.[2] But the Church is also understood in an extensive creative way in the sense that what is true in Christ is reaching out into the history of humanity renewing the human community in accordance with its own instrinsic newness and perfection. Union with Christ, i.e. union with the Church, is, then, the real basis for the renewal of the human community. In this light, how could one speak of the renewal of the Church? This could only be done on the basis of a different ecclesiology. And this is, in fact, what seems to me to lie behind the shift from the original perspective to the new one in this study programme.

2. Two ecclesiologies

Already in document No. 1 of the background material — though the same applies to all the documents to a greater or lesser extent — we observe the promotion of a certain ecclesiology which operates with a juxtaposition (in some cases we could even speak of a disjunction) between God and Christ on the one hand and the Church and human community on the other — the last two being closely related to but not actually identified with each other. Once this distinction is established one can then envisage God and Christ being the basis for the unity and renewal of church and human community (or society), and therefore of unity and renewal not as an ecclesiologically established reality, but as a *desideratum* which awaits to be worked out and realized in history in the future. In this perspective the "unity-renewal project is welcomed... as of strategic importance for the orientation of the whole work of the WCC"!...[3] and most of the conclusions and suggestions made follow on as logical consequences. There is one very striking statement in document No. 1 which can serve best as an illustration of the juxtaposition that I have been expounding. "The source of unity, community and new life, both for a sinful world and for a church of sinful men and women, in fact, the source of ultimate hope for all God's creatures, is this sovereign rule of God as revealed in Christ Jesus, crucified and risen. The quest for visible unity in the church, and for the renewal of that human community to which the church belongs, therefore stands always under the righteous judgment and redeeming grace of the triune God. It is a quest never to be fully or permanently achieved in time, but conducted with trust in him for eschatological fulfilment."[4]

Here the "sinful world" and the "sinful church" are joined together and it is, indeed, said explicitly that the Church "belongs to the world". On the other hand, the unity and renewal of the Church and the world is a "quest" and, what is even more startling (!), "a quest which is never to be fully or permanently achieved in time" for it can only be an "eschatological fulfilment"!

I do not wish to press this point any further. I must, however, make it absolutely clear that this kind of ecclesiological perspective does not belong to the experience of the Orthodox Christian. From an Orthodox dogmatic theological perspective, which is rooted in the experience of the saints and fathers of the Church, such a perspective denies the Incarnation and presupposes at best a Nestorian Christology and at worst a Jewish ebionitic understanding of Christ. For the Orthodox the Church cannot be properly spoken about or viewed without a primary reference to the humanity of Christ and a secondary reference to our participation in this humanity. It is only with *this* humanity in mind (of Christ and His own) that we can truly appreciate the grace of the Holy Trinity and the sovereign rule of God. In this light, I hope that my claim will be understood, namely, that an Orthodox finds it unacceptable to shift from the perspective of the unity of the Church as the basis for the renewal of the human community to the perspective of the unity and renewal of the Church and the world on the basis of an ongoing and constantly changing work of God which never achieves its end in the midst of history because this end lies beyond history and time in an eschatological realm which is transcendent and destined to be revealed after the end. Is it unjust to call the former the Orthodox perspective and designate the latter as modernist Protestant? But whatever labels we care to give to these perspectives and whatever views we may ultimately entertain about them, should we not take them absolutely seriously in the context of the present dialogue and study programme? I fear that if we fail to do so, in other words, if we fail to be frank about our experiences (the ecclesiological ones in particular) and to persist in discovering the minds which shape our identities and our experiences, our orientation will not lead us to the achievement of our ultimate aim.

I could go on and single out many more unacceptable statements in the background material to this present study from an Orthodox perspective — e.g. the notion of "brokenness and renewal within the Church", or of "failures in the world which hinder renewal in the Church", or of "the Church in its need to overcome human sinfulness and division in its members", or of "the creative renewal of the world which challenges the Church", or of "the Church as sign of a *coming* unity of mankind", or of "many transformations which must take place in the church if it is to be renewed and moved into the offered life of unity", or of "an ecclesial community which is more inclusive" (!), or of "a church that must be restored and move deeper into life in unity", or of "confessing that the Church is divided, theologically and emotionally, by divisions within the human community, since social-dividing issues are church-dividing issues", or of "the ecumenical task of renewing the church", etc., etc. In the last analysis, however, I would return to the same general assessment about the divergent ecclesiological perspectives: that which sees the Church in Christ and the grace of the Trinity and that which sees in it close proximity with the world and humanity independently of the humanity of Christ. There is, however, one more area in the background material to this study that also needs to be critically looked at from an Orthodox theological perspective. This is the area concerning methodology.

3. The question concerning methodology

The methodology envisaged in this study is twofold. In the first instance it has to do with what is called "method of theological reflection" (the general aspect) and secondly, it has to do with "a working method". The former is identified as "an integrated theological method" which integrates four points: (1) the biblical, (2) the traditional, (3) the secular, and (4) the new theological approach implied in actions related to issues of unity and renewal. In fact, a closer look at what is said about these points reveals that (1) and (2) are subordinated to (3) and (4) to the extent that they are denied. This is especially seen in the distinction between *inductive* (credal) and *deductive* (liberal or liberational) approaches and in the claim that the former should be replaced by the latter. Even more striking for an Orthodox is the claim that *Tradition* (presumably the Bible and the Creeds) should have to pass *the test of relevance in every context* (see p.326 of document No. 1, ER). This means, in effect, that the Christian norms should be tested by other norms which determine the relevance of the former! These other norms are produced by the contemporary general sociological context within which the Christian Tradition finds itself. I am afraid that such a *testing* implies, if I am to put it rather bluntly, that the judge should be judged by the convict! — something which could not be defended as Christian, even if one is prepared to misquote Matthew (9:6 and 1 John 4:1 and blatantly abandon *exegesis* for *eisegesis*.[5] From an Orthodox point of view what is given to us here as method of theological reflection is ecclesiologically very negative inasmuch as it questions the normative nature of the Church and her Tradition (the Pillar and Foundation of the Truth against whom no gates of hell can prevail) from a non-Christian norm.

Particularly confusing and misleading is in this connection the emphasis on *experience*, most eloquently presented in Mary Tanner's paper (Document No. 3).[6] Dr Tanner speaks of "a new emphasis on experience" without telling us what this experience really is and without tackling the obvious dictum of experience that not all experience is normative and Christian. Statements like "what we make of the Christian story and tradition and what we make of contemporary life should be brought together so that a growing understanding of theology may emerge", or that "new truths about the nature and being of God may be seen", or that "the community interprets and articulates the vision of church unity and therefore needs to be wider and more inclusive", are quite strange to Orthodox experience which is rooted and seeks to be rooted in the experience of the Prophets, the Apostles and the Fathers and Saints of the Church of Christ throughout the ages. It is obvious that such a methodology which relies heavily on the dialogue between the church and the world rather than on the dialogue between man in Christ and His Church with God, is the logical corollary to the ecclesiology which understands the Church in sociological terms or in terms of its relationship and interaction with the world.

The special aspect of the methodology envisaged in the background documents consists in the promotion of topics suggested by the interaction between Church and world. Such a topic is the present one concerning *the community of women and men in church and society*. What is advanced here is consistent with the above-mentioned ecclesiological context and its theological methodology. However, what is regarded as renewal and unity in church and society finds no biblical or traditional warrant.

This is clearly to be seen in the demand for the equality of the sexes which is pushed forward as a point of church renewal against an alleged inequality in the traditions of the Church. Here we see that the integrated method with a new emphasis on experience renders results which stand in blatant contradiction with the biblical, the credal-canonical, the liturgical and generally the traditional patterns of the Christian Church. I do not wish to go into details, or to make a traditionalist plea here. But I cannot help thinking that it is unscientifically presumptuous, to say the least, to criticize the traditional understanding and order of the community of men and women in the church as implying *sexism* and *inequality* of sexes before you have made serious enquiry as to the logic enshrined in the traditions of the Church and, indeed, before actually testing the Christian character or status of such terms as *equality of sexes, inclusive community* (as opposed to a *traditioning community*).

The very term "sex" implies natural male and female differentiation and distinction which cannot be described by the abstract and ideological term of equality. The traditional teaching of the Church, at least as the Orthodox Christians perceive it, entails a spiritual identity between women and men and a biological distinction which implies complementarity as opposed to inequality. It is within this context of the biological differentiation that we find not only in man-woman relations (in the context of family and marriage in particular) but also in ma(e)n-ma(e)n[7] and woma(e)n-woma(e)n[8] relations a certain order which is useful and even necessary for the performance of certain functions and the achievement of certain aims. Similar orderings of a biological natural character are observed in the rest of creation.

There are hierarchies in the world which do not imply inequality but complementarity and the retention of their integrity constitutes the guarantee of their wellbeing and fulfilment. Such is also the order in the Church (I mean the ordained priesthood as distinct from the laity) which has been under attack in the present Study programme through the claim of the alleged "equality of women and men", which demands the ordination of women to the priesthood. The restriction of ordained priesthood to men only does not imply inequality, since the gift administered by the priest is *equally* available — to the same measure — to priests and lay people, men and women. In the Orthodox perspective significant differentiations between Christians arise not from the positions or functions that one occupies or performs in the Church, but from the measure of one's participation in and consistency with the grace of God which is *equally* made available to all.

Since my intention here is not to enter into a thorough discussion of all the points made in the background material but to speak generally and in an introductory but fundamental way, I shall not delay any more in discussing the special aspect of methodology, but go on to discuss the special topic of the Community of Women and Men in the Church and the World from the Orthodox perspective as I indicated in the opening statements of this paper.

4. The Community of Women and Men

In Orthodox doctrine women and men are both identical and distinct. They are identical inasmuch as they are both made *in the image and likeness of God*, and they are distinct inasmuch as they are respectively endowed with *peculiar male and female characteristics* which are not exchangeable or interchangeable.

In traditional language the former perspective of identity of image and likeness refers (properly or principally) to the soul, the inner aspect of the human being, whilst the latter, the perspective of distinction, refers to the body. In more contemporary language we could say that the identity of women and men is psychological or spiritual, and their diversity is biological or bodily.

The Orthodox tradition supplies us with a number of profound elaborations on these perspectives, which can be understood both internally and externally, separately and together as forming an indissoluble unity.

The identity of the "in the image and likeness of God" is understood externally as referring to human lordship and dominion over the rest of creation. Internally examined, however, the undifferentiated image of men and women refers primarily to the rational, mindful and self-determining (αὐτεξούσιον) capacities of their souls which enable them to participate in God's nature and perfection (i.e. God's powers and energies).

The external and internal aspects of the image and likeness are likewise interconnected inasmuch as the one interprets the other. The dominion of men and women over the rest of the creatures is realized in terms of understanding the latter (mind), articulating the reasons of their nature (logos) and using and guiding their life-movement (will). In this perception women and men belong to a community which is actively engaged in the life of creation and which can, in turn, be described in the last instance as a participation in (μετοχή) and cooperation with (συνεργεία) God the Almighty Creator and Sustainer of all things.

The somatic or biological differentiation of male and female does not automatically suggest incompatibility or contradiction, but implies natural complementarity. It calls for a union which results in life, in effect, an increase and multiplication of the human race which enjoys God's blessing. Now the psychological-spiritual and the somatic-biological perspectives are again profoundly interconnected inasmuch as the former always expresses its activity through the latter.

So far, so good... But there is a serious problem, or rather, problems, which amount to a certain loss or confusion in the community of men and women in creation. I say a *certain* loss because the problem, namely, the Fall, is neither total, nor final, and therefore not irredeemable. There are three basic levels to this problem, (a) the theological, (b) the anthropological, and (c) the cosmological, which can be distinguished in the context of analysis but not in the context of existence.

Another way of describing the problem of the Fall of women and men from the original design of their communion in the church and the world is by saying that the psychological aspect has been subjected to the biological aspect so that the identity of women and men is lost, as it were, by being subjected to the distinction of the biological make-up of both. Thus the identical souls become "male" and "female" and their spiritual and hegemonic powers are subjected to and serve the powers of the body which are merely led by instinct. This is a traditional problem which has resulted in terrible strife between women and men. It is part of God's economy for dealing with this problem that has given rise to a certain ordering or structuring of the community of women and men in their fallen state. There is in other words a law which is to be traced both in the Old and the New Testaments even though some minor modifications do appear in the two biblical contexts.

The problem can also be seen in exactly opposite terms, i.e. as the subjection of the biological difference to the psychological or spiritual identity. The actual result of this is the suppression, misuse and even subversion of male and female sex — the case that seems to be more dominant in our present time. Here again appropriate laws are introduced with the view to preventing further aggravation of the problem and procuring repentance and restoration.

Experience has shown how such laws, though good, are hard to fulfill. But Christian experience shows that at this point we have God's intervention in Christ and his Church which exerts a healing effect upon those in need. In Christ and his Church there is no male and female but a new man, a new creation. This is an eschatological reality firmly established in the Risen Lord Himself and especially in the new body which He brought to light through His glorious and mighty resurrection. In the first instance this means that Christ's human soul is not subjected to his body but the opposite is the case. Since His soul is neither male nor female, it follows that the maleness of Christ's body is not a point of contradiction but of reconciliation and complete and real renewal. But it may also mean — and this is most probably the case — that Christ's risen body is no longer male, as it was before, but resembles that of the angels who are not male or female for they do not marry nor are they given to marriage. If this is the case, then, those who participate in Christ are inwardly restored to the former identity and will overcome the biological distinction of the present body in heaven. The practice of Christian virginity linked with Christian ascetism bears witness to this. However, as long as we Christians on earth have not yet participated in the bodily resurrection of Christ, we still need the law (OT and NT) with all its regulations to guide us and prepare us for the final journey and perfection. Fulfilling the law in our life is precisely restoring the image of Christ's soul to our soul, becoming identical with it, neither male or female. This is the witness of Mary and the Saints as the chief members in the Church. In the Orthodox Tradition, however, there is a very strong sense of the participation of the body in the renewal which is in Christ. The cult of the relics of the Saints is a certain demonstration of the above.

5. Some specific conclusions

1. The sacramental/liturgical dimension of the Church with its Trinitarian, Christological and soteriological foundation should be recovered and made primary. Otherwise the fundamental distinction between *society* (secular) and *koinonia* (Christian) may be lost.

2. The biblical/traditional theological perspectives should be restored to their primary place in our methodology. We need to hear the Tradition clearly before we attempt to criticize it from new points of view which may also be questionable. Although all experience should be taken seriously and critically examined, not all experience is Christian and normative.

3. The biblical/traditional perspectives on male and female should be examined not only "negatively" from modern general sociological points of view but also "positively" from their primary normative intention, before critical assessments are made.

In all three directions the Orthodox have a lot to contribute and their voice should be sought persistently by their Protestant fellow-Christians, not only because the Orthodox are usually reluctant in formulating their views, but also because their views represent the wisdom of the Christian Tradition.

NOTES

[1] This background material includes the following: (1) "Minutes of the Meeting of the Standing Commission 1984, Crete", *Faith and Order Paper No. 121*, Geneva, WCC, 1984 (hereafter *Crete Minutes*). Also: "The Unity of the Church and the Renewal of Human Community: Programme Outline", in *The Ecumenical Review*, Vol. 36, No. 3, July 1984, pp.323-329. (2) "Unity/Renewal: Proposed Consultations", in *Crete Minutes* pp.43-52. (3) Mary Tanner, "Unity and Renewal: the Church and Human Community", in *The Ecumenical Review*, Vol. 36, No. 3, July 1984, pp.252-262. (4) Paul A. Crow, Jr, "Unity and Renewal: Introductory Reflections", in "Faith and Renewal: Commission on Faith and Order, Stavanger, 1985", ed. Thomas F. Best, *Faith and Order Paper No. 131*, Geneva, WCC, 1986. (5) The Church — Women and Men in Community, excerpts from Janet Crawford and Michael Kinnamon, eds, *In God's Image: Reflections on Identity, Human Wholeness and the Authority of Scripture*, Geneva, WCC, 1983; and Constance F. Parvey, *The Community of Women and Men in the Church*, Geneva, WCC, 1983 (hereafter *The Community*). (6) "The Letter from Sheffield to the Churches" and Bibliography, in *The Community*, *op. cit.*, pp.90-93 and 195. (7) Madeleine Boucher, "Authority-in-Community", *Mid-Stream*, Vol. 21, No. 3, July 1982, pp.402-417.

[2] References include Gal. 3:28.

[3] Cf. *Crete Minutes, op. cit.*, p.34; *ER, op. cit.*, p.323.

[4] *Ibid.*, pp.36-37; p.325.

[5] *Ibid.*, pp.38-39; p.326.

[6] Mary Tanner, "Unity and Renewal", *op. cit.*, pp.254f.

[7] For instance, father to son, or elder brother to younger brother, or, indeed, generally older man to younger man.

[8] For instance, mother to daughter, or elder sister to younger sister, or, indeed, generally older woman to younger woman.

Report of Group I

A. Post-Sheffield

The eight members of our group had differing experiences of, and reactions to, the Community of Women and Men in the Church Study. Several had been deeply involved in the process and in follow-up of various kinds; some had never heard of the Study nor of Sheffield, but were deeply concerned with the same issues; one noted that the CWMC issues had little relevance in her situation and that "feminism" is not a term acceptable to the Orthodox Church.

Members of the group found it impossible to single out the effects of Sheffield within a whole longer process of change, to which many factors have contributed. But we noted that a number of changes *have* occurred in some of our churches, and that Sheffield had undoubtedly contributed to some of these. In particular we noted the increased participation of women in many of our churches, in ordained and lay ministries, theological education, decision-making bodies and denominational structures, and in the ecumenical movement. We spoke of an increased attention to women's questions and to feminist theology. In the words of one member: "Women in the church are now on the agenda."

However we also noted that in some cases there is continuing opposition to such changes and that many women still experience problems within their churches. The comment was made that the process begun at Sheffield is always under threat.

We noted with some disappointment that so far the only published translation of the Sheffield report is that in German. *We therefore recommend* to the Standing Commission of Faith and Order that all possible steps be taken to facilitate translations of the Sheffield report into Spanish and French.

B. Insights and implications of the CWMC study for the understanding of the church

1. Power and powerlessness

The question of power and powerlessness is one of the key issues that arises from the Community Study. The study points to possibilities of being the church in a non-imperialistic way, of being a church-in-community. One of the chief values of the Community Study is the fact that it reflects the experience of that part of the community that sees itself as powerless.

Some see in socio-political structures the presence of demonic elements ("principalities and powers") that must be overcome. In situations where the church itself enjoys power the crucial question is, how is this power used, and on behalf of whom? Often those in power are "power-blind". The improper and negative uses of power always entail violence.

However there is for Christians an understanding of a good way to use power. Jesus Christ used his power to heal, reconcile and release (liberate). His was a power that made people whole. The church is commissioned to continue Christ's ministry of healing, reconciling and liberating. As people appropriate their dignity as children of God, beings made in God's image, they are empowered.

2. Expressions of pain

In our discussion frustration, pain and agony were expressed by a number of group members on issues relating to women and men in the church. These included:
— the gap that exists between the vision of community and the reality of life as actually experienced in the churches;
— the seeming incompatibility between the commitment to visible church unity and the commitment to the community of women and men in the church;
— the continuing sense of voicelessness and exclusion felt by many women in different areas of church life;
— the exaltation of the "given unity" of the church despite our continuing experience of eucharistic exclusiveness;

— the use of exclusive language, and categories of thought and expression that divide Christians from one another;
— our inability to communicate that which is important to us.

3. Unity and the vision of renewal

The search for unity and the vision of a renewed community of women and men in the church require a process of ecumenical learning. The process of our group taught us all that, because partners in ecumenical dialogue come from a variety of cultural and ecclesial contexts and have different understandings about the nature of the church, great sensitivity is essential in listening, explaining and discovering the contribution of each participant.

We affirm our commitment to both the unity of the church *and* the renewal of the community of women and men in the church, and draw attention to what we see as the danger of playing one against the other. Care must be taken to ensure that progress towards church unity not be sought at the expense of those who are voiceless and marginalized in church structures.

At the same time, we wish to affirm that an understanding of the church as mystery and prophetic sign and as a redeemed human community are complementary, and that polarization of these understandings impedes renewal.

In moving towards the vision of renewed community, we find that our incarnational understanding of the church is very helpful. Our understanding of incarnation as God-becoming-human gives value and dignity to every person and mobilizes us in the direction of participation and partnership.

We also understand the church as a eucharistic community. In the eucharist we celebrate the presence of Christ with us here and now. Yet at that very table some of us are painfully aware that the unity which Christ has given us in the church is not yet fully manifested. In our commitment to unity and renewal we are reminded that the powers of evil are definitely defeated in Christ's death and resurrection, but they also have to be overcome again and again both personally and as Christians in society.

4. Implementing the vision

The compelling vision of the renewed community which was articulated by the CWMC study challenges us to take steps towards its realization. In the Gospels the announcement of the reign of God does not simply point to a dream. Its power and presence *are* among us. The vision of the renewed community challenges relationships that are characterized by domination, oppression and exclusion. It calls us to change and commitment.

What are the forces that hinder the realization of the vision? What powers and traditions are we up against? What are the structures that resist movement towards community, and why? To what extent have the concerns and impulses from the CWMC study been taken up? Can we point to any experience in the Christian community of men giving up positions and power in order to allow women to participate? Can we see any progress towards the implementation of the vision of renewed community in those churches which are hierarchical in their structures?

Whatever the answers to these questions, we should not be discouraged but should continue to press on, asking: "Given the vision and accepting our limitations, what concrete steps can we take even now?"

C. The case studies

We see the case study methodology as of value inasmuch as it takes human experience as its starting point and as a reality that is reflected upon in the light of faith. By telling us what sort of community women and men actually experience in their churches, a contribution is made to our understanding of ecclesiology. This methodology permits us to discern the incarnational presence of Christ in the hopes, struggles and achievements of the people of God in certain specific situations.

We also appreciate that this methodology is closely tied to that of the CWMC Study, as it involves the inter-relation between doing theology and implementing change, interpreting traditions and envisioning renewal. We regretted that more time was not available for group discussion of the different case studies.

1. Case study from India

a) Ministry: In our discussion appreciation was expressed for the insights that emerged about new forms of ministries for both women and men. We saw that these are often, though not exclusively, of a pastoral nature; that is, they enable the various members of the body of Christ to attain the maturity and mutuality sustained by the vision of the renewed community. Significant ecumenical opportunities open up in many cases through such new ministries. However we also noted that in some other contexts new forms of ministries for women become "special ministries", which then function to exclude them from traditional ministries.

A question was raised about models of ministry. In view of the fact that these are often drawn from old, static models of society, can we not recover the rich variety of ways in which Jesus Christ served? What ministries relate to the way people live today?

b) Mission and unity: Appreciation was expressed too for the fact that the bold venture of church union in the case of the Church of South India was primarily for the sake of the world, that is to say, for the sake of making known the reconciliation of the world initiated by God in Christ. We saw that this missionary concern and impetus to personal and corporate renewal also lay at the heart of the CSI decision to ordain women as presbyters.

We noted that as it tried to live out its unity and its purpose to be the sign of God's mystery and God's people, the CSI modified previously existing structures. This raises the problem of the tension between faithfulness to eternally-valid "revealed structures", and the recognition that some aspects of church structure have developed historically in the course of the church's life in the world.

c) Societal structures and roles: It was pointed out that in a situation of societal stratification, such as in India, the church as an inclusive community is a powerful sign of reconciliation and unity not only for the church itself, but for humankind.

We also discussed the fact that in many societies with rigid role definitions the functions of child-nurturing are often not valued. The vision of renewed community impels us to see that human beings can worthily fulfill a variety of roles and that child-nurturing is an important and valuable task which should be recognized as such and affirmed.

2. The Orthodox presentation

Our group appreciated the depth of theological thinking in the two papers which made up the Orthodox presentation. We observed the difference in method from the other two presentations and suggested that in future it would be important to have more information about the particular situation of women and men in the Orthodox church, in the form of a descriptive picture and more experiential material.

Further explanation of the Orthodox perspective was given as follows:

a) Many opportunities are given for women to participate and serve in the church and Orthodox women have no feeling of exclusion. Many women are studying theology and teaching theology in schools and also at university. But more important than being active in the church is to become a saint in the body of Christ. The focus must always be Christocentric.

b) Theology and a true understanding of the church are more important than the study of society because the presence of the body of Christ will change society through a process of transfiguration. Because the church is seen primarily as the body of Christ, and not as a socio-political reality, many issues dealt with in the CWMC Study seem seriously imbalanced from an Orthodox point of view.

Group members appreciated the development of the concept of *koinonia*, a true community of women and men, in the paper of Father Limouris. This concept of *koinonia* as communion in Christ, a community based on a relationship to God, where love rules, offers a theological basis for a vision of a community of women and men living in mutuality in the church.

3. Case study from the United States of America

a) *"Men's church, women's church"*: This study dealt with a specific local church in which the concerns of the Community Study have been taken up (in terms of leadership and the use of inclusive language). Of particular interest to our group was the reflection that in the past it was as if there were two churches: a "male church" that gave structure and leadership ("it wrote the books"), and a "women's church" that sought money for the church and its work, studied the Bible, ministered to its own members, was committed to mission, and was asked to look after the practical details of church life. The women could only exert influence or bring about change through their husbands who held positions of power within the "men's church". Single women thus had no influence.

The present stage in the life of this congregation is characterized by a coming together of the "men's church" and the "women's church". It is a process of finding out what mutuality means. It is a long, hard road to create a community of women and men in mutuality. We noted that the congregation, in the preparation of this case study, undertook an arduous process of self-study. This helped it to understand both the problems and the possibilities inherent in its efforts to create a more inclusive community of women and men within its own life.

b) This experience seems to be true in at least some other parts of the world. The challenge is that as we begin to travel the road towards renewed community, we often become aware of our divisions in a fresh way. The roles of laymen and laywomen in the various tasks of service, mission, administration, teaching, etc. of the church should be examined to see how they limit, or enhance, the use of each person's gifts. It is essential to ensure the full participation of all. However this should not turn into a power struggle in which, tragically, the loss is felt to be greater than the enrichment brought about by a new vision of partnership among the whole people of God.

Report of Group II

I. On from Sheffield

Every member of the group had something to contribute from their own situation about the development of the issues of the Community of Women and Men Study. In some cases, like England and the United States of America, this was a direct result of the World Council study and in response to the challenge of the Sheffield recommendations sent to all the member churches by Central Committee.

— In *England* the British Council of Churches responded to the Sheffield consultation by producing a study guide, *Circles of Community*, for local groups; it also funded a two-year project to consider the impact of the feminist movement on the churches. The United Reformed Church and the Methodist Church both set up working groups on the Sheffield recommendations while the Church of England has had a major study on the participation of women in local and national synodical structures and in the boards and councils of the Church. In addition a growing number of women's groups are emerging: the Catholic Women's Network; Women in Theology; the Christian Women's Resource Centre; Women in Inter-faith Dialogue.

— In *Japan* the United Church of Christ has tried new ways of Bible studies for women. The National Christian Council Women's Committee set up a dialogue between Christian feminists and women in other religions, as well as a study on Christian feminism. Recently the fiftieth anniversary of the ordination of women was celebrated and women ministers organized theological research. There is generally a growing interest in feminist theology but not, in Japan, as a direct result of Sheffield.

— In the *German Democratic Republic* it seemed that after Sheffield and Dresden questions were too quickly answered about the controversial 50 percent participation of women and other issues. Now there seems a certain stagnation and the issues are hardly discussed, especially by the church leaders. Women's questions are not being heard and feminist theology is only alive amongst a small group of women. Opposition to feminist issues often comes from women themselves, as was seen in the Lutheran World Federation Conference in Budapest where women said they "didn't understand the issues".

— In the *United States of America* major shifts are taking place in the roles of men and women, raising fundamental questions for the institution of the family. The National Council of Churches has a primary commitment to the issues of the Community Study. Its major work, much debated, has been the publication of an inclusive language lectionary. In the Roman Catholic Church the question is intensifying as women begin leaving a church in which they feel there is no role for them. The Disciples of Christ continue their long commitment to the issues as seen in a major consultation in Iowa in 1985, which selected the community of women and men as one of its leading themes.

— In *Czechoslovakia* there has been some attempt to work on inclusive language and feminist theology. It was the good experience of women in teaching, preaching and pastoral care that led, thirty years ago, to the ordination of women. In the last years the situation of women in the ordained ministry has improved greatly. However, the inter-related "web of issues" pointed to by the Community Study are only beginning to be addressed.

— Amongst the *Orthodox* the issues are little discussed. Some research has been completed by individual writers. The exception is in the United States, where the Orthodox Church of America produced in 1980 a study document on the Community Study called *Women and Men in the Church*. Many Orthodox women continue to be critical of Sheffield. They feel that the issues formulated by the Community Study do not impinge upon them and that the way the questions are formulated are foreign to their understanding the church.

These examples are very limited but they do suggest that the issues of the Community Study in general, and the Sheffield recommendations in particular, have had differing impacts in the various parts of the world represented in our group. Nevertheless, in some form or other, issues relating to the Community Study are surfacing almost everywhere. This led the group to observe:

a) The importance of exchange of perspective and insights amongst different churches and different regions of the world. Only the World Council of Churches is in a position to ensure that this happens through consultations, publications and its Assemblies.

b) The need for the study on unity and renewal to stimulate (1) discussion in areas where this study has had little chance to take root (our group welcomed the plans for regional development proposed at Stavanger),[1] and (2) case studies amongst the Orthodox churches in different parts of the world.

II. Reflection on three case studies of the Prague consultation

The group expressed their gratitude for the three so-called "case studies" and the two introductory reflections on the Community Study. While recognizing the very different nature of the contributions, each presented in their very different ways ecclesiological issues arising out of the experiences of the community of men and women in the church.

A. The method of the Community Study as a valid way of discovering truths about the nature of the church

The Prague consultation was set up on the basis of listening to case studies and asking what insights these had for an understanding of the nature of the church. This followed the underlying method of the Community Study, which was based on the exploration of the experience of being women and men in community and upon bringing what was discovered from that experience into dialogue with scripture and Tradition. The method was described as "a double dynamic" in which scripture and Tradition sometimes affirms experience, sometimes judges it, and experience enables us to discover new depths in the Tradition. The Community Study provided many case studies, indeed it was itself "a case study of case studies" which contained many ecclesiological insights (cf. the paper presented at this consultation by the Rev. Janet Crawford). Our group found the case studies presented at Prague to be a significant and refreshing departure from the normal style of Faith and Order work, offering us new ways of thinking and working ecumenically. The Rev. Sandra Winter Park took us existentially into the life of a specific congregation and showed us how, in this particular local church, new modes of behaviour and new patterns of living in the community of the church had emerged.

While agreeing that this method of action-reflection — the bringing together of scripture and Tradition with experience — is a valid way of engaging in ecumenical theology, some reservations about the way it was followed were expressed by some members of the group:

— There needs to be a greater recognition of liturgical experience as the central and unique part of the experience of a Christian community as distinct from any secular group. Here the Orthodox have an important contribution to make. In liturgical experience the whole community enters into "kairos", "saving time", "another realm", "redemptive time" which is constitutive of the life of the Christian community.

— Any future work should ensure that the experience of a wider community, both ecclesially and regionally, is brought into the study.

— Descriptions of the method of the study should make clear that experience is itself a part of both scripture and Tradition and not something separate or distinct from it.

— Greater clarity needs to be sought on the understanding of Tradition and the relation between scripture and Tradition. This, of course, is a question lying behind much ecumenical study. Following on the Montreal report (*Scripture, Tradition and Traditions*),[2] the Community Study has fruitful insights to offer for a theological method in which both experience and reflection (reason) are given a proper place.

— Our group also recognized that some people are not "comfortable" with the part of the method that explores experience, and others are not "comfortable" with the emphasis on reflection on scripture and Tradition. While agreeing that all need to be engaged in both aspects, it was acknowledged that some persons, because of their particular skills and sensitivities, will have more to contribute to the analysis of experience, and others to the explication of Tradition. The study on unity and renewal needs to continue to encourage each side to take seriously the contribution of the other, and to hold the two in creative balance. To show the need for *both* aspects was one of the values of the Prague consultation.

B. *The central ecclesiological challenge*

From the ecclesiological insights of the Community Study, as presented by both the Rev. Dr Constance Parvey and the Rev. Janet Crawford, as well as the three case studies there surfaced again and again the question of two different "ecclesiological models". These were caricatured as an "Orthodox/Catholic model" which defines the church as the church "in essence", where the liturgical community is the primary expression of the church and "church activities" are seen as "ecclesiastical affairs"; and a "Protestant model" which seemed to some to take the sociological structures of the people of God within human history as its primary starting point. In the first model the emphasis is upon participation in the mystery of Christ and the church as his body, understood sacramentally. In the second model the emphasis is upon the organizational activities of the church, understood as a community in the world.

Our group wrestled with the fundamental question of whether the Community Study in general, and the case studies in particular, were based exclusively on the *second* model in such a way as to deny the first. We came to recognize the danger of too hastily placing others into one or another polarized ecclesiological position. We became aware of the urgent need to learn each other's "ecclesiological language". We began to ask, "is it not possible, instead of setting one ecclesiology over against the other, to discover within the Community Study an integrated ecclesiology, a balanced ecclesiology which might draw and hold together the divided churches, and draw women and men together within the community of the church?" What became clear was the need to watch our language in talking on the one hand about the church itself, which in its being (essence) is the body (humanity) of Christ, the divine mystery, the koinonia, and cannot be divided (we are already one in our common baptism); and on the other hand the "human face of the church", the "society of the church", the community (as distinct from koinonia) which shows signs of brokenness.

When we move towards an "integrated ecclesiology" the divisions and brokenness that we recognize in the stories of the Community Study, and in Rev. Sandra Park's case study, are seen for what they are — a denial of the oneness we already have in baptism. One Orthodox member of our group suggested that the "narrower" definition of the church "in essence" had great possibility for changing the broken structures and relationships in the church. The Orthodox view of the church allows for a variety of "models". It allows for different structures and patterns of organization of ministries (diaconia) to emerge, according to the particular cultural context and structure of society in which the church finds itself. The principle of "economy" allows for change in structures and order without changing the liturgical structures of the priesthood which are rooted in the Christian history of salvation. While maintaining the "core" of the faith, the "legacy of the undivided church", "what is essential", the principle of economy allows structural change and a variety of models of the church's ministries (diaconia) in the world to emerge.

Our group experienced painfully how difficult it is to find ways of talking about the church which do not deny the insights and faith of other Christians, thus blocking discussion. Nevertheless we came to see that with patience and determination it is possible to move forward together. We agreed that in the continuation of the Community Study issues, and by bringing a wider group into the study, significant progress can be made not only in healing the divisions in the ordered life of the community but in reaching a common understanding of the nature of the church. All of the other ecclesiological issues which emerged from our reflections on the case studies were bound up with this fundamental ecclesiological discussion.

C. The nature of the unity we seek

In reflecting upon the experience presented to us by the Rev. Dr Padmasani Gallup of the Church of South India, we are reminded that the *desire* for unity is essential. Only a genuine desire for unity will bring about that metanoia (repentance) needed both for bringing churches together and for healing the divisions in human community. We are reminded that our case studies, and the Community Study, always viewed the church from inside. We need to be aware of how Christian division is interpreted by those outside the church. From Japan, from the perspective of India, from socialist and non-socialist countries, we learned that the church needs to be visibly united to face external challenges, to be effective in mission and to give credible witness and, most of all, to offer united worship to the Triune God. The goal of visible unity was always affirmed by the Community Study, but Dr Gallup's reflections on the Church of South India underlined for us that visible unity has profoundly to do with the quality of *relationships* between those united in the eucharist: it has consequences for the equal participation of women and men in the structures of the church, in the sharing of "power". She also made it clear that for her and for the Church of South India the ordination of women to the priesthood, at least in appropriate cultural situations, was a necessary part of the outward expression of the church's unity. Many in our group wanted to affirm these signs of visible unity of the church, and felt that "ecclesiastical joinery" — even agreement on the common confession of the faith, on baptism, eucharist and ministry and on the structures of the church — can never be sufficient for visible unity. There must be expressions of the obliteration of brokenness in the community of women and men in the church, as well as the obliteration of all other forms of brokenness — of the whole "interlocking web of oppression" described at the Sheffield consultation.

D. *Women and the priestly ministry*

Both the case study from the Church of South India and that from the United States of America underlined once more the question of the relation between the ordination of women to the priesthood and the unity of the church. Our group asked the familiar questions: is it a matter of economy; is it a church-dividing issue; can we move closer together despite our divided practices in this areas; is the acceptance of the ordination of women to the priesthood necessary for the visible expression of the church's unity? However, a prior question kept surfacing in the group: what priesthood *has* the ministry? To the Orthodox in particular, achieving a common understanding of the priesthood in relation to the ministry is a prerequisite for resolving the question. Here the convergence on the understanding of priesthood/ ministry in the Lima text ("Baptism, Eucharist and Ministry") was welcomed. Our group looked for further work on the relationship between the unique High Priesthood of Christ, the priesthood of the whole people of Christ in the local church, and the priesthood of the ordained ministry. The Community Study had much to contribute to this discussion, and here the experience of women in those churches that do ordain women to a ministry of word and sacrament is an essential element in the discussion, as well as the experience of congregations who call forth, support and experience that ministry.

E. *Participation and determining the life of the community of the church*

We recognized that the Community Study and the Rev. Park's case study both raised questions of participation in the life of the church, of sharing in the "power", "authority", and the "determining of the life of the community". Here again we must choose very carefully the language we use to describe the experience, of some women, of those structures which women experience as oppressive and excluding. Equally, the language with which we respond to such testimonies from experience has to be carefully chosen. The Community Study suggests that the participation of men and women is not of the same quality, and that there is unequal participation in the ordering and decision-making structures in the life of the community. How do those without a voice, whether they are marginalized because of sex, class or colour, find a voice in the places where the life of the community is determined?

How should the church live in such a way that it *embodies* its belief that all are equal? These questions, born out of the experience of many women, need to be related to our understanding of participation in the liturgical life of the community as well as its organizational structures.

They also have to be seen in relation to different roles, and the assignment of roles in the Christian community. Here again the Community Study, with its case studies and testimony from experience, should influence any work Faith and Order undertakes on structures of authority and decision-making.

F. The church, the imago Dei and the place and role of Mary

Genesis 1:27 was a foundational text in the Community Study and our group recognized that the Orthodox presentation had important material worthy of further study and reflection in relation to our understanding of the image of God. For Orthodox the *imago Dei* is the same in women and men. The image is to be interpreted in a "spiritual" and not "bodily" sense. It is Christ who restores the image in us. Although he is a "male icon" the image is the image of male and female. Mary is the first of the community of redeemed humanity to realize the work of Christ in a unique way. While not far from us she, in a unique way, tells us of the image restored through the incarnation of her Son. Any follow-up to the Community Study should reflect on the place and role of Mary, for the Orthodox see Mary as providing a role model for both women and men and also as restoring a "feminine" dimension to the church.

NOTES

[1] See "Faith and Renewal", ed. Thomas F. Best, *Faith and Order Paper No. 131*, Geneva, WCC, 1986, p.211.
[2] "The Fourth World Conference on Faith and Order: the Report from Montreal 1963", eds P.C. Rodger and L. Vischer, *Faith and Order Paper No. 42*, London, SCM Press, 1964, pp.50-61.

Report of Group III

Group III had eight members and included a Roman Catholic Domini-can from France, an Orthodox from Greece, a Lutheran from America, a Methodist from Argentina, a Presbyterian from the Cameroon, a Reformed from France, an Evangelical Brethren from Czechoslovakia and a member of the Church of South India — altogether three men and five women. (A member of the United Reformed Church in the United Kingdom was present initially.) Our cultural, linguistic and ecclesial diversity was a blessing in the sense that it affirmed the urgent necessity for a high level of trust and openness in order to be able to speak, hear and listen. However, we recognized that formal discussion of the presenta-tions was hampered by language barriers within the group.

I. Sheffield — a postscript

1. Whether we liked it or not, acknowledged it or not, Sheffield affected us all in our own situations. The reports ranged from "total ignorance" of Sheffield, to its "considerable effects". "Sheffield had stimulated a re-examination of the constitution of our churches in terms of ordination of women and fairness of representation of the constituent members on councils and committees where the power of decision-making is lodged," was one report. Sheffield was also perceived nega-tively as giving a "fixed image of the church according to North America". It seemed to be generally true, especially in Africa and Asia, that Sheffield provided the impetus for the churches to look critically at their own situation, just as the International Women's Decade had

encouraged secular organizations to examine themselves in terms of male-female participation.

2. The Roman Catholic (France) and Orthodox (Greece) members of our group affirmed that all avenues of active, recognized ministry are open to women except that of ordained ministry in the church. The Roman Catholic member related that in the total catechetic ministry of the church in France, women outnumber men by nine to one. This participant regretted that, in the discussions around the community of women and men, too much emphasis was placed on the traditional ordained ministry. He suggested that further study should be made on biblical texts that could broaden and renew our understanding of women's ministry in the church. The Orthodox member acknowledged that women are the pillars of their church. Both reported from their situations that lay leaders are encouraged within the church's ministry and that there are a large number of lay women leaders, a situation unthinkable twenty years ago. Both the Roman Catholic and Orthodox members reported that there is a move to revive the ordained diaconate for women. In neither situation was there an acknowledgment of brokenness in the community of women and men in the church.

3. In Czechoslovakia, several of the Protestant churches have recognized the pastoral gifts of their women and have called them to the ordained ministry for decades. In addition, some are moving, albeit slowly, to invite and allow women into places of decision-making. However the scripture, written in a patriarchal historical context, is not to be touched in any kind of effort at introducing a greater level of equality in human relationships. A Czechoslovakian participant quoted the church's position as follows: "There must be a good reason why the language of the Bible is not inclusive."

4. In Cameroon (French) the women's organization within the church is very strong. When the pastor is overworked with many parishes, women do everything necessary for the worship and ongoing life of the church. "Why can't we do the one thing when we do everything else?" is a painful query from the women. "If being Christian is renewal, we have to *do* something," is an understanding of ecclesiology which goes beyond structural unity to the renewal of the whole *ecclesia*.

5. The Church of South India is struggling to be the body of Christ witnessing to the unity in Christ in the midst of persons of other faiths. It has begun to call women to the full ordained ministry of its church, and is consciously moving towards fair representation of women and men in its councils and committees, in a recognition of the church as a community of women and men.

6. The member from the Methodist Church in Argentina celebrates the fact that her church has a commitment to the principle of the priesthood of all believers. It attempts, in its study and programme, to practise the collegial authority of a circle rather than the hierarchical one of a pyramid, so that in the equality of women and men their respective experience, and the wisdom of their reflection, is shared fully.

7. The Reformed Church in France has no problems with the leadership of women in the church, was the report from one group member. The church concentrates now on teaching and "not losing persons from the church". A rigid ecclesiology is not known; women lead worship as often as men. In the absence of a pastor, the delegated woman leader may consecrate and distribute the elements of the eucharist, a situation unthinkable twenty years ago. "Now it is natural," was the happy affirmation of this member — a positive move towards healing the brokenness in the church.

II. Sheffield and the third world

Africa, Latin America and Asia were represented in our group by three women. In an attempt at articulating an ecclesiology we were forced to look at our ecclesial histories, at the peculiarities of having been brought to birth as "mission churches". "Mission" carried an inevitable cultural pattern which alienated the early mission churches from both their own cultural roots and their neighbours. The church was foreign to the culture. But this is changing. Conscious, unconscious and spontaneous expressions of the experience of liberation through the gospel of Jesus Christ are giving distinctive characteristics and identities to the churches in the third world. We have felt free to respond to the "raw fact" of Christ, and to build and articulate our faith around the body of Christ.

III. Sheffield and ecclesiologies

As we began to move into ecclesiology there were more questions than answers: what is the church? which church? how do you identify the church? what is the identity of the church in Africa and Asia? Two basic definitions or descriptions of the church became acceptable as starting points for an ecclesiology. One is the understanding of the church as a "given", somewhat static; the other is the church as unfolding, dynamic, changing in structure as well as nature.

If the CWMC study did nothing else, it drew attention to the tragic extent to which ecclesiologies have become polarized. It is as if the men/women polarization is but a symptom or a symbol of other polarizations:

the nature-structure polarization of the church as a continuing "given", in tension with the church as called, gathered and constantly renewed; the emphasis on tradition versus experience; the eucharist/ministry-mission dichotomy; the focus on theology *or* sociology; the authority of tradition and the authority of scripture.

The church was variously described according to the understanding and experience of the traditions represented in our group: we spoke of the church as a sacramental, mystical, Trinitarian community; of the church as first-fruits with an eschatological dimension which is salvific, requiring adherence to a moral and spiritual discipline; of the church not to be identified with society or the world, but to be perceived as the leaven therein; of the church as present in all Christian churches, but not fully present until an eschatological fulfilment in God's time (an affirmation of the uniting churches); of the church as a community celebrating the sacraments of baptism and eucharist, which can be seen as both an invitation and "fertilization" to find God around the eucharist, and to "give birth" to new community.

Sheffield focused both on the church as a broken community of women and men and as a sign of renewed community. The understanding of the *nature* of this community, or in formal terms "ecclesiology", emerged gradually as we began to listen to the specific experiences which group members revealed about their own church's attempts at obedience to the Lord, and faithfulness to scripture and Tradition.

If the fundamental purpose of Sheffield was indeed to explore issues of gender in community, and if the "essential nature of the study was ecclesiological", pertaining to inclusive community of women and men in the church, then for those in the third world it added another dimension to the issue of community. We had to ask how to be and to become the body of Christ, the eucharistic community in the midst of, as well as removed from, our neighbours and relatives who subscribe to a different faith. The ecclesial community has to be conscious at the same time of an extended *inclusiveness* (of caste, tribe, clan), as well as tighter *exclusiveness* in terms of discipline. The eucharistic community of the church mandates an unequivocal affirmation of faith, an uncompromising discipline of scripture-based spirituality/morality, and an unrelenting pursuit of evangelism, as well as witness within the community. Along with issues of the community of women and men in the church, the *mutuality* required within the body of Christ opens up issues of the community of rich and poor, high and low caste, tribal and language groups within one and the same ecclesial community which meets at the table of our Lord and at the foot of the cross. Within this *ecclesia* we seek unity and renewal. Our sources of renewal are Jesus at the cross, the Christ of the resurrection, the eucharist of the broken body, the scripture fulfilled in Christ and the relationship of the koinonia, the worshipping community gathered together and renewed by God.

The ecclesiologies represented within our grasp were diverse, if not polarized. There is ample evidence that the church as the body of Christ has responded to the social changes taking place around it, resulting in a new equality of women and men. These changes are not attempted randomly, but are a consequence of attempting to live by faith and in faithfulness to the Christian values of the gospel of Jesus Christ. It is an outcome of both repentance and faith, and a response to God's call to obedience to God's will for women and men in community.

Recommendations

1. More extensive and in-depth study of the scriptures is necessary to provide a fuller theological framework for ecclesiology.
2. Interpretation of scripture needs to follow a methodology that takes into consideration the nature of the group involved, its theological background and cultural variety.
3. The explorations of ecclesiology need to hear and incorporate the experience of the church as a minority in the midst of people of other living faiths, as well as case studies from other cultures.

A Personal Theological/Ecclesiological Reflection on the Prague Consultation

MARTIN CRESSEY

This reflection was developed as a personal overview of the consultation at the request of the participants. It began as a draft text for the elaboration of a concerted account of the process, but there proved to be insufficient time for its completion in that sense. It is written from the perspective of a participant in the Sheffield, Chantilly, Stavanger and Prague meetings — that is its claim to a certain objective subjectivity about the process!

Two theological approaches

The work of the consultation focused on the three studies of Christian experience presented. Study of experience had also been a vital element of the World Council of Churches' programme on "The Community of Women and Men in the Church". Participants in the CWMC programme who shared in this consultation showed, by their recollections and evaluations of that programme, how important it was that contemporary experiences of women and men who shared in the Study were taken as a starting-point for theological reflection.

Already in the reports of the groups which studied the three cases it is clear that the approach to theological reflection from this direction, i.e. from study of experience, must be related to the approach which begins from scripture, and from the Tradition which embraces the scriptural

● Rev. Martin Cressey (United Reformed Church) is principal of Westminster College, Cambridge, UK.

revelation. It was for the same reason that the first consultation of the Faith and Order study "The Unity of the Church and the Renewal of Human Community" at Chantilly, France, January 1985, worked on its statement concerning "The Church as Mystery and Prophetic Sign", which was further intensively discussed at the meeting of the Faith and Order Plenary Commission in Stavanger, Norway, August 1985. (This statement is, by decision of the Stavanger meeting, under editorial revision for later distribution.[1])

The Chantilly/Stavanger statement is an example of the attempted inter-relation of theological methods. Its title alludes to theological themes which have played a great part in Christian tradition; "mystery" *(mysterion)* is a New Testament word for the "open-secret" of God's eternal plan in Christ for the reconciled life of humankind. "Mystery" has also been used to refer to the sacramental life of the church. "Sign" has been applied by the Second Vatican Council and the Uppsala Assembly of the WCC to the church as sign and instrument of God's unitive purpose. At the Vancouver Assembly of the WCC the sign was characterized as "prophetic", that is, as sign given by Christ, which provides both a pre-vision of God's fulfilled purpose and a judgment on both the human community and the ecclesial community, whenever the divine purpose has been resisted.

These concepts of "mystery" and "prophetic sign" were discussed both at Chantilly and Stavanger in relation, on the one hand, to the scriptures (and in particular the scriptural testimony to the sovereign rule of God, the kingdom) and, on the other hand, in relation to contemporary issues of human alienation and of human renewal struggling to overcome that alienation. This combination of themes and styles of discussion produced at Stavanger considerable theological tension and consequent dis-agreement, but it focused attention on the need to receive God's revela-tion *in* particular situations, *through* particular experiences.

Receiving God's revelation

Such reception (and "reception" is a key word in Faith and Order study today) is essential to the theme of unity and renewal. The CWMC consultation on "The Authority of Scripture in the Light of the New Experiences of Women" (Amsterdam, 1980)[2] highlighted the issues. How do new experiences relate to the givenness of God's self-revelation? From a Christian viewpoint, new experiences are certainly to be evaluated by seeing how they kindle insight upon the given revelation, and are in turn illuminated and corrected by the revelation. Of course the range of experiences considered must include the experience of believers, in the eucharist and in the life of discipleship. But is it possible for such experiences not only to challenge misunderstanding and misuse by Christians of the revelation, but even to challenge the form of that revelation, mediated through patriarchal societies, whose male perspective distorted God's self-communication? Such a question must seem radical in the setting of Faith and Order work, but it is one form of a question about the authority of scripture which has been agitating the churches ever since critical scrutiny of the scriptures began in the struggle to relate the mission of Jesus to the structure of Jewish and Greco-Roman traditional societies.

The Prague consultation again engaged with this issue as it followed day by day the Bible studies led by Prof. Elisabeth Schüssler Fiorenza (Federal Republic of Germany and the USA) on a feminist theological reconstruction in New Testament hermeneutics and, through the second presentation, reflected on the Orthodox understanding of the roles of women and men determined by the being of the church in Christ.

In relation to CWMC, the presentation by the Rev. Janet Crawford made it clear that the Community Study had been "essentially biblical, Christological and Trinitarian"; yet it had also raised controversy over hermeneutics, over the significance of Jesus, the saviour of women and men, being male, and of Mary being a woman, yet also forerunner of all future Christians, men and women; it had raised debate also over the language of the creeds in glorifying God as Father, Son and Holy Spirit. The study of the fourth world conference on Faith and Order (Montreal 1963) on "Scripture, Tradition and Traditions"[3] needs to be brought back into active consideration by the churches in relation to the recent developments of ecumenical debate on exegesis and hermeneutics.

The question of hermeneutics

To return to the Bible studies, these presupposed the critical feminist-theological hermeneutics of liberation set out in Prof. Schüssler Fiorenza's books *In Memory of Her*[4] and *Bread, not Stone*.[5] They sought to elaborate, with the help of historical-critical analysis, two distinct paradigms of the church in the New Testament. Prof. Schüssler Fiorenza has herself summarized their approach as follows: "In such a critical feminist-theological teaching the story of the 'woman bent double' in Luke 13:10-17 becomes a paradigm for the societal and ecclesial 'bondage' of women in patriarchy. It challenges us to focus our attention on these women on 'the bottom of the patriarchal pyramid' oppressed by racism, classism, imperialism and sexism. It calls us to solidarity with them in conversion and repentance."

"Patriarchy" was carefully defined in the Bible studies as a historical-sociological-theological concept that was first articulated by Aristotle and has decisively influenced Western culture and Christian theology. By using patriarchy as a heuristic concept for analyzing New Testament texts and reconstructing the Jesus movement and early Christian missionary movement, the church as "the discipleship of equals" becomes historically and theologically visible. Inclusiveness, wholeness and "equality from below" characterize the "new family of disciples" in the Jesus movement; "equality in the power of the Spirit" is foundational for the early Christian missionary movement. The pre-Pauline baptismal formula Galatians 3:28 expresses this theological self-understanding of the early Christian missionary movement, which rejects all patriarchal status-stratifications and religious privileges as constitutive for the body of Christ, the church. The so-called Household Code texts of the Deutero- and post-Pauline literature (for example, Col. 3:18-4:1 and 1 Tim. 2:11-15) seek to impose the Aristotelian ethos of patriarchal submission first on the members of the household — slaves, women, young persons — and then on the whole community, in order to lessen the tension with their Greco-Roman patriarchal society. However, the Gospels of Mark and John, which were written around the same time, "reject all structures of domination and insist that Christians should not avoid suffering caused by the tension between the discipleship of equals and Greco-Roman patriarchal society and culture".

Serious historical and exegetical and hermeneutic engagement with the position thus set out in the Bible studies will be an important part of future work by the Faith and Order Commission, since agreement on the scriptural basis for the roles of women and men in the church will be essential for the resolution of questions which now seriously divide Christians and churches from one another. This feminist hermeneutic addresses the need of Christian women (and men who support their hopes) who have felt they might have to abandon scriptural authority in order to be liberated. A direct appeal is made to the Jesus movement and the early Christian missionary movement. One might compare the ecclesiological argument of Emil Brunner in *The Misunderstanding of the Church*[6], contrasting a spirit-led *ekklesia* with the so-called "early Catholicism" of the pastoral Epistles. To call for serious attention to such arguments is not of course to see them as other than controversial.

Context and correction

Yet there are common aims involved in the study of scripture and Tradition. Receiving God's revelation in context is an aim common to all Christians. Removing misunderstanding of the revelation is a task common to all Christian education. There has to be continuing reflection on the way in which God the Holy Spirit is still at work among humankind, as the guide for this contextualization and correction.

Thus the Orthodox presentation by the Very Rev. Dr George Dragas and the Rev. Dr Gennadios Limouris (Ecumenical Patriarchate) offered an understanding of the Christological context and criteria for Orthodox reflection on the church and on the roles of women and men. The richness of these papers did not permit a full consideration of them, and there was a procedural difficulty in considering two presentations of national and local church experience (Church of South India and St John's Church, Berkeley, USA) alongside a presentation of the Orthodox theological *position* in which, for Orthodox Christians, any reflection on experience should be grounded. Something of the concerns put to the consultation may be grasped through two citations.

From Father Gennadios: "The church is 'theandric' in *nature* (or constitution), the union of all that exists, or rather destined to embrace all that exists: God and the creation. It is the body of Christ and therefore both one with him and distinct from him. The church is immanent and has within it the transcendent community of the Persons of the Trinity, which is filled with boundless love for the world."

From Father George: "The traditional teaching of the church, at least as the Orthodox Christians perceive it, entails a spiritual identity between women and men and a biological distinction which implies complementarity as opposed to inequality... In Orthodox perspective differentiations between Christians arise not from the positions or functions that one occupies or performs in the church, but from the measure of one's participation in and consistency with the grace of God which is equally available to all."

From the other case studies came a plea to the traditional Christian, whether Orthodox, Roman Catholic or conservative Protestant, to be open to what is happening in the world around, not abandoning the tradition but seeing how in the context of developing patterns of human life and relationship there may be corrected not the gospel itself, the treasure (2 Cor. 4:7), but the shape of the earthen vessels in which the gospel is held by the church, vessels which are earthen not only in their fragility but also in their character as culturally and historically determined and therefore sometimes distorted, sometimes freshly illuminating. Such reshaping was described, for example, by Mrs Mabel de Filippini in relation to the "base communities" of the churches in Argentina.

Two ecclesiological emphases drawn from experience

This dialogue on ecclesiology, only begun in the Prague consultation, requires for its fruitful continuance a reflection on the two ecclesiological emphases underlying the two main positions which were implicit in our deliberations.

On the one hand, exemplified by the Rev. Dr Padmasani Gallup's future-oriented account of the coming to unity of the Church of South India, there is a vision of the church as in constant pilgrimage, moving through a history of the world in which the risen Christ ever calls it to respond to the divine presence, to the creative work of the Holy Spirit. Such a vision is not indifferent to the past; it recognizes the (literally) vital importance of the source of the church's life in Christ, but it does not identify any particular moment of the church's pilgrimage through history (e.g. the Reformation) as determinative, normative for its future. That which gives identity to a river (see Ezek. 47) is its source, not any one part of the configuration of its channel and banks.

Thus in the Church of South India the union of 1947 has opened the way to further steps in overcoming divisions within the church. The ordination of women to the ministry of word and sacrament has been one of these steps, arrived at by a long process of consultation in the church and now being implemented as each diocesan council is ready to make the relevant decision. Those involved in these ordinations have experienced them as a renewing act of the Holy Spirit.

Over against this picture stands another vision, primary for some Christians but by others held alongside the first. This perceives the church as the given place of Christ's risen presence in the mystery of the sacraments, and the gospel as having a context which was defined, under the guidance of the Holy Spirit, in the foundational period of the church.

In such a perspective "the restriction of ordained priesthood to men only does not imply inequality, since the gift administered by the priest is equally available — to the same measure — to priests and lay people, men and women" (from Father George's paper).

It was evident, with regard to this question of ordaining women to the ministry of word and sacrament and in other ways, that these two ecclesiological emphases led participants in the consultation to different initial responses to particular "cases" of Christian experience. The emphases are not to be contrasted as respectively subjective and objective — both rest upon a faith in the objectivity of the risen life of Christ. They are not to be contrasted as ontological and functional — both speak of *being* in Christ and *acting* in Christ's service. They are not to be contrasted as depending respectively on experience and revelation — both claim to experience God's self-revelation in the process of history. Yet there *are* distinct emphases in the understanding of the divine/humane encounter, of the divine/human reality in which the mystery of the gospel finds its active expression.

This is the point at which the third case study presented by the Rev. Sandra Park (USA) had such an important role to play. She enabled us to enter, through the experience of one local church in Berkeley, California, into the way in which this dialogue between the two ecclesiological emphases has taken place for "ordinary" Christians over the past thirty years.

Her interviews with members of St John's Presbyterian Church revealed many aspects of this dialogue. For instance:

a) the way in which individuals, e.g. one of the first women to be elected elder, had to work through their own hesitations over such matters as participating in the distribution of the communion elements;

b) the possibility of involvement in such a study of those opposed to change, but still firmly rooted in the church as a family;

c) how difficult it is, even when women share in representative groups, for them to achieve the leadership roles within such groups, e.g. responsibility for budgeting and financial control;

d) the difficulty of the inclusive language issue, especially in reading from scripture in worship and in using inclusive language for speaking of God;

e) the importance of women in creating community care programmes;

f) the feeling among some women that male leadership in ministry is part of the familial pattern of church life and possibly essential to retain male participation in the church.

The feature of the St John's experience which found the widest echo from others in the consultation was the reality of "two churches" in the one local church, a "men's church" and a "women's church"; a men's church with token participation of women but generally male leadership, and a women's church in the women's organizations and projects, responsible for many auxiliary and supportive roles throughout the whole range of church life. The recognition of this reality is most important for the present phase of St John's, which is the hard struggle to bring together the "two churches" in the one body of Christ. There is a grieving for the past that has to be worked through before there can be a creation and celebration of a church of true mutuality.

Truth and pain

The presentation of local and personal experiences highlighted the emotional commitments that affect the dialogue about ecclesiology. The perception of conservative positions of *any* tradition as "rigid" and "unjust" can easily lead to an equal and opposite dogmatism in those seeking change. The question is acutely raised of how to introduce into the issues of the struggles against oppression — the struggles against sexism, racism and all the other forms of oppression — how to introduce there the patience and mutual openness between "radical" and "conservative" that have been found essential for such theological tasks as the development of the *Baptism, Eucharist and Ministry* study.

There have been moving glimpses in the consultation of such openness and patience. Yet while such patience may keep a dialogue in process, it may alienate others who feel that patience delays justice (cf. the World Alliance of Reformed Churches debate about an attitude to the South African member churches who support apartheid). Those thus alienated in the debate about sexism have abandoned a reconstructive feminism for a feminism which has rejected the Christian church and tradition as incorrigibly patriarchal, and finds positive value in an alternative "women's spirituality".

The issues here are not confined to the sexism debate, but are relevant for the whole ecumenical movement and the strong feeling in some quarters that there are *two* movements, one reconciling (to the point of being too conciliatory?); the other striving for justice (to the point of being too destructive/aggressive?). It is necessary that this question be explored in all units of the WCC, not only in the Faith and Order Commission. But the Commission has an opportunity in the Unity and Renewal Study to address the question directly. As was pointed out in one of the groups at the consultation, to be patient about the role of women (to allow the churches to make progress with unity issues such as those of *Baptism, Eucharist and Ministry*, or the search for "A Common Expression of the Apostolic Faith Today") may betray *both* the women who are denied effective participation in the search for unity *and* the search for unity itself, which will reach false solutions of problems unless there is a fuller development of the community of women and men in the church. Only an "impatient patience" will serve the purpose.

Hurting and healing

What is this "impatient patience"? Much was learnt about it at Prague. It is a combination of understanding, will and emotion. It is not simply an attitude but a part of ecclesiology, a reflection on the ecclesial community, where hurting and healing both take place within the circle of God's love and so healing can prevail. It is an attitude which enables people to recognize what hurts and what heals; so at Prague we found that:

— It hurts when you need to pursue an issue of deep inner concern and it gets turned into an inter-confessional argument.
— It hurts when you are not heard because your whole theological approach is misunderstood as just an argument.
— It hurts when you ask a question and someone weeps or laughs.
— It hurts when you weep or laugh and all someone does is ask questions.
— It hurts when a consultation with so much input from women concentrates on issues which men select from the agenda.
— It hurts when a consultation on the community of women and men neglects marriage and the family as a place of that community.
— It hurts when single people are invisible and inaudible in a "family" conversation.
— It hurts when the sun goes down on our anger.

Wrong ideas about God hurt.

— It heals when hurts are seen for what they are and openly tackled.
— It heals when those who are hurt can go aside for a while together.
— It heals when methods are planned together to meet the perceived needs of the whole group.
— It heals when there is time for explaining yourself.
— It heals when there is time and will to hear the explanation.
— It heals when there is time simply to discover one another as Christians.
— It heals when prayer and worship are not only the framework for a meeting but also its "atmosphere".
— It heals when we forgive one another.

The love of God heals.

A way forward

A possible way forward lies in the concept of conciliar fellowship which was elaborated before, at and after the Nairobi Assembly of the WCC. The Rev. Janet Crawford's paper spoke of the way in which the study of "The Community of Women and Men in the Church" produced "an envisioning of renewed community". It is instructive to set this "envisioning" alongside the description offered at Nairobi of conciliar fellowship:

A renewed community would be:
— an inclusive community in which no individual or group would be excluded, oppressed, subjugated or exploited;
— a community in which relationships would be characterized by love and mutuality;
— a community of equals without domination and subordination, superiority and inferiority;
— a community embracing and celebrating diversity and difference;
— a community encouraging the full participation of all its members and the development of the gifts of each individual;
— a community of women and men, living together as equal partners.

"The one church is to be envisioned as a conciliar fellowship of local churches which are themselves truly united. In this conciliar fellowship, each local church possesses, in common with the others, the fullness of catholicity, witnesses to the same apostolic faith, and therefore recognizes the others as belonging to the same Church of Christ and guided by the same Spirit."[7]

The left-hand text refers primarily to local situations, the right-hand to the worldwide church; yet this comparison indicates how important for both statements is *community*. The Chantilly/Stavanger statement on the church as "mystery and prophetic sign"[8] needs to be elucidated in terms of the community and communion of the church, in order that the ecclesiological issues discussed at Prague may be treated in a way that engages with contemporary Christian experiences. Such experiences are not only those reflected in "The Community of Women and Men in the Church" study but also those involved in other aspects of what Sheffield called "the web of oppression". The Rev. Dr Constance Parvey's paper reminded us that it was an important step forward at Sheffield to recognize sexism as part of the interwoven complex of racism, classism, economic exploitation and other forms of oppression.

The Community Study reflected experiences of women and men in a way that showed what it is like to feel powerless. The church is commissioned to exercise a ministry of healing, reconciliation and release towards the powerless and with them. Such a ministry is carried on in the distinctive power of Jesus Christ, a power that makes people whole.

Release from the web of oppression by that power involves a painful turning to Christ in penitence for the many ways in which Christians have taken part in oppression. Yet despite the many failures of Christians, there are victories in the struggle against the web of oppression, victories that may be celebrated as part of our life in Christ. Just as the unity of the church is a given reality and also a task before us, so the victory of the risen Christ is a present reality as well as the ground of hope.

Jesus Christ, bringer of life

In one of our worship services the consultation was reminded of Jesus' bringing of life to the widow's son at Nain (Luke 7:11-17). The weeping woman became the focus of Jesus' attention: he had compassion on her. The outcome of that compassion restored community; Jesus gave the son to his mother and the crowd was led to praise God and to disperse to witness to Jesus' act. Yet it is following that act that the imprisoned John the Baptiser is introduced by Luke as struggling with the question: "Is Jesus the coming one?" (Luke 7:18-20). Today there are many places of human struggle, places where the web of oppression is very strong, where after moments of breakthrough long years of frustration erode hope. So people are asking: "Where is deliverance to be found?" The church is called to be the community where Jesus the life-giver is at work by the Spirit in healing power; in the church the relationships of women and men can be renewed by Christ. In this and in every upsurge of new life in Christ the unity of the church can focus the mystery of God's eternal plan and provide the sign of a coming renewal of human community.

NOTES

[1] "The Unity of the Church and the Renewal of Human Community: the Church as Mystery and Prophetic Sign" (FO/85:4) is now available in its latest form for study and comment from the Faith and Order Commission, 150 route de Ferney, 1211 Geneva 20, Switzerland. The original (Chantilly) version is printed in "Church, Kingdom, World: the Church as Mystery and Prophetic Sign", ed. Gennadios Limouris, *Faith and Order Paper No. 130*, Geneva, WCC, 1986, Appendix 2, pp.163-175.

[2] The report of the consultation is published as "The Authority of Scripture", in *In God's Image: Reflections on Identity, Human Wholeness and the Authority of Scripture*, eds Janet Crawford and Michael Kinnamon, Geneva, WCC, 1983, pp.79-108.

[3] See "The Fourth World Conference on Faith and Order: the Report from Montreal 1963", eds P.C. Rodger and L. Vischer, *Faith and Order Paper No. 42*, London, SCM Press, 1964, pp.50-61.

[4] New York, Crossroads, 1983.

[5] Boston, Beacon, 1984.

[6] Translated by Harold Knight, Philadelphia, Westminster Press, 1953.

[7] *Breaking Barriers: Nairobi 1975*, ed. David M. Paton, London, SPCK, and Grand Rapids, Wm. B. Eerdmans, 1976, p.60.

[8] See note 1.

Report of the
Prague Consultation

An international consultation on the theme of the Community of Women and Men and the Unity and Renewal of the Church and Human Community was held in Prague, Czechoslovakia, from 25 September to 2 October 1985. The 27 participants, 15 women and 12 men, came from 16 countries and 11 churches. We wish to record our gratitude to the Czechoslovak Ecumenical Council for its generous and sensitive hospitality. We welcomed the opportunity to meet and discuss with church leaders of the Ecumenical Council and to share our hope for the ecumenical movement. In particular we record our thanks to the following persons: Dr Anezka Ebertova, Dr Jaroslav Ondra and Dr Josef Smolik. Sharing in worship with local congregations, and taking part in a service of holy communion in a church packed with young people, were moving experiences for the members of the consultation. The conference found time to explore and enjoy the beautiful city of Prague bathed in the autumn sunlight. However, the painful history of the division of the churches in this city and this land across the centuries made us aware of the need we all have for the healing and reconciliation of our past and present divisions.

The life of the consultation was grounded in prayer from the opening service in the Lutheran Church of St Michael, at which we were joined by representatives of the Czechoslovak Ecumenical Council, to the closing act of worship. Morning by morning, meditations led by consultation participants from different regions helped us to feel a part of a wider worshipping community. And, at the moment when the consultation experienced the greatest tension in committing its reflections to paper, the group testified, by joining hands in prayer, to its shared belief that the Holy Spirit will lead us into all truth. In this experience we discovered afresh that prayer and theology are one.

The Prague proceedings

The consultation was the second to be held as part of the Faith and Order Commission's Study on Unity and Renewal, one of the three major studies of the Commission. The first consultation, held at Chantilly, France, in January 1985, produced a paper which was further developed at the Faith and Order Plenary Commission meeting in Stavanger, Norway, in August 1985, entitled "The Church as Mystery and Prophetic Sign".[1] The intention of this second consultation was to recall the ecclesiological insights of the Study on the Community of Women and Men in the Church, the results of which were gathered together in the Sheffield conference in July 1981.[2] Thus the Prague consultation, under the moderatorship of the Rev. Dr Paul Crow, was concerned to explore and develop the ecclesiological insights of the Community Study. It is planned that these insights will, at a later stage, interact with the Chantilly/Stavanger work on "The Church as Mystery and Prophetic Sign". In a similar way a consultation on ideologies, planned for September 1986, will contribute to the ecclesiology of the unity and renewal study. The Rev. Dr Constance Parvey, director of the Community Study from 1978-1982, and the Rev. Janet Crawford reflected in different ways on the Community Study.

From the outset the Community Study was based upon experience, the experience of as inclusive a community of Christians as could be drawn into the study process. Experience was always understood as a valid, indeed an essential, part of theological exploration. This was reflected at the Prague consultation in the three central presentations as well as in the presentation of biblical material by Dr Elisabeth Schüssler Fiorenza. Her material was extremely challenging, and the group felt that in future consultations it will be essential to allow adequate time for dealing with both the technical and the personal demands offered by such presentations. The group is grateful for the privilege of having Elisabeth present throughout the entire meeting.

The three presentations which formed the centre of our work were very different in style and content. This proved important not only for the content each one contained, but for helping us understand the different yet complementary methods involved in theological reflection.

The first presentation, by the Rev. Dr Padmasani Gallup, described in a personal way her experience in the Church of South India. Padma emphasized the need for the visible unity of the church in a culture where Christianity is very much a minority religion. She described also the developing role of women in the church's ministry, including the presbyterial ministry, and her own pilgrimage towards ordination.

The second presentation, by Orthodox participants the Very Rev. Dr George Dragas and the Rev. Dr Gennadios Limouris, included first an evaluation from an Orthodox perspective of the method of the Community Study, its ecclesiological insights and the understanding of male and female, masculine and feminine. The second part was a major contribution by Father Gennadios entitled "Men and Women: Equal Partners in the Christian Community: an Orthodox Point of View".

The third presentation, by the Rev. Sandra Park, was closest to being a "case study" in the social-scientific sense of the term. We found it to be a refreshing departure from the customary style of Faith and Order work. It took us existentially into the life of Sandra's congregation in Berkeley, California, and showed how, in that very particular church, new modes of behaviour and new patterns of living in the community of the church have emerged.

As in so many consultations, the pressure of time made it hard for small groups to feel that their response did justice to the richness of the presentations. Interpretation and language and agenda affected the nature and shape of our discussions. Considerable discussion time was occupied with issues prominent in the North Atlantic regions, particularly between Protestant and Orthodox members from North Atlantic churches. As a consequence situations of women and men coming from churches in socialist and "third-world" contexts, which raise other urgent concerns and essential perspectives, were often not heard. However, an important part of the report of the Prague consultation is contained in the ecclesiological insights delineated by the three groups in their reports. In addition, Principal Martin Cressey was asked to present an overall personal reflection upon the consultation. This was not an easy task, and the group records its gratitude for Martin's patience in attentive listening and skillful recording. We hope that this reflection, together with the three reports, will enable others to understand the discussions and insights of the Prague consultation.

It is the following recommendations, agreed upon by every member of the consultation, which will ensure the influence of the insights of this major international consultation upon the future work of Faith and Order

— not only on the Study on Unity and Renewal, but also on its study programme work upon "Towards a Common Expression of the Apostolic Faith Today" and upon "Baptism, Eucharist and Ministry".

Recommendations

The Prague consultation recommends that:

1. The Steering Group on Unity and Renewal consider how best to stimulate discussion among those whose voices were not heard in the Community Study. In particular, "case studies" should be carried out among Orthodox groups in different parts of the world.

2. The Steering Group ensure that the study guide recommended at the Stavanger meeting of the Faith and Order Commission include issues such as marriage, family life, the role of Mary, monasticism, etc. This study guide should be oriented towards regional groups in order that cultures other than Europe and North America be taken seriously. The Steering Group should seek case studies from those people who suffer exploitation and oppression and who struggle for peoplehood, for they often point to fresh ecclesiological understandings.

3. The Steering Group on Unity and Renewal ensure that the ecclesiological insights of the Community Study, and in particular the formulation of these at the Prague consultation, interact with the study and further development of the Chantilly/Stavanger text on "The Church as Mystery and Prophetic Sign".

4. The Steering Group on Unity and Renewal see that the explorations of ecclesiology listen to and incorporate the experience of the church where it lives as a minority in the midst of people of other living faiths. This theme, out of those proposed at Stavanger for a fourth consultation, now seems to us to be the most important (see the report of Group II, 7 at Stavanger).[3] This should be undertaken in collaboration with the WCC Sub-unit on Dialogue with People of Other Living Faiths.

5. The Faith and Order Standing Commission consider how to develop work on the Montreal report on "Scripture, Tradition, Traditions"[4] in such a way as to contribute to a fuller theological framework for ecclesiology. In particular these reflections should take up for exploration and evaluation the report of the Amsterdam consultation (1980), entitled "The Authority of the Bible in the Light of new Experiences of Women"[5], and the approaches to the interpretation of the Bible reflected in the biblical presentations at the Sheffield and Prague consultations.

6. The Steering Group on "Baptism, Eucharist and Ministry"

(a) take into account the work of the Community Study on "power", "authority", and "determining the life of the community" in any future work on common structures of decision-making and teaching authoritatively;

(b) undertake a study on the priesthood in relation to the ministry of the whole people of God, in the light both of the BEM convergence (not consensus) on priesthood and the experience of women, and of congregations, in those churches that ordain women to a full ministry of word and sacrament;

(c) undertake a study on the eucharist as transformation/transfiguration in the body of Christ and its implications for renewal vis-à-vis the insights of the Community of Women and Men in the Church Study.

7. The Faith and Order staff ensure that the materials from the Prague consultation, and from Chantilly/Stavanger, be published soon as Faith and Order papers (cf. a suggested outline for the publications of material from the Prague consultation).

8. The Faith and Order Standing Commission see that all possible steps be taken to facilitate the translation of *The Community of Women and Men in the Church: the Sheffield Report* into French and Spanish, as was stated in the recommendations passed to the churches by the Dresden Central Committee. Fulfillment of this recommendation will help the Community Study to be more widely reflected upon, and will promote the necessary continuing study and deeper research into women's concerns in theology.

NOTES

[1] This text, which is undergoing continuing development, is available from the Faith and Order Commission, WCC, Geneva.

[2] See *The Community of Women and Men in the Church: the Sheffied Report*, ed. Constance F. Parvey, Geneva, WCC, 1983.

[3] "Faith and Renewal", ed. Thomas F. Best, *Faith and Order Paper No. 131*, Geneva, WCC, 1986, pp.208-214.

[4] "The Fourth World Conference on Faith and Order: the Report from Montreal 1963", eds P.C. Rodger and L. Vischer, *Faith and Order Paper No. 42*, London, SCM Press, 1964, pp.50-61.

[5] See "The Authority of Scripture in Light of New Experiences of Women", in *In God's Image*, eds Janet Crawford and Michael Kinnamon, Geneva, WCC, 1983, pp.79-108.

Appendix 1

Participants

Beaupère, Father René, (Roman Catholic), 2 Place Gailleton, 69002 Lyon, France

Crawford, Rev. Janet, (Church of the Province of New Zealand, Anglican), The College of St John the Evangelist, 202 St John's Road, Auckland 5, New Zealand

Cressey, Rev. Martin, (United Reformed Church in the United Kingdom), The Principal's Lodge, Westminster College, Madingley Road, Cambridge CB3 0AB, England

Crow, Rev. Dr Paul A. Jr, (Disciples of Christ, Moderator of Study on "The Unity of the Church and the Renewal of Human Community"), President, Council on Christian Unity, P.O. Box 1986, Christian Church (Disciples of Christ), Indianapolis, IN 46206, USA

Desroches, Prof. Rosny, (Methodist Church in the Caribbean and the Americas), Nouveau Collège Bird, B.P. 22, Port-au-Prince, Haiti

Dragas, Very Rev. Dr George, (Greek Orthodox, Ecumenical Patriarchate, Archdiocese of Thyateira and Great Britain), Abbey House, Palace Green, Durham DH1 3RS, England

Ebertova, Dr Anezka, (Czechoslovak Hussite Church), Hviezdochavora 1, 10100 Prague 10, Czechoslovakia

de Filippini, Ms Mabel Lidia Sardon, (Methodist Church in Argentina), Segurola 4240, 1419 Buenos Aires, Argentina

Gallup, Rev. Dr Padmasani J., (Church of South India), 122B., T.T.K. Road, Alvarpet, Madras 600 018, India

de Garcia, Mrs Ana Langerak, (Lutheran Diocese of Costa Rica and Panama), CELEP, Apartado 1307, 1000 San José, Costa Rica

Gerka, Rev. Prof. ThDr Milan, (Orthodox Church in Czechoslovakia), Orthodox Theological Seminary, V Presove, u1. Sladkovicova 23, 080 01 Presov, Czechoslovakia

Heiling, Rev. Inge, (Ev. Lutherische Landeskirche Mecklenburg), Burgseestrasse 3, Schwerin, 2755 German Democratic Republic

Hiller, Rev. Hilga, (Ev. Landeskirche in Württemberg), Morikestrasse 6, 7014 Kornwestheim, Federal Republic of Germany

Isshiki, Mrs Yoshiko, (United Church of Christ in Japan), 29-6 Kyodo 2-chome, Setagaya-ku, Tokyo 156, Japan

Koukoura, Dr Mrs Dimitra, (Church of Greece), 37 Vas Konstantinon Ave., 54622 Thessaloniki, Greece

Ondra, Dr Jaroslav N., (Evangelical Church of Czech Brethren), u1. 2 Wintra 15, 16000 Prague 6, Czechoslovakia

Opocenska, Rev. Jana, (Evangelical Church of Czech Brethren), Nepomucka 1025, 15000 Prague 5, Czechoslovakia

Opocensky, Rev. Dr Milan, (Evangelical Church of Czech Brethren), Nepomucka 1025, 15000 Prague 5, Czechoslovakia

Park, Rev. Sandra Winter, (Presbyterian Church, USA), 2514 Dana Street, Berkeley, CA 94704, USA

Parvey, Rev. Dr Constance F., (Lutheran Church in America), c/o Lutheran Theological Seminary, 7301 Germantown Ave., Philadelphia, PA 19119, USA

Roy-Bremond, Mrs Arlette, (Eglise réformée de France), 9 allée des Champs Balais, 86000 Poitiers, France

Schüssler Fiorenza, Dr Elisabeth, (Roman Catholic), 7, Phillips Place, Cambridge, MA 02138, USA

Smolik, Prof. Dr Josef, (Evangelical Church of Czech Brethren), Belgicka 22, Prague 2, Czechoslovakia

Suvarsky, Archpriest Prof. Dr Jaroslav, (Orthodox Church in Czechoslovakia), V. Jame 6, Prague 1, Czechoslovakia

Tanne, Prof. Bio, (Roman Catholic), Institut catholique de l'Afrique de l'Ouest, 08 B.P. 22, Abidjan 08, Ivory Coast.

Tanner, Mrs Mary, (Church of England, Anglican), Highclere, Camp End Road, Weybridge, Surrey, England

Zoe-Obianga, Mrs Rose, (Presbyterian Church of Cameroon), P.O. Box 352, Yaoundé, Cameroon

Faith and Order Commission staff

Best, Rev. Dr Thomas F., (Disciples of Christ, Christian Church)

Chapman, Mrs Eileen, (Uniting Church in Australia)

Gassmann, Mrs Ursula, (Evangelical Church in Germany, Lutheran), coopted

Limouris, Rev. Dr Gennadios, (Ecumenical Patriarchate of Constantinople)

Sbeghen, Mrs Renate, (Lutheran/Eglise nationale de Genève)

Appendix 2

An Orthodox Statement
on the Prague Consultation

VERY REV. DR G. DRAGAS, DR (MRS) D. KOUKOURA
AND VERY REV. DR G. LIMOURIS

The inclusion of such a brief statement was requested by the small minority of the Eastern Orthodox participants in the above consultation. The final plenary approved the inclusion of such a statement, to be written at a later date. It represents some critical remarks about certain procedural and methodological aspects of the consultation.

On the whole we felt that the consultation was imbalanced and one-sided. There was a predominance of women participants who were concerned with women as such, in most cases from a feminist point of view. This is manifested in the choice of topics for presentation and discussion and especially in the daily lengthy feminist reflection on the Bible to which no response was allowed in spite of strong objections from several participants especially the Orthodox. In the opinion of the Orthodox such a reflection not only did not take seriously the traditional stance of the churches, but was openly offensive inasmuch as it distorted the historical teaching of the Bible, explicit and implicit, by imposing value judgments of feminist ideology on the biblical data.

The strong commitment to feminist ideology of many of the participants meant that critical theological discussion in a spirit of mutual respect was often replaced by an unprecedented emotionalism which opted for particular contexts, cases and concerns at the expense of common basic experience. Thus the women's plea for inclusiveness was made in such a way that it excluded the traditional Catholic and ecumenical Orthodox perspectives. Women's rights and concerns tended to determine most of the agenda and the discussions and thus the actual subject of communion of women and men in church and society was partially treated. The attempt of the Orthodox participants to direct attention to the central theme of the consultation was greatly resisted and unfairly criticized. As a result of this one-sided feminist approach, there was no discussion on such central topics like family, divorce, the children, the young people and the elderly. Such topics central to the theme of the consultation and of central concern for the churches today were replaced by partial modern and general ideological and sociological concerns including women's rights, the ordination of women and other related subjects. Though particular concerns and issues are important, the central concerns which bring out the mind of the participating churches should be given priority.

From the methodological point of view the consultation was yet another example of the trend that seems to be dominant in several contemporary secular/sociological and religious contents, which involves the promotion of positivist tactics, which push for this or that particular case or cause. The imbalance which results from such an approach leads to false pretences which neither enjoy any special value nor carry any authority among the Orthodox. Even more seriously such approaches undermine the significance of Faith and Order as such, and transform it into a source of independent challenges to the member churches of the WCC rather than proving it to be an effective instrument in promoting a profounder and more objective understanding of the common and uncommon stances of the member churches which might lead the churches to appropriate constructive ecumenical actions.

The Orthodox are very firm on the catholic Christian perspectives (apostolic and patristic) which constitute sine-qua-non's of Christian integrity. By structuring the agendas of consultations having in mind the concerns of all the member churches we can be more successful in achieving the true objectives of the Faith and Order movement. Exposure of difference is not easy either to do or accept. It is necessary, however, if more positive and long-lasting results are to be attained to, not only to expose but patiently to investigate the exact presuppositions which lie behind them, so that real advance in mutual understanding and mutual undertaking of responsible action might be taken.

The Prague consultation exhibited most of the possible problems which beset the modern approach to the dialogue — inadequate or one-sided or preliminary treatment of the subjects in question by emphasizing specific/ limited cases and contexts and giving the impression of deliberately ignoring the total picture (including the historical/traditional dimension of the case). Yet it ended with a sense of optimism. The unhappiness, frustration, disappointment and tension which were experienced at the beginning of the consultation, were transformed by clear indications of a willingness to understand, to appreciate and to integrate the particular and general concerns.

This statement may still retain something of the sharpness and tension which emerged at Prague, but it can certainly conclude with a sign of optimism and hope. Whatever the inadequacies of us Christians are, the mystery of the church is so great and adequate that we can be healed by it especially when we are exposed. Dialogue, serious dialogue, and faith and commitment will indeed lead us to the conquest of the truth, for Christian unity.

Appendix 3

Overview of the
Unity and Renewal Study Programme

The understanding of the Study on "The Unity of the Church and the Renewal of Human Community" has been sharpened and deepened since the initial programme outline developed at the Faith and Order Standing Commission meeting in Crete in 1984.[1] The following is adapted from the programme overview as adopted by the Faith and Order Standing Commission at its meeting in Madrid, August 1987.[2]

1. The Unity and Renewal Study has four major components or programme elements, as follows:

1) the text on "The Church as Mystery and Prophetic Sign";

2) study of the theme: "Unity and Renewal and the Community of Women and Men in the Church";

3) study of the theme: "Unity and Renewal and Issues of Justice";

4) local study groups on issues of unity and renewal (social and political context, women and men, the church, interfaith context).

2. Each element will be developed towards the next meeting of the Faith and Order Plenary Commission (1989).

1) "The Church as Mystery and Prophetic Sign": consultation, Chantilly, 1985. The text will undergo continuing review by Standing and Plenary Commissions, and benefit from contributions by consultants.

2) Community of Women and Men: consultations: Prague 1985 and Africa 1988; "integration" of results, November 1988.

3) Justice: consultations: Singapore 1986 and Brazil 1987; "initial integration" of results, February/March 1988; consultation with black churches, USA, August 1988; further "integration" of results.

4) Local study groups using the Unity and Renewal *Study Guide*: 1987 onwards; initial evaluation of reports: small consultation, December 1988/January 1989. Continuing reception of reports.

3. The various programme elements will be integrated for presentation to the Faith and Order Plenary Commission (1989)

Preparation of Report for Plenary commission: consultation, March 1989 (Steering Group, Commissioners, consultants, consultation participants, representatives of local groups)

4. The Faith and Order Plenary Commission (August 1989) will review the Unity and Renewal Report and provide directions for further work.

5. This will focus on preparation of input to the World Council of Churches Assembly at Canberra, Australia (February 1991). It could include the following elements:

1) further results from the continuing study process in local study groups;

2) responses from churches to the initial Unity and Renewal report;

3) possible additional work in critical areas, in coordination with other WCC and Faith and Order programmes:
   a) Unity and Renewal and the Brokenness of Creation
   b) Unity and Renewal in an Interfaith Context

4) final revision of the Unity and Renewal report for input to WCC Assembly.

6. The Unity and Renewal report will provide major input for the WCC Assembly (1991), which will give direction for future work in this area.

NOTES

[1] "Minutes of the Meeting of the Standing Commission 1984, Crete", *Faith and Order Paper No. 121,* Geneva, WCC, 1984, pp.33-52. Reprinted in "Church, Kingdom, World: the Church as Mystery and Prophetic Sign", ed. Gennadios Limouris, *Faith and Order Paper No. 130*, Geneva, WCC, 1986, pp.186-203.
[2] "Minutes of the Meeting of the Standing Commission (Majadahonda, Madrid, Spain, 1987)", *Faith and Order Paper No. 141*, Geneva, Commission on Faith and Order, 1987, pp.83-89.

DATE DUE

HIGHSMITH   # 45220

THE DILEMMAS OF TRUSTEESHIP

THE
DILEMMAS OF TRUSTEESHIP

ASPECTS OF BRITISH COLONIAL
POLICY BETWEEN THE WARS

*The Reid Lectures delivered at Acadia University
in February 1963*

by

KENNETH ROBINSON

*Director of the Institute of Commonwealth Studies
and Professor of Commonwealth Affairs in the
University of London*

with a Preface by

WATSON KIRKCONNELL

President of Acadia University

LONDON
OXFORD UNIVERSITY PRESS
NEW YORK   TORONTO
1965

Oxford University Press, Amen House, London, E.C.4.

GLASGOW NEW YORK TORONTO MELBOURNE WELLINGTON
BOMBAY CALCUTTA MADRAS KARACHI LAHORE DACCA
CAPE TOWN SALISBURY NAIROBI IBADAN ACCRA
KUALA LUMPUR HONG KONG

Printed in Great Britain by
Butler & Tanner Ltd, Frome and London

CONTENTS

AUTHOR'S FOREWORD

This book contains the Reid Lectures delivered at Acadia University in February 1963. I am most grateful to the President and his colleagues for honouring me with the invitation to give them and for their gracious hospitality during my stay in Nova Scotia. I have restored to the second chapter some administrative detail which would have overloaded a lecture and made minor revisions elsewhere but the lectures are substantially as delivered.

In the first lecture I have made use of one or two passages from a chapter on the Commonwealth of Nations 1917–1949 which I contributed to *L'Europe au XIXe et XXe Siècles,* Volume 6. I am obliged to the publishers, Messrs Marzorati of Milan, for permitting this. I am also grateful to Professor G. S. Graham, Dr A. F. Madden, and Professor P. N. S. Mansergh for their kindness in reading and commenting on the manuscript, and to Miss Margaret Beard for reading the proofs.

K. E. R.

Institute of Commonwealth Studies
  London, February 1964

PREFACE

The Reid Lectures were established in 1958 by Harvey T. Reid, B.A. (Acadia and Oxon), D.C.L. (Acadia), of St Paul, Minnesota. Their purpose is to bring to Acadia University, at least every second year, an eminent scholar or man of affairs who will give a brief series of lectures on some important phase of history or political science. Their founder expressed a basic preference for a theme related to the British Commonwealth of Nations, but did not rigidly so restrict the lecturer.

Dr Reid was born in Hartland, New Brunswick, in 1891 and entered Acadia in 1908. On graduating in 1912, he was chosen as Rhodes Scholar for Nova Scotia and took an Oxford degree two years later. In the first world war he served as a captain in the Royal Field Artillery and was wounded in action. In due time he became a member of the Minnesota State Bar Association and the American Bar Association. He has been president of the West Law Publishing Company since 1948 and of the American Law Book Publishing Company since 1952.

An invitation to deliver the first Reid Lectures was given early in 1958 to His Excellency Norman A. Robertson, Canadian Ambassador to the U.S.A. and formerly High Commissioner to the United Kingdom. His lectures were entitled 'Some Thoughts on the Commonwealth'. Charles Edmund Carrington, Professor of British Commonwealth Relations in the Royal Institute of International Affairs, delivered the second series of lectures in October 1959, on 'The Liquidation of the British Empire'. Nicholas Mansergh, the Smuts Professor of the History of the British Commonwealth in the University of Cambridge, delivered the third series of lectures, in December 1960, on 'South Africa 1906–1960: The Price of Magnanimity'. Kenneth Robinson, Director of the Institute of Commonwealth Studies in the University of London, delivered the fourth series of lectures at Acadia University in February 1963 on 'British Colonial Policy between the Wars' and, with minor revisions, these are printed here.

WATSON KIRKCONNELL

Acadia University
  February 1964

I

THE IMPERIAL CONTEXT
OF 'TRUSTEESHIP'

At the end of the first world war, the British Empire
reached its greatest territorial extent. Although still
generally, and even officially, so called, the Empire
included the five self-governing communities known as Dominions, whose actual relationship with Great Britain, if somewhat obscure, was evidently very different from what the word
'empire' implied elsewhere. For at least a quarter of a century
people had been arguing that this new relationship called for
a new name.[1] This was soon to result in the official use, to
describe their association with Britain, of a new expression, the
'British Commonwealth of Nations'.[2] In the widest sense
in which either name could be used, the political entity so
described included more than a quarter of the world's surface
and more than a quarter of its population. Moreover, in the
peace settlement, the British Empire, as cynics did not fail to
notice, acquired control of the greater part of the German
colonies and of much of the Turkish Empire, though these
additions, made under the new Mandate system of the League
of Nations, were held to imply something short of annexation
and, in the former Turkish territories at any rate, called for the
early realization of self-government.

Hardly more than a quarter of a century later, in 1949, this
British Empire had given place to a group of eight independent
states, Great Britain, Canada, Australia, New Zealand, South
Africa, India, Pakistan, and Ceylon, which, in that year,
declared themselves to be 'united as free and equal members of

the Commonwealth of Nations'—the adjective 'British' now disappeared—'freely co-operating in the pursuit of peace, liberty and progress'. Outside this unique association, various parts of the world, which in 1919 were under the effective ultimate control of the British government in London—Iraq, Egypt, Jordan, Israel, Burma, and Ireland—had become independent sovereign states. Of what was left besides these two groups of independent states, many territories were in the process of achieving internal self-government and were recognized as destined to emerge, sooner rather than later, as independent states, either within or outside the Commonwealth. Southern Rhodesia, or rather its tiny white population, had indeed enjoyed internal self-government since 1923 subject only to ineffective British control of certain aspects of the treatment of 'native affairs'.[3] The Gold Coast and Nigeria were discussing new Constitutions which would give them elected African assemblies enjoying a very large amount of control of their internal affairs, while the ancient colonies in the West Indies seemed at last to be accepting the idea of federation as the pre-requisite of full independence within the Commonwealth. Internal self-government had just been restored in Malta. Even if all such territories, which were nearly self-governing but not quite, were included in the term, the British Empire, in the sense of territories under the ultimate political control of Great Britain, now included only some seventy-five million people, no more than half as much again as the United Kingdom itself.

There are some large questions that will be asked about this great process of decolonization. Was it, after all, no more than the reflection of the declining power of Great Britain in the world, a decline whose consequences in the Imperial sphere it has been the principal merit of that much-vaunted British realism to admit before it was, in the fullest sense, forcibly compelled to do so? Or was it only the concession of the forms of political independence, the better to maintain, as long and as much as possible, the commercial advantages of that economic dependence which was the frequent accompaniment if not indeed, as Marxists contend, the major purpose of political subordination? Or was it, again, if properly understood, the inevitable working out of what has frequently been asserted to be the central purpose of British rule, 'the government of men by themselves', a preoccupation so deep-seated as to amount to something like a habit, persistent if often fitful? It must be doubtful whether processes so numerous, carried out through so varied a network of relationships, and over such widely differing parts of the world, are ever likely to lend themselves to such summary assessment. But in any event it is certain that our present knowledge of the actual consequences of many decisions, no less than of the motives which led to them, falls far short of what would be needed to arrive at conclusions on matters such as these, even in particular instances, much less in their totality. Whatever its motives, this earlier phase of the transformation of the British Empire preceded the end of colonialism elsewhere. In this, as in much else, the British have been pioneers, even if it was in spite of themselves.

Six major themes can be distinguished in this earlier phase of the transformation of Empire. Three of them were formally announced as early as 1917 when the Imperial War Conference resolved that 'the readjustment of the constitutional relations of the component parts of the Empire' should be considered after the war but that any such readjustment 'should be based on a full recognition of the Dominions as autonomous nations of an Imperial Commonwealth, and of India as an important portion of the same, should recognize the right of the Dominions and India to an adequate voice in foreign policy and in foreign relations, and should provide effective arrangements for continuous consultation in all important matters of common Imperial concern, and for such necessary concerted action, founded on consultation, as the several

Governments may determine'.[4] The emphasis on Dominion autonomy as involving 'an adequate voice in foreign policy' reasserted Dominion interest in extending their own control in this field and indicated one dominant preoccupation of the next twenty years. The recognition of the position of India, reversing the decision of 1907 excluding India from the Imperial Conference, paralleled the British government's declaration in August 1917[5] that the object of British policy was 'the progressive realization of responsible government in India as an integral part of the British Empire'. The decision to include India in the new machinery gravely underestimated the period which would elapse before it achieved the fully self-governing status which alone could fully justify that decision, and for the next thirty years the implications of the 'most momentous utterance ever made in India's chequered history'[6] remained the most crucial of British imperial themes. The use of the new expression 'Commonwealth' coupled with the old adjective Imperial presaged not only the transformation of the relations between the Dominions and Great Britain which 'full recognition of the Dominions as autonomous nations' would necessitate, but also the ambiguity of expression by which this new multiplicity of states would, for some time yet, seek to retain an 'Imperial' unity.

The fourth theme is one which even today finds all too little place in much British thought and writing about Empire. It is the sorry story of Ireland's struggle for independence: the British Algeria. Like the three earlier themes, its roots reach far back beyond the first world war, but its last phase began with two events of that period which finally destroyed the old Home Rule party: the Unionists' proclaimed intransigence in 1914 and the Easter Rising of 1916. If the first went far to make the Partition of Ireland certain, the implacable suppression of the futile gesture of 1916—Arthur Griffith, the Sinn Fein President, wrote of the British execution of fifteen of its leaders 'I had not believed they would be stupid enough to do it'[7]—finally won Sinn Fein to the Republic. Together, they doomed the characteristic but too facile hope that the imposition of Dominion status in 1921 might somehow reconcile Irish nationalism and Imperial unity, for they ensured that the freedom it conferred would be doggedly used by the Irish to achieve that true republican freedom they had been denied. In the process, Dominion status was itself dismantled.

But if the lessons alike of Partition and of the limited appeal of Dominion status in countries which were not 'daughter nations' for long went unremarked in British policy elsewhere —as for example in Palestine and India—one lesson of Irish experience remained. 'Ireland was', Dr Conor Cruise O'Brien has written, 'the first instance in modern times where a nation long-subdued won its freedom from a Great Power which had not been defeated in war.' As he goes on to point out, 'the framework within which Irish nationalism was contained, the framework of Anglo-Irish relations, was and is like nothing else in the world' since those relations are 'so ancient and so close—not merely in a geographical sense—that they have created both bitternesses and tolerances of unusual refinement'.[8] But the experience of 1920 and 1921 left one conviction widespread if often unspoken; there were evidently limits to the extent to which British opinion might be counted on to tolerate the use of British force to suppress nationalism. As Amery, no shamefaced imperialist, wrote of Malta 'we have enough with one Ireland, without creating another'.[9]

In the development of the fifth theme, the rise and decline of British power in the Middle East,[10] the first world war assuredly marked a decisive stage. The declaration of a British Protectorate in Egypt may juridically have done no more than substitute for a nominal Turkish suzerainty an anomalous British one. But it was accompanied by the deposition of the pro-Turkish Khedive and the installation of a Sultan more acceptable to the British. The facts of British occupation since 1882 could hardly have been more strongly underlined and the stresses of a war in which Britain assumed full responsibility for the defence of a neutral Egypt resulted in a noticeable increase in the evidence of British control and an equally noticed decline in its effective supervision of Egyptian agency in meeting unpopular wartime needs. The result was to be seen in popular support of the demand for independence punctually presented in November 1918 by Zaghlul. All British attempts to satisfy this demand finally broke down, partly because of the ambiguous politics of the Egyptian monarchy but mainly because, while ready to concede the label of independence, the British were determined to retain the substance of power in all they deemed vital to their Imperial needs. What they proposed was in essence only another version of the dyarchy that Congress rejected in India. The defeat of the Turks which ultimately resulted in British control of Iraq, Palestine, and Transjordan, under the new Mandate system, set up in a vast area new definitions of British responsibility. But the most decisive single event in the history of British power in the Middle East occurred on 2 November 1917 when the British government issued the Balfour Declaration that they 'viewed with favour the establishment in Palestine of a National Home for the Jewish people', and would 'use their best endeavours to facilitate the achievement of this object, it being clearly understood that nothing shall be done which may prejudice the civil and religious rights of existing non-Jewish communities in Palestine'. Though it was to take more than a quarter of a century before the British admitted complete failure in Palestine, that failure was not in Palestine alone. British policy in the Middle East lay in ruins.[11]

The sixth, and last theme—and the one which we shall be considering in these lectures—the redefinition of policies in the dependent Empire, and especially in Africa, is scarcely to be found in any general pronouncements of policy before the second world war. This theme has to be traced largely in the interstices of administrative practice and in individual instance. And if it is impossible to point to any convenient signal that a new note had come into the development of this theme with the end of the first world war, the outbreak of the second equally marks no clear end of a phase in its evolution. For that, the decisive event is to be found in the Labour government's public acceptance in 1949 of 'self-government within the British Commonwealth' as the immediate, rather than the remote, object of British policy in the Gold Coast. The implications of that decision elsewhere, but particularly in Africa, the colonial continent *par excellence,* were by no means immediately admitted, if, indeed, they were perceived. But even if the pressure of international hostility to colonialism, then already evident, had not so greatly and so rapidly increased in the ensuing years, those implications would, in my judgement, have been no less profound, though they might not have been so quickly manifest. For the quarter of a century between the end of the first world war and the end of the second, the feature of British colonial policy that stands out in retrospect is the tranquil assumption of the long-term character of colonial rule. It was an assumption accepted by many, perhaps most, of the radical critics of that policy who were often more concerned to purify, supervise, or even internationalize, such rule than to advocate its rapid replacement by independence.

Taken together, these six themes may fairly stand as summarizing that earlier phase in the transformation of the British Empire which came to an end just after the second world war. That phase is now often presented in a perspective very different from that of even a few years ago. The almost exclusive preoccupation of some earlier discussions with its domestic dynamics is judged oddly parochial; for it is presented not as the outcome of any peculiar idiosyncrasy of British

rulers or of the settled communities of the older Commonwealth countries, but rather as the earlier phase of a much
larger and more deep-seated change in the whole structure of
relations between the western European states and the rest of
the world, begun by the first world war and vastly accelerated
by the second. From this point of view, the 'failure of nerve' increasingly unconcealed in Britain and France in the 'thirties,
which made it impossible to prevent or limit the second world
war, is much more important than any ideology of self-government. And even apart from the decline of European power,
fundamental changes in the relations of the whole western
world with Asia and Africa were an inevitable consequence
of the ever-increasing impact of western modernity on their
traditional societies, an impact of which European imperialism
was the principal, though often involuntary, agent. That the
social and economic consequences of the spread of modernity
could not for ever have been politically contained by European
imperialism—particularly in view of its original maritime
basis—need not be disputed. None the less the effective power
to make themselves independent actually possessed by many
of the new states at the moment of decision in their emancipa-
tion can easily be exaggerated—and, not infrequently, has been.
In the pressures that have resulted in the headlong retreat from
Empire in recent years, some weight must, all the same, be
given to this second factor and to an increasingly general
realization that its strength could only be expected to grow.
More must surely be accorded to the change in the relative
power of the European imperial states so drastically brought
about by the second world war. It takes time, of course, before
the full implications of so vast a change can be realized and
their consequences absorbed in day-to-day policy. Yet one may
hesitate to accept this plausible thesis as a wholly satisfactory
explanation even of the more recent phase of decolonization if
one recalls post-war French policy in Indochina, the long

struggle to retain Tunisia and Morocco, to say nothing of Algeria (a special case by any standards) or Dutch policy in Indonesia or, more striking still, that of the Portuguese in Angola.

However they may be interpreted, the developments of the *last* decade do little to justify the view that those of the *earlier* phase in the transformation of the British Empire were no more than inevitable concessions from weakness. Whatever importance history may assign to an intelligent anticipation of that inevitability, we need not deny the significance of a pervasive conviction among many in Britain, whose political outlook might otherwise have led them to rally to the assertion of Imperial power, that the representatives of British democracy would not in such contexts persist in a policy of repression long enough for success. 'Unionist policy died' Austen Chamberlain had told the House of Commons in 1922 'not because it was . . . wrong' but because 'to be successful it needed continuity, patience, perseverance—and our people would not pursue it connectedly through the changes of party warfare.'[12] The lesson may not have been without its influence in those interminable debates which finally resulted in Baldwin's supporters putting the Government of India Act on the statute book in 1935, in spite of Winston Churchill—and much else. There was, however, something more, something which was the unique achievement, until then, of the British Empire: the existence of the Dominions.

It may be true, as Professor Thornton asserts in his brilliant, if sometimes perverse, analysis of *The Imperial Idea,* that 'no emotional capital was invested by imperialists in the idea of the Commonwealth'.[13] It depends on whom you count as imperialists. But no one who has seriously studied the end of other contemporary empires can fail to realize the immense difference that the 'Dominion model' made in the British case, merely by existing at all. For a time, it is true, the steady development of 'colonial self-government' and the widening realization of its implications on the relationship between Britain and the Dominions served only to underline the gulf that existed between what Milner in 1906 had described as 'The Two Empires', 'the one', to quote an Indian historian, 'white and self-governing, the other non-white and dependent. The former was "Greater Britain", an "expansion of England", "the sphere of settlement", "an empire of dwelling places"; it was not really "empire" in the strict sense of the term but a "commonwealth". The latter belonged to "the sphere of rule", the English were in it but not of it; it was the true "empire" in the classic continental tradition.'[14] But even as this division was becoming more pronounced it was being undermined at its most crucial point. While Imperialists argued what in retrospect seems a phantom debate about the merits of Federation and Tariff Reform as a means of reconciling Dominion freedom with Imperial unity, 'colonial self-government' provided the somewhat prosaic wagon to which Indians hitched their nationalist star. 'The cases of the French in Canada and the Boers in South Africa showed', said the Congress leader, Gokhale, 'that there was room in the Empire for a self-respecting India.'[15] No doubt Indians had largely turned away from 'colonial self-government' as a programme when the British at last brought themselves in 1917 to proclaim it as their aim in India. But for their British rulers, that declaration in the end proved to be the critical turning point. Some, of course, still hoped that it might somehow be possible to undo that fatal step or at least to delay indefinitely further progress on a road they were convinced could only lead—the phrase is Churchill's—to 'measureless disasters'.[16] But others had some glimpse of what had once moved the young Philip Kerr (the later Lord Lothian) who had been one of the select band in Milner's kindergarten to tell a Toronto audience in 1912 'If we manage to create in India a self-governing, responsible dominion, and if India, when it is responsible and self-governing, elects to remain within the British Empire, we shall have solved the greatest difficulty which presents itself to the world today'.[17] The vision faded in the long years of frustration and resistance but when independent India elected—for in this the two new Indian Dominions, divided in almost everything else, were agreed—to remain within the Commonwealth, the decision did much to promote British acquiescence in the transformation of what remained of that second, Dependent, Empire in almost all of which self-government had until the second world war seemed no more than a comfortably remote contingency.

The rosy glow that attended Asian membership also did something to encourage the British to overlook the full import of those major changes that had meanwhile come about in the nature of the Commonwealth itself. These were the outcome partly of Afrikaner and Irish determination to resolve the skilful ambiguities of the Balfour report, partly of the national growth of the older Dominions, greatly accelerated by the second war, and partly of the military and economic weakness which was the price Britain had to pay for failing to prevent the war she eventually won. In sum, the Commonwealth changed from being a community into which you were, so to speak, born into an association which for the present at least you decided not to leave. By helping for a time to cushion the British from any clear appreciation of the nature and limitations of this new Commonwealth, Asian member-ship no doubt contributed considerably to the readiness with which they came to contemplate the emergence of new member states in West Africa and Malaya—a considerable service to the world, as well as to Britain. But, assisted by the monu-mental error with which they crowned their disastrous failures in the Middle East in the Suez operation, this British failure of full understanding of the new Commonwealth was even-tually to play its part in producing that delayed reaction to the loss of imperial power, the full measure of whose consequences cannot yet be estimated.

But, to return to the earlier phase in the transformation of Empire, it was not of course only through Indian example that the model afforded by colonial self-government, the old Dominion model, influenced the character of political demands in the Dependent Empire, or, what is possibly more important, the response to them. Until Indian independence had shown that a similar development really could take place in the Coloured Empire, just as it had, long before, in that other Empire of the White Dominions, the full force of the example was limited. None the less, the notion that British colonies had progressed by stages to full self-government and that others might move along the same road even if not to the end of it undoubtedly influenced the politically minded in more than one dependency. Especially, perhaps, was this true in the West Indies, indubitably coloured but in historical fact, if not in legal theory, colonies of settlement, the place, if anywhere, where the two Empires met. Here was to be found the widest assortment of examples. Some, like Barbados, had never lost the old representative system though its significance as a measure of 'the government of men by themselves' is brought into a juster perspective if we realize that, as late as 1938, the electorate nunbered 5,000 in a population of 200,000; others, like, Jamaica, after surrendering their old assemblies in the second half of the nineteenth century had again advanced to a legislature, partly official, partly nominated, partly elected, in this case by an electorate which in 1935 numbered 66,000 out of a total population of 1,122,000. In Jamaica, not only were officials in a minority but any nine of the fourteen electives could veto a financial bill. Others, again, like Trinidad had never had an assembly and the Governor's casting vote still, in 1938, ensured an official majority in the legislative council. West Indian history afforded as many examples of political retrogression as of advance; but their relationship to the earliest stages in the evolution of the 'Dominion model' seemed obvious and undeniable. To British settlers in East and Central Africa that model seemed a no less obvious and undeniable 'natural right'. If it was only in Southern Rhodesia that they attained fully responsible government, their campaigns elsewhere focused attention on the implications of their political objective for Asians and, more remotely, Africans.

But the most important impact of the Dominion model was, perhaps, its 'demonstration effect' on the British themselves. The suitability of 'responsible government', the 'parliamentary system', the 'Westminster model', for such alien environments as the tropical dependencies provided was long and seriously questioned. More far-reaching, perhaps, were the doubts that Milner, still preoccupied with his 'two Empires', confided to his journal in 1923. 'We probably took a wrong road', he wrote, 'in trying to convert India into a Dominion. There is no natural basis for such a relationship between India and Great Britain or Australia or Canada, as there is for the relationship now in process of development between those predominantly British communities among themselves. On the other hand, the more important units of the Dependent Empire will not be content, as they grow up, to remain Dependent. And if we cannot successfully attempt to convert them into Dominions, and yet do not want them to become Foreign Nations, what is to be done? Political wisdom has to find a means, a new form of organization, a new tie which will keep them connected.'[18]

Milner's question remained unanswered. If the subsequent history of Dominion status in Ireland suggested the limitations of British 'political wisdom' in so completely rejecting the alternative scheme of external association propounded by De Valera, that of the newly independent states in the Middle East was, before long, to show the limitations of treaties

between evidently unequal 'partners' as a means of legitimizing
a special relationship, that 'something in the nature of a new
element in Imperial relations'[19] of which Amery had hopefully
spoken at the Imperial Conference of 1926. Meanwhile the
notion that some form of self-government must one day come
about 'at least in the more important units', however remote
that day might be, was in marked contrast to other imperial
habits of mind. When as late as 1944 General de Gaulle called
a conference to reappraise French colonial experience and
policy in Africa it began by declaring 'La constitution even-
tuelle même lointaine de self-governments dans les colonies
est à écarter.'[20] That such a declaration would have been
unthinkable in Britain no doubt owed something to the
American Revolution but far more to the history of colonial
self-government in what were then called the Dominions. However remote the prospect might seem for most of the Colonial
Empire in the inter-war years, it was not inconceivable. To
some it might portend the destruction of an Empire, but to
others it would rather signal its fulfilment. Even in 1933 a
distinguished British historian could, after all, say to a Canadian
audience 'A Dominion of Nigeria, for example? Why not?'[21]
It was the possibility and, in a sense, the concreteness of such
an idea that made the difference.

Some points of contact there were, then, between the six
major themes that, looking back, we can detect in imperial
policy during what Churchill has called 'another Thirty Years
War'. Part at least of the climate of opinion in which colonial
policy was developed and applied was provided by a world
in which, especially after 1930, these themes were becoming
more insistent. But their inter-relationship, so far as it was remarked at all, would seem to have been mainly in the world
of ideas or at any rate of conversation in clubs rather than that
of power and responsibility. Of course the institutions of
British government were not such as wholly to isolate the

discharge of at least the highest responsibilities involved in each of these major themes from one another: in Parliament, as in the Cabinet, the same people considered and, so far as Britain was concerned, decided them all. That, however, by no means meant that the bearing of one thing on another was necessarily in mind. Even if it had, it would have affected only that small proportion of major issues which ultimately found their way to such exalted seats of decision and then only at a point at which they had been largely shaped by innumerable plans and decisions earlier arrived at in departmental or territorial isolation. No doubt the sheer magnitude and variety of the problems of the Commonwealth and Empire would always have precluded their being the primary responsibility of any single organ of the British government. In fact, historical accident, British conservatism, the natural distaste of the Dominions for having their evolving relationship with Britain handled by the Colonial Office, decreed that four separate Departments of State, the Dominions Office, the India Office, the Foreign Office, and the Colonial Office, should divide, rather than share, that responsibility.

The new Dominions Office was not established until 1925 and it was not until 1930 that the two posts of Colonial Secretary and Dominions Secretary were for the first time held by different people while all but the most senior of the staff of the two offices was in theory interchangeable until after the war. None the less they naturally became steadily more distinct and the movement of administrative staff between them ceased except, and then rarely, in the more junior posts.[22] There was also a small block of work in the Dominions Office which some thought should have remained, where it properly belonged, in the Colonial Office, namely the oversight of administration in the three small territories under United Kingdom rule in South Africa, Basutoland, Swaziland, and Bechuanaland. The assumption that underlay this arrangement was the possibility of their eventual transfer to South Africa. As that possibility slowly receded, the arrangement inevitably became politically more difficult to change, while its administrative conveniences became more entrenched. Its share in the neglect the territories suffered at least until the later 'thirties may have been exaggerated but it is doubtful whether it is altogether unfounded. That the Dominions Office should retain responsibility for Newfoundland, when in 1934 it reverted to what was in fact Crown Colony government, was no doubt inevitable. The experience offered some evident lessons about the limitations of the mere absence of responsible, or even representative, government as a means of solving the problems of a colonial economy. Whether they altogether escaped notice in the Colonial Office, we do not know, though that Department was responsible for British Guiana whose ancient constitution had in 1928 been replaced on somewhat similar financial grounds.

India remained—how could it be otherwise?—an Empire by itself, the responsibility of a third Secretary of State and an entirely separate India Office; Professor Mansergh, who himself served for some years in the Dominions Office, has recorded that 'Between these two departments, divided geographically only by the width of a Whitehall quadrangle, there was surprisingly little contact and a marked difference of outlook'. To this he ascribed some part in the reasons why the lessons to be learnt from experience in Ireland about 'the adaptability of dominion status to countries which were not *natural* dominions' . . . 'were in fact almost wholly ignored'[23] in guiding British policy in India. That same quadrangle divided the India Office from the Colonial Office: perhaps that was one reason why the lessons to be learnt from experience in India seem seldom to have been considered either, except on relatively technical matters such as finance, irrigation, forestry, or co-operation, where the Colonial Office sometimes employed on expert missions to particular territories men with Indian experience. What might have been gained by some more systematic and persistent attempt at such a confrontation of Indian experience and the more general issues of colonial policy may be glimpsed from one example. Lord Hailey, the almost mythical example of Indian Civil Service brilliance, was persuaded on his retirement to turn his attention to Africa. Published in 1938, his massive *African Survey* made an outstanding contribution to the more dynamic and broadly based policy of colonial development and welfare defined in 1940. It was only the beginning of his impact on African policy; but, what, we may ask, if he had come to African affairs a little younger, or if there had been several, lesser mortals no doubt, who in the prime of their Indian experience could have been involved in African problems?

In the Middle East, British responsibilities were eventually divided[24] in 1921 between the new Middle Eastern Department of the Colonial Office, responsible for 'Iraq, Palestine, and Aden, and the Arab States under British influence' and the Foreign Office which remained the Department concerned with Egypt and with the Sudan, a territory which had everything in common with the tropical African colonies except its political status as an Anglo-Egyptian condominium. The main practical consequence of this Middle Eastern arrangement was to deflect much of the energy of successive colonial ministers into the hopeless politics of Palestine and to ensure that too much of the constructive talents of some of the abler men in the Colonial Service were exhausted in its cynical frustrations. If there was any truth in the allegation of Arab sympathies that Zionists and their supporters increasingly brought against both the Office and the Colonial Service, it is unnecessary to deduce that these were wholly or even mainly the outcome of the Department's brief association with Iraq or of its responsibilities in Transjordan or the Aden

Protectorate. There was, after all, quite enough in the historic, as well as the contemporary, experience of the Colonial Office elsewhere to account for such a bias against the claims of immigrant European settlers. The decision to assign these Middle Eastern responsibilities to the Colonial Office was almost certainly a mistake. That it failed to bring about any measure of unity in British policy in the Middle East can hardly be considered an important part of the count against it. The decision to allot Syria to the French and their expulsion of Feisal in 1920 had already put paid to what little chance of any such unity had been left by the Balfour Declaration—before the Middle Eastern Department of the Colonial Office had even been established.

No more than a series of administrative no-man's-lands poised uneasily between the well-defined 'Empires' of the major Departments of State, such marginal areas could hardly be significant in promoting that more comprehensive and co-ordinated Imperial programme which Imperialists only gradually tired of demanding and which foreign critics, especially the French, were prone to believe must exist. The major development of the earlier years between the wars was the gradual replacement of Milner's 'two Empires' by three. 'The Colonial Empire', Amery told the Imperial Conference in 1926, 'has, in fact, during the last generation, evolved as a separate constituent element in the Empire, different on the one side from the Dominions, in which I include for that purpose Great Britain as well . . . different also in very many respects . . . from the Empire of India.' For all its variety, this Colonial Empire, he claimed, none the less possessed 'a certain unity'. Although the numerous territories that made it up enjoyed, he was careful to mention, 'autonomous institutions in varying degree and ever-increasing measure', their governments were all, in the last resort, the responsibility of Parliament and the Secretary of State, they were nearly all in the tropics, and they were 'mainly inhabited by populations of a non-white character'.[25]

When the first world war broke out, considerable parts of the immense areas in Africa that had been brought within British jurisdiction in the last quarter of the nineteenth century had barely come under a settled administration. Tanganyika, with an area slightly larger than Nigeria, had only come under Colonial Office rule with the end of the war, its administration to be reconstructed practically from scratch. But as the period of incorporating these new territories within the effective area of British rule drew to an end in Africa, as it had a little earlier elsewhere in the newer tropical dependencies, an increase of production and trade began to show itself, and the revenue that followed began to be sufficient to support a somewhat more elaborate and developed administration. With the slow growth of this development, with an increasing realization of the possibilities, as well as the problems, of tropical medicine, agriculture, and education, and with better understanding of the intricacies of native social organization, colonial policy began to be considerably more complex, more specialized, and more active. But alike in the economic and the political sphere, the number of British people with direct personal interest in these areas was still relatively small, even if it was growing. As the Colonial Empire emerged as a distinct and recognizable entity, it also became one for specialists. It was a world of its own but a world apart.

In that world, a single 'blessed' word at once expressed the aspirations of policy and concealed their conflicting practical implications: Trusteeship. It was a word with a long and chequered history in British thought and practice about the problems of empire. But its contemporary elevation as the touchstone of policy in the inter-war years owed something to the international recognition it achieved in the Covenant of the League of Nations. It was the principle to be applied to those ex-enemy territories which were 'inhabited by peoples not yet able to stand by themselves under the strenuous conditions of the modern world'. Their 'well-being and development' formed 'a sacred trust of civilization'. What this principle implied for those of these territories whose peoples had not 'reached a stage where their existence as independent nations can be provisionally recognized' was administration by a Mandatory Power, subject to internationally prescribed conditions designed to ensure the absence of certain abuses to which experience (and especially, it must be said, British views of that experience) suggested colonial rule (and especially in British eyes, that of other powers) was regrettably liable: the continuance of slavery and the slave trade, the use of forced labour for private advantage, the demoralizing traffic in arms and spirits, the obstruction of missionary (and especially foreign missionary) activities, the use of colonial territories and colonial manpower to reinforce the armed strength of the colonial power. Except in the Pacific Mandates and South West Africa which, on the insistence of the Dominions governments concerned, were to be administered as integral portions of the Mandatory states, there was added the obligation to maintain the Open Door, 'equal opportunities for the trade and commerce' of all members of the League.

All these essentially negative injunctions were spelt out in more detail in the Mandates themselves which enjoined the Mandatory to respect the rights and safeguard the interests of the native population in regard to the holding or transfer of land, to ensure proper public control of its alienation to non-natives, to protect natives from fraudulent labour recruitment. They expressly prohibited the grant of monopolistic concessions or, in general, of economic privileges on a preferential basis to nationals of the Mandatory power and prescribed in detail the other requirements of an Open Door policy. Trusteeship, from this point of view, was a code designed to prevent the Trustee from acquiescing in certain kinds of abuse or indulging

in others, to his own advantage. But the Mandates themselves added a more positive condition; the Mandatory was to
'undertake to promote to the utmost the material and moral
well-being and the social progress of the inhabitants'. Its
generality was in marked contrast to the detail in which the
prohibitions were prescribed, and it omitted any reference to
the training of the inhabitants for the exercise of political
responsibility.[26]

The code applied of course only to the Mandated territories.
But this should not lead us to underestimate its significance
as an exposition of what in the years immediately after the
war, British authorities regarded as at least the minimal requirements for good colonial administration. After all they had,
to all intents and purposes, written it themselves. Amery's conviction that it was not likely that any mandate would 'impose
upon us any conditions . . . we have not been in the habit of
imposing upon ourselves'[27] was well founded. That was in
1919. Twenty years later, Governor Cameron looking back on
his Tanganyika service recorded that the terms of the Mandate
'did not trouble or preoccupy my mind in any way': they were,
he said, 'the ordinary and recognized principles of British
Colonial Administration'.[28] No doubt, but Cameron had
found them useful enough in his successful opposition to
Amery's plan for establishing an East African Dominion
under settler influence.

But it would be a gross travesty of either the ideas or the
practice of trusteeship, at any rate in the inter-war years, to
suggest that this largely negative code was all there was to them,
as some recent critics have come near to implying, who,

> look at the end of the work, contrast
> the petty done, the undone vast.

Milner, Amery, Ormsby-Gore, the leading men at the
Colonial Office for the greater part of the formative decade after

the war, were all profoundly convinced that the great task
ahead was the positive one of economic and social, especially educational, development and they all knew, especially
Ormsby-Gore, a great deal of what this meant in detail in the
Colonial Empire. Even if they had not, there was another
event in the early 'twenties which greatly influenced the contemporary definition of Trusteeship. In 1921 Lugard, the most
famous of British African governors, published *The Dual Mandate in British Tropical Africa,* in which he reflected on his life's
work and propounded the theme that Europe was in Africa
for 'the mutual benefit of her own industrial classes, and of the
native races in their progress to a higher plane; that the benefit
can be made reciprocal, and that it is the aim and desire of
civilized administration to fulfil this dual mandate'.[29] This
long, highly personal, repetitious, but immensely powerful
book provided ample justification, largely from Lugard's own
experience, of the importance of those negative—perhaps it is
fairer to say protective—aspects of the doctrine of trusteeship as
the Mandates attempted to define it. The abuses they sought to
prohibit had in large part been the accompaniment of that
relatively short but decisive period of European Imperial expansion in Africa and the Pacific that took place in the last
quarter of the nineteenth century and of its consolidation in the
first decade of our own. That period had been characterized
by a widespread emphasis on the urgency of rapid economic
development for the advantage of the European countries and
some impatient contempt, even in Britain, for the principles
of the humanitarian period that preceded it. European enterprise, whether by settlers, plantations, or mining enterprises, had
for a time been represented as the only effective form of development in the tropics. J. A. Hobson's powerful critique of
Imperialism, first published in 1902, however it may be assessed
as a contribution to economic history, had done much, aided
by the publicity given to the Congo scandals in the years that

followed, to discredit that conception and not only in the more radical flanks of the rising Labour Party. It still, of course, survived, especially in the small but influential group which had sunk so much emotional capital in the South African idea but it was soon to be progressively weakened by the actual development of 'native policy' in South Africa especially after the first Nationalist government of 1924. Lugard's *Dual Mandate* not only supplied much evidence of its dangers but, more important, offered an alternative approach: 'Develop resources through the agency of the natives under European guidance, and not by direct European ownership of those tropical lands which are unsuited for European settlement.'[30] Apart from the problem of countries like Kenya, parts of which *were* suitable, many conflicts were, of course, inherent in the conception of the Dual Mandate.

Any prospect there might be of reconciling them clearly depended on the maintenance of colonial rule, the final authority of the trustee, for an unspecified period. 'The era of complete independence', Lugard wrote, was 'not as yet visible on the horizon of time.'[31] This would have been so even if his conception of indirect rule—rule by native chiefs subordinate to the control of the protecting power—had not appeared to offer an alternative to the development of representative government as the basis of a policy more suited to African genius. If such an alternative, whatever its potentialities, was to be reconciled with 'the dual responsibility of controlling powers in the tropics viz. as trustees to civilization for the adequate development of their resources and as trustees for the welfare of native races' it was evidently a long-term prospect.

In one perspective, the Dual Mandate was a far more realistic restatement of a much older approach to the problem, one with a continuous history from the mid-nineteenth-century humanitarian vision of Buxton and Venn that if Africans were not deprived of their land or their freedom to engage in 'a just and legitimate trade' and were helped in a programme of agricultural development, they could do it for themselves, the vision that Dickens had satirized as Borrioboola-Gha in *Bleak House*,[32] and that Mary Kingsley and E. D. Morel, whose great campaign finally brought the Congo atrocities to an end, had sustained at the turn of the century. In another perspective, it was the very doctrine that Chamberlain himself propounded. He had proclaimed in 1895 the task of development in the dependencies 'for the benefit of their population and for the benefit of the greater population which is outside'.[33] Too many of his ardent disciples put all their emphasis on the second aim with a perfunctory assertion that it *must* benefit the natives. Even the best of them were suspiciously ready to applaud the *arrière pensée* in Milner's contention that the natives of Tanganyika (and elsewhere) 'might easily find themselves worse off under a just but penurious and unprogressive administration than under one which, while less careful of their rights, was more zealous in developing the resources of their country'.[34] It was nevertheless true that, in hands less forceful and dynamic than those of Lugard, the weakness of this approach was its tendency to relapse into complacent satisfaction at the absence of traditional abuses and to overlook the stagnation of native society, or the social and other dangers that might be concealed even by successful economic growth.

The emphasis of trusteeship was then, in the first place, 'protective' and that, especially among the critics of colonial policy, in a somewhat negative fashion. In the second place, it was on the promotion, so far as might be consistent with that protective character, of economic and social development. Whether that development was to be brought about 'by the agency of the natives through European guidance' or by more direct European enterprise and what was the appropriate scope of state action continued to be warmly debated, especially in relation to East and Central Africa. But, at least among those who had not written off the whole enterprise as a more than unusually sordid example of capitalist exploitation, there was an increasingly general realization that development, and research, on which it must depend, were the two great needs of the Colonial Empire and that both would have largely to be promoted by government. Development by the agency of natives through European guidance called more obviously than development by direct European enterprise for much more extended and more expert agricultural, forestry, and medical services in the colonies. Lugard recognized the claims of development but he also emphasized the case for careful study and adaptation of native society to the new needs in such matters as land tenure, labour recruitment, education, the development of mineral resources and of industries processing raw materials or supplying the simpler needs of local markets. The exponents of trusteeship recognized in short, in the jargon of a later age, that development required an economic infrastructure and technical assistance. That in retrospect they seem to have grappled so slowly and so inadequately with these more positive tasks is, of course, the result of many factors, most of all the climate of economic fact and opinion in an era during the greater part of which the effective demand for the primary products of the Colonial Empire was low because industrial economies, more especially that of Britain, remained chronically below full employment.

But there was a more long-term obstacle which assumed greater importance during the brief period of relative prosperity, between the first post-war slump and the great depression, that coincided with Amery's tenure of the Colonial Office. It was the continued dominance of the doctrine that French writers rather engagingly call 'le self-supporting', a doctrine succinctly defined by the third Earl Grey in the middle of the nineteenth century: 'the surest test of the soundness of measures for the improvement of an uncivilized people, is that they should be self-supporting'.[35] The trustee was not to use his own money to make the ward's estate more productive. The most he might do was to use his own credit to guarantee a loan. Colonial revenues must be able to meet the service of any loans they were permitted to raise and the salaries of any staff they were permitted to employ. If a breach was at last made in this doctrine in 1929 when the first Colonial Development Act was passed, it was a small one and the great depression ensured that its practical effects were even smaller than its authors had expected. Throughout the inter-war years, the day-to-day consequences of this accepted attitude towards colonial finance were numerous and obvious. But even more important than the practical limitations it imposed were its pervasive but more subtle consequences on the thinking of almost all who were at all actively concerned with those institutions in which colonial policy was shaped.

NOTES TO CHAPTER I

[1] S. R. Mehrotra, 'On the Use of the Term "Commonwealth"' (*Journal of Commonwealth Political Studies*, Vol. II (1963), pp. 1–13), shows that, among others, Bernard Shaw, Campbell-Bannerman, Goldwin Smith, and Merriman (the Cape statesman) advocated 'Commonwealth' in place of Empire at various times between 1885 and 1905.

[2] First officially used in the Anglo-Irish 'Treaty' of 1921. *Ibid.*, p. 12.

[3] The word 'ineffective' may be criticized on the ground that discriminatory legislation, such as the Land Apportionment Act of 1931, was discussed with the British Government before its introduction in S. Rhodesia. It remains true that the veto was never used and that 'Any British Government would clearly have been reluctant from the start to intervene in the affairs of a self-governing colony, and after the first few years intervention became progressively more difficult' (P. Mason, *Year of Decision* (London, 1960), p. 3).

[4] *Minutes of the Imperial War Conference* (Cd. 8566), 1917, p. 5.

[5] 20 August 1917. *Report on Indian Constitutional Reforms* (Cd. 9109), 1918, para. 6.

[6] *Ibid.*, para. 7.

[7] Quoted by T. de Vere White, 'Arthur Griffith', in C. C. O'Brien (ed.), *The Shaping of Modern Ireland* (London, 1960), p. 67.

[8] O'Brien, *op. cit.*, pp. 9–10.

[9] L. S. Amery, *My Political Life*, Vol. II (London, 1953), p. 194.

[10] These Lectures were delivered before the publication of Elizabeth Monroe's brilliant book *Britain's Moment in the Middle East 1914–1956* (London, 1963).

[11] Miss Monroe writes 'Measured by British interests alone' the Declaration 'was one of the greatest mistakes in our imperial history', *op. cit.*, p. 43.

[12] Commons *Hansard*, 17 February 1922, c. 1461–2, quoted by A. P. Thornton, *The Imperial Idea and its Enemies* (London, 1959), p. xi.

[13] Thornton, *op. cit.*, p. xi.

[14] S. R. Mehrotra, 'Imperial Federation and India 1868–1917'. *Journal of Commonwealth Political Studies*, Vol. I (1961), p. 34.

[15] G. K. Gokhale, *Speeches* (Madras s.d., ?1909), p. 782.

[16] Sir W. S. Churchill, *The Second World War*, Vol. I (London, 1948), p. 27.

[17] Mehrotra, *op. cit.*, p. 38.

[18] Viscount Milner, *Questions of the Hour* (new edition, London, 1925), p. 204.

[19] *Imperial Conference, 1926. Appendices to the Summary of Proceedings* (Cmd. 2769), 1927, p. 134. As Miss Monroe puts it, 'the plans adopted for immediate use were various but the end was the same—to evolve a compromise between the Middle Eastern wish for independence and the British wish to retain partial control', *op. cit.*, p. 71.

[20] *La Conférence Africaine Francaise, Brazzaville 1944* (Paris, 1945), p. 32.

[21] Sir R. Coupland, *The Empire in These Days* (London, 1935), p. 179.

[22] In 1940, Sir Cosmo Parkinson, then Permanent Under-Secretary at the Colonial Office, was transferred to the corresponding post in the Dominions Office when Sir George Gater, the Clerk of the London County Council, was brought in to the former post. But he returned after four months when Sir George Gater was temporarily transferred to the new Ministry of Home Security.

[23] P. N. S. Mansergh, *Survey of British Commonwealth Affairs: Problems of External Policy 1931–1939* (London, 1952), p. 271.

[24] According to Lord Beaverbrook, *The Decline and Fall of Lloyd George* (London, 1963), pp. 40–41, Sir W. Churchill had intended that the Colonial Office should also take over Egypt from the Foreign Office but was baulked by Lord Curzon.

[25] Cmd. 2769, p. 111.

[26] The best discussion of the Mandate arrangements is H. D. Hall, *Mandates, Dependencies and Trusteeships* (London, 1948).

[27] Commons *Hansard*, 30 July 1919, c. 2175.

[28] Sir D. Cameron, *My Tanganyika Service and some Nigeria* (London, 1939), p. 20.

[29] Sir F. D. (later Lord) Lugard, *op. cit.* (third edition, London, 1926), p. 617.

[30] *Ibid.*, p. 506.

[31] *Ibid.*, p. 198.

[32] For the reality behind this see Professor J. F. A. Ajayi, 'Henry Venn and the Policy of Development', *Journal of the Historical Society of Nigeria*, Vol. I (1959), pp. 331–42, and his unpublished London Ph.D. thesis, 'Christian Missions and the Making of Nigeria, 1841–1891'; also P. D. Curtin, *The Image of Africa* (Madison, 1964), pp. 300–4.

[33] Commons *Hansard*, 22 August 1895, c. 642.

[34] Milner, *op. cit.*, pp. 172–3.

[35] Earl Grey, *The Colonial Policy of Lord John Russell's Administration*, Vol. II (London, 1853), p. 281.

II

THE INSTITUTIONS OF COLONIAL POLICY

In 1897, Sir George Goldie, the head of the Royal Niger Company, told Chamberlain 'whatever may be the present activity of the Colonial Office, it cannot be permanently a creative machine. Its main business . . . is that of control—the "governor" of the steam engine and not the boiler. Its officials are brought up from the first in this all-important work of control, which develops an entirely different habit from that of initiating and administering.'[1] Even Chamberlain's galvanizing activity could not greatly change these habits of an able but increasingly overworked bureaucracy or the ingrained distaste of a still Gladstonian Treasury for imperial expenditure on which those habits largely rested. Margery Perham's great biography of Lugard makes that clear though it certainly does not support the harsher verdict of Chamberlain's private secretary, a Colonial Office man himself, who told a younger colleague just before the first war, 'Oh, Joe was a great man. He woke the office up and it has been going to sleep ever since'.[2] All the critics, then and later, conceded the ability, the industry, and the knowledge of its officials—at least so far as knowledge could be acquired in Downing Street. What was wanting was variously described: the touch of reality that only practical experience, or at least some first-hand appreciation, of colonial conditions could bring, sympathy and a more lively sense of partnership with the 'men on the spot', and, more fundamental, as an outstanding governor, Sir Donald Cameron, put it, 'constructive thinking where large issues are involved'.[3]

Some of this criticism was of the kind which is endemic between men at headquarters and men in the field. Some of it was the inescapable result of the functions of the Colonial Office as a supervisory and controlling organ and one, more-over, obliged, whatever its own views, to work within a system whose dominant assumptions for long precluded any direct financial assistance from the metropole to the colonies unless in dire need and as a last resort. Some of it reflected the fact that the administrative staff of the Office formed part of the Home Civil Service, recruited by the stiffest of competitive examinations, while those of the colonies, except in Ceylon, Malaya, and Hong Kong, where they were chosen by the same method, were appointed by the patronage of the Secretary of State. Colonial Office men were widely suspected (not always unjustly) of thinking themselves very much the in-tellectual superiors of most of the colonial administrators, some of whom returned the compliment by pointing to the lack of practical experience in Whitehall.[4]

In 1919, the Office[5] was still much as it had been in Chamberlain's time, although since 1907 there had been a separate division for the Dominions. The Colonies division consisted of seven geographical departments, each dealing with a par-ticular area like the Far East or the West Indies, and one general department which handled a variety of miscellaneous sub-jects, mostly of minor importance, which affected the colonies generally. Apart from a legal adviser, all the superior staff was 'administrative'. No medical, agricultural, technical, or scien-tific staff were employed in the Office itself. The Crown Agents for the Colonies acted as commercial and financial agents for all the non-self-governing territories and were financed en-tirely by the payments those territories made for their services. In their offices there was a permanent engineering staff, pri-marily concerned with the supervision of contracts and the design and inspection of equipment ordered by the colonies,

whose advice in engineering problems was of course available
to the Colonial Office. There were long-established contacts
between the Office and experts working in such places as the
Imperial Institute, the Royal Botanic Gardens (whose Director,
since 1902, had had the title 'Botanical Adviser to the Secretary of State'), and the London and Liverpool Schools of
Tropical Medicine. In the London School of Tropical Medicine a Tropical Diseases Bureau had been established. It was
maintained by contributions from the British government and
from Dominion and Colonial governments, and managed by a
committee responsible to the Secretary of State, including a
number of distinguished medical authorities as well as members of the Colonial Office staff. Similar arrangements applied
to the Tropical Diseases Research Fund, established in 1904,
and the Imperial Bureau of Entomology (to whose income of
£4,570 the British government contributed £500). There were
also two Advisory Committees whose members included
'outside experts' as well as officials, the Colonial Survey Committee (established in 1905) to advise on survey problems and
the Advisory Medical and Sanitary Committee for Tropical
Africa, established in 1909. For all these bodies, the Colonial
Office provided the secretariats. With such an organization,
the Colonial Office was not conspicuously suited to playing
any effective part in setting up 'a new and more positive standard of our duty and obligation towards the peoples to whom
this house is in the position of trustee'[6] which Amery, then
Parliamentary Under-Secretary for the Colonies, had told the
House of Commons as early as July 1919 would be the task of
reconstruction in the Colonial Empire.

The history of the Colonial Office (and of the Colonial
Service) in the inter-war years could be written in terms of their
gradual, though by no means complete, adaptation for such a
task. That it was so gradual no doubt owed something to the
conservatism of some officials. It owed far more to the prevailing

climate of ideas about what was sound economic and financial policy for colonies and to the effects of economic depression: the retrenchment that followed the first post-war slump of 1921 provided a kind of rehearsal for the more desperate setback that followed in 1931. And, although this cannot be fully assessed until the records are available to scholars, it owed a good deal to Treasury parsimony in instances where, even by the standards of the day, the expense involved was trifling. Soon after he ceased to be Colonial Secretary in 1921, Milner bluntly asserted that the Colonial Office was 'the Cinderella of the great public departments. In the annual autumnal battle of the Treasury with all the other Offices over the preparation of the Estimates, Cinderella stands a poor chance. When "economy" is in the saddle, she stands no chance at all.'[7]

Yet, between 1919 and 1929 'the British government spent on the Colonies (including Palestine and Iraq) a total of £81·8 million in all kinds of assistance' (a sum which may be compared with their total annual expenditure which, in 1929, was something over £72 million). Of the £81·8 million, however, no less than £51 million represented military and air force expenditure in Iraq which also accounted for a further £7·5 million of other 'kinds of assistance'. British expenditure on all the other territories that made up the Colonial Empire was thus about £23 million. In the period 1929–1940, that of the first Colonial Development Act, expenditure outside the Act was £19·9 million while advances totalling £8·8 million were approved under the Act, of which about £6·5 million was actually spent in these years. Loans totalling £8·6 million were also written off under the Act of 1940 but £5·5 million of this represented the cost of building the Uganda railway in the last years of the nineteenth century. The conclusion of a distinguished authority that 'the habit of finding large sums for expenditure in the colonies was well established long before it became a formal policy'[8] thus requires qualification. Over the inter-war years as a whole such sums averaged, if Iraq is excluded, just over £2 million a year.

Milner, indeed, spoke with the bitterness of experience. For what he had 'without hesitation' affirmed was 'the most urgent and vital' question in the colonies—'the adequate application of science to the conservation and development of their resources'[9]—the Office had in 1919 obtained a Parliamentary grant of £20,000 a year to be spent on research in the poorer territories, only to see this reduced to £2,000 in the 'economy' campaign of 1921. The modest expenditure needed to make a start in equipping the Colonial Office (and, as we shall see, the Colonial Service) for setting that 'new and more positive standard' of the duties of trusteeship of which Amery had spoken seems to have been forthcoming only with great difficulty.

Already in 1919 Members of Parliament had urged that the Office should be freed from its Dominion responsibilities to concentrate on the task of development in the Colonial Empire. The political arguments for such a change were of course reinforced by the new position assumed by the Dominions during and immediately after the war but it was only in 1925 that Amery succeeded in getting this done when he became Secretary of State. Even then, the decision was delayed for months because the Treasury declined to pay the new Permanent Under-Secretary of the Dominions Office the normal salary of such a post.[10] Although the separation of the two offices was no doubt a prerequisite of the adaptation of the Colonial Office for a more positive role, the full effect can only have been delayed by the arrangement by which Amery and, for a time, his successor, Sidney Webb, held both portfolios while the decision in 1921 to assign to the Colonial Office Britain's new responsibilities in the Middle East was to deflect much of its energies to the intractable politics of Palestine.

But gradually the Office was equipped and organized to meet some of the needs of the enlarged conception of its task in the Colonial Empire. Specialist advisers began to appear on its staff. The first, in 1921, was a personal (and unpaid) post of 'adviser on business matters' which lapsed in 1923.[11] In that year an Advisory Committee on Education in Tropical Africa was set up, with a full-time secretary, Hanns Vischer, the remarkable Swiss missionary, who had become in 1908 the first Director of Education in Northern Nigeria.[12] This, incidentally, was made possible by the support of the African governors and was paid for jointly by the African colonies themselves. Vischer was in effect an educational adviser for tropical Africa. Five years later the Committee's scope was extended to the whole Colonial Empire and Arthur Mayhew from the Indian Education Service became joint secretary and responsible for educational advice for the non-African colonies. The later twenties saw the appointment of a succession of advisers: Medical (1926), Economic and Financial, Fisheries (1928), Agriculture (1929), Animal Health (1930). The last three were paid for by contributions from the colonies or from other funds not under normal Treasury control.[13] The depression brought a halt to this, as to many other consequences of the rethinking of the problems of colonial development which took place between the first post-war slump and the great depression. It was not until 1938 that the next such post was created, that of Labour Adviser, a direct consequence of the series of labour 'disturbances' in the West Indies. Almost all the advisers—many more followed after 1940—were men who had had outstanding careers in the Colonial Service. They travelled extensively and helped to bring the Office into much closer contact with the men in their own branches of the Colonial Service.

There was a somewhat similar development of Advisory Committees. To those concerned with medicine and education, others were added, notably the Colonial Advisory Council on Agriculture and Animal Health set up in 1929.[14] Through them the Office was also brought in touch with a wider range of expert knowledge and opinion in Britain itself. Both Advisers and Advisory Committees have of course been criticized and it is certainly arguable that eventually the Colonial Office had too much of a good thing.[15] But in the inter-war years, the Advisory Committees played an important part in bringing more and more of British scientific and professional expertise to bear on colonial problems and so helped to build up a small but powerful body of informed opinion in Britain.

After 1930 a new development began. Amery had considered, but rejected, the possibility of reorganizing the Colonial Office completely, substituting for the traditional geographical distribution of work a wholly functional arrangement. He had seen in the development of the adviser system the best method of combining expert knowledge in the various technical problems of development with the need for continuity in policy and regard for the widely differing political and social circumstances of individual territories. But as the sphere of government widened, and the scope of international action[16] increased, the advantages of a functional organization of the administrative work itself became more and more evident, in the Colonial Office as elsewhere. Nowhere was this more striking than in economics: the problems of marketing rubber or oilseeds, or of settling the basic principles on which mineral exploitation could be most advantageously organized in the interests of the community, were matters in which a general knowledge of the particular circumstances of an individual territory was by no means enough.

Until the second world war, when they rapidly overtook geographical departments and advisers in importance, the development of functional departments was very slow. Three departments concerned with the recruitment and training, promotion and conditions of service of the Colonial Service itself were the first to appear in 1930. The next, in 1932, was an Economic Section which became in 1934 an Economic Department, partly the outcome of the great depression, the extension of Imperial Preference, and the development of commodity restrictive schemes, but also of the appointment in 1932 as Secretary of State of Sir Philip Cunliffe Lister, previously four times President of the Board of Trade.[17] One of its first members actually was an economist, Sir Sydney Caine, later Director of the London School of Economics. In 1938, a Social Service Department followed, and soon after a Development Department, intended for the financial and administrative problems of the new Colonial Development and Welfare Act of 1940. By 1960 there were still only nine geographical departments but twenty-one specialist departments, thirty scientific and technical advisers, and twenty-three advisory committees. A cynic might add that the Colonial Empire was fast ceasing to exist, but it is perhaps more to the point that almost the entire organization of scientific and technical advisory services was in the following year transferred to the new Department of Technical Co-operation where it has been redeployed to meet the needs of newly independent states both within and outside the Commonwealth, as well as continuing to serve those of the remaining dependencies.

Other changes were made in the 'twenties and 'thirties which show that some Ministers at least felt that there was something in the reproach of aloofness from the colonies which, especially in the earlier years, had been so frequently levelled at the Office. Between 1921 and 1947 only one of the Permanent Heads of the Office had himself been a member of its staff.[18] Amery records that his 'first concern' was to bring the Office itself into more direct contact with the colonies. To this end he was 'determined that the new head of the Office should be someone who knew what it felt like, when toiling away in stifling heat, to get a stuffy dispatch from Whitehall',[19] so he appointed the Governor of Jamaica to that post. He, in turn, was succeeded in 1933 by the Governor General of the Sudan, while between 1930 and 1942 several other governors were brought in as Assistant Under-Secretaries. Amery also adopted a deliberate policy of arranging that his Parliamentary and his Permanent Under-Secretary should get away from the Office on visits to the colonies and of sending other members of the staff on special missions as secretaries of commissions of inquiry, or in a few cases for spells of service. By 1930 twenty-four of the administrative staff of fifty-four had made such visits or served in the colonies. Increasing numbers of colonial civil servants were also being attached to the Office for short periods. The two Colonial Office Conferences[20] of 1927 and 1930 attended by Governors or the most senior officials from almost all parts of the Colonial Empire exemplified both the new tendency to treat the Colonial Empire as a single entity and the attempt to improve contact between the Office and the men on the spot. Their main preoccupations were the reorganization of the Colonial Services, especially the scientific services, and the development of communications and transport.

In 1930 it was finally decided, as the result of a report by a committee presided over by Sir Warren Fisher, the Permanent Secretary of the British Treasury, not to amalgamate the Office with the Colonial Service because its work was 'in its essentials different from the work of Colonial Administrations'.[21] Instead a more organized and regular system of interchange was adopted under which new entrants to the Colonial Office staff would normally serve a two years' secondment to a colonial administration after their first few years in the Office while a number of colonial civil servants would serve a similar period in the Office.

Strictly speaking, the Colonial Service, to which we must

next turn, did not exist, in 1919 or even in 1930. Each territory was a separate unit of government, with its own administrative and technical services, its own scales of pay and conditions of service. These administrative systems, it was true, were 'sometimes described as The Colonial Service, as though they constituted a single Service'. 'Such an illusion', the Warren Fisher Committee remarked, 'does not survive the most cursory examination.'[22] All appointments were made by the Governor. The lower levels were filled locally, but vacancies requiring new appointments in the higher grades had to be notified to the Colonial Office. The Governor might of course recommend the appointment of someone in the territory, whether a native or not. But the Secretary of State normally selected a candidate and the Governor then appointed him. Before the first world war, candidates were interviewed by two of the assistant private secretaries who recorded their particulars and when a vacancy was notified produced a field of possible candidates from those on their books and made a proposal to the Secretary of State. One of the private secretaries was a Colonial Office official, the other was a personal appointment by the Secretary of State. The latter post was comparatively junior and also temporary, since a new Secretary of State might not wish to retain his predecessor's nominee.

In 1911 a new incumbent had been appointed to the latter post, a man of utter integrity and remarkable vision such as an otherwise hopelessly indefensible system of this sort occasionally throws up. He was a young man, just down from Oxford and, partly because of the oddity of the system, he was to remain in charge of the recruitment and training of the Colonial Service until his retirement as Sir Ralph Furse in 1948.[23] When he came back to the Colonial Office in 1919 after war service the increasing scale and widening scope of colonial government evidently demanded an altogether new approach to the problem of recruitment. Especially in agriculture, forestry, and veterinary work, the supply of men with the qualifications required did not exist. It had to be created. There were three distinct but related problems.

First, Furse was convinced that qualities of character and temperament were of such special importance in colonial conditions that for all appointments, specialist as well as administrative, it was essential to maintain and develop a system of individual selection which would seek to give full weight to such qualities, however difficult they might be to assess, rather than to turn over to a system of competitive examination such as that which had been adopted, following the Indian model, for administrative and police posts in the Far Eastern territories, Ceylon, Hong Kong, and Malaya. This was no easy task since the system Furse had inherited was obviously vulnerable to accusations, however unjustified, of jobbery and some at least of his own colleagues, themselves the product of competitive examination, were convinced 'there was nothing like leather'. This problem was not finally settled until 1930 when the Warren Fisher Committee endorsed the system of selection by interview but recognized that it was 'open to criticism first and foremost as being one of patronage', which 'could not, in theory be defended'. Furse and his three assistants should accordingly be incorporated in the permanent staff of the Colonial Office and the final recommendation of a candidate for a colonial appointment should in future be made by a Board nominated by the Civil Service Commission. These proposals were accepted by Sidney Webb (Lord Passfield) who had become Secretary of State in the Labour government while, as Amery had foreseen, Warren Fisher's support ensured Treasury agreement. Two years later the administrative posts which had been filled by competitive examination since the eighteen-seventies were brought within the new system.[24] As the opportunities available elsewhere in the Colonial Empire without examination became better known, there had been increasing difficulty in securing enough candidates for them by the old one.

Secondly, the scope and possibilities offered by the Colonial Empire must somehow be presented to the young men of Britain in a way which would enable them to compete, as offering a career comparable with the other great public services in Britain and India and especially with the All India Services. This, as Furse had long argued, and Amery and Ormsby-Gore, his political masters, fully agreed, called for some degree of standardization of salaries and conditions of service for similar jobs in different territories so that officers could be transferable between them without necessarily being offered promotion. This was most important for the smaller and poorer territories which otherwise had little chance of ever getting the best men. Chamberlain had proposed a unified Colonial Service in the 'nineties: in this, as in so many other things, he anticipated developments which it took nearly half a century to achieve. Furse himself had put the idea to Milner as early as 1919. For the next ten years, he worked through a series of expert committees set up to consider what could be done to improve recruitment and provide for training in forestry, agricultural, veterinary, medical, and scientific research services.[25] All of them urged the importance of unifying the miscellaneous appointments in their respective fields but those which were most specific about how this was to be done thought that the new unified services would have to be financed by a central fund to which all colonies contributed. On that rock these schemes foundered. The Warren Fisher Committee strongly urged unification which would, it said, raise the prestige of the Colonial Service and secure, 'so far as is humanly possible that the best officers should have the chance of rising to the top'. Though this would involve some scheme of related salary scales, it need not be financed from a central fund. Unification would bring substantial benefits to all colonies and special advantages to the smaller ones. It was, the Committee said, 'an issue of the very first importance from the point of view of Colonial Development'.

For the next decade the new Colonial Service Division of the Office, which the Warren Fisher Committee also recommended, was busy with the creation of the new Unified Services, like the Colonial Administrative Service set up in 1932 and followed by the Colonial Medical Service, the Colonial Agricultural Service, and so on. For most of them specific professional qualifications and further special post-graduate training were required of all new entrants. The standard, as well as the number, of candidates undoubtedly improved. It was not the fault of those responsible for colonial policy that, far from the continuing expansion they could reasonably expect in the late 'twenties (between 1924 and 1929 new recruitment for these administrative and professional appointments averaged over 450 a year), the world economic depression and the catastrophic fall in colonial revenue it produced made it impossible even to maintain much of what had so laboriously been achieved. In 1932 when the revenue of most colonies was only half what it had been in 1929 the total recruitment fell to 70; although it recovered, it never again equalled the 1924–9 average until the second world war ended in 1945.[26]

But the most far-reaching result of this era was in connexion with the third problem, the development of new forms of training and the establishment of new institutions both to provide that training and to direct and stimulate the research needed if it was to be relevant to tropical problems. To create the supply of suitable men which the early twenties had shown did not exist, scholarships were established to enable men with a basic scientific or professional training to equip themselves in forestry, agricultural, and veterinary work. To train them new institutions were established in the Colonial Empire or in

Britain. The Imperial College of Tropical Agriculture where the agricultural scholars took a year's post-graduate training was opened in Trinidad in 1922. Once again the cost was at first met mainly by colonial governments though there was an imperial contribution and substantial grants were later made by the Empire Marketing Board and the Empire Cotton Growing Corporation. A proposal for an Imperial Forestry Institute, for post-graduate training of forestry officers for British as well as overseas service, had been turned down by the Treasury in 1921. In 1924, mainly as a result of Furse's intervention at the Empire Forestry Conference held in Canada the year before, it was opened in Oxford. Its annual cost was then put at £5,000, the greater part to be met by colonial governments.[27] Such examples (there are many others) surely go far to substantiate Amery's description of the Treasury as a 'surly watchdog'.[28]

In 1925 Amery accepted another proposal, which Furse had also originally suggested to Milner in 1919, that the 'rather sketchy' three months' training at the Imperial Institute for men selected for administrative posts in tropical Africa, which had originally been established in 1909, should be replaced by longer courses at Oxford and Cambridge. Such courses would also serve to publicize in those two vital centres of recruitment the opportunities offered by the Colonial Service. Except to the extent that the universities were able to provide teaching staff, these courses, which were enlarged in 1933 to include Malaya, and in 1945 extended to all colonies, were financed until 1945 wholly by colonial funds. The setting up of the Advisory Committee on Education in Tropical Africa led to the opening in 1928 at the London Day Training College of what was probably the first course of teacher training designed exclusively to meet the special needs of developing countries.[29] This later became the Department of Education in Tropical Areas of the Institute of Education at London

University. By 1938 80 per cent of the new entrants to the Colonial Service received special training before taking up their appointments, the majority for a year or longer.[30] In a few years all this had a profound effect on the awareness of the needs and problems of the Colonial Empire among many of Britain's leading scientists and academics.

There was one aspect of these changes in the organization of the Colonial Service which deserved more attention than it ever received and whose importance was bound to increase as the years passed. In recommending unification, the Warren Fisher Committee had thought it well to say that it did not 'suggest that the system should be carried to the length of becoming a positive hindrance to the local promotion of officers of first-rate ability'.[31] Yet it was surely inevitable that at the very least it should make it less likely that there should be such officers to promote. If they had the initial qualifications required, which roughly speaking amounted to a university degree or its equivalent, they would not be attracted to the subordinate ranks of the local civil service, while if they had not and joined the local civil service from school, they were most likely to find the way blocked, unless indeed their 'first rate ability' was phenomenally evident, because they were not so qualified. Until 1942 indeed candidates presenting themselves for selection for first appointments in the Colonial Administrative Service were required to be of 'pure European descent' though there was no regulation precluding the appointment of local men to posts in a colony normally filled by officers of that Service and a few were. Nothing is more striking in retrospect than the absence of any attempt to encourage the people of the colonies to equip themselves for public employment at the levels of the unified services.

Had it been considered, the experience of Ceylon was in fact particularly instructive on this point. Some Ceylonese had been appointed to the administrative service even in the

middle of the nineteenth century and when the new competitive examination was introduced in 1856, designed for university graduates, some continued to be appointed locally
by the Governor. After 1870 the examination was held
simultaneously in London and Ceylon but as there were very
few Ceylonese with British university degrees it was now more
difficult for Ceylonese to compete and in 1880 the Ceylon
examinations were discontinued. In 1891, however, a separate
Local Division was established in the civil service and some of
the administrative posts were actually reserved for its members,
with the result that by 1920 eleven of the ninety higher administrative posts were held by Ceylonese. This Local Division
was abolished in 1920 and it was decided that one-third of all
new appointments to the administrative service should be filled
by Ceylonese. The proportion was increased to a half in 1923.
If sufficient Ceylonese were not forthcoming from the London
examination a local examination was to be held. But it was
soon clear that there was now a sufficient supply of local
graduates, partly as a result of the opening of the Ceylon
University College, and the examination was, after 1924, again
held simultaneously in London and Ceylon. By 1930 fifty-five
of the administrative posts were held by Ceylonese and eighty-
three by Europeans. Recruitment of Europeans was suspended
in 1931, resumed in 1935, and again suspended after 1937.
By 1940 the figures were almost exactly reversed.[32]

Ceylon, of course, was the most advanced colonial territory
and any such prospects might be thought quite remote in
tropical Africa. So no doubt as a general rule they were in the
'thirties, yet in the Gold Coast Guggisberg, the most far-
sighted Governor of the age, had produced in 1926 a twenty-
year plan under which the number of Africans holding what
were termed 'European appointments' which was then twenty-
eight should rise to 148 in 1936 and 229 in 1946. By that time,
he calculated, they would represent nearly half the total. Such

precise planning is no doubt impracticable but by 1938 there were actually only forty-one. The failure was partly due to the changed outlook brought by the world economic depression and especially the fact that facilities for local higher education were not developed as Guggisberg had hoped.[33] Yet even in 1927 the Director of Colonial Scholars told the Colonial Office Conference that there were forty-six West Africans then studying at British universities, and when in 1942 two Africans were appointed to the district administration of the Gold Coast one was an Oxford, the other a Cambridge, graduate and both measured up to the highest standards of British or Dominion recruits to the Colonial Administrative Service.

The reorganization of the Colonial Service undoubtedly improved its quality and efficiency as an instrument of development. But it is hard to believe that its concentration on the requirement for British officers did not adversely affect the opportunities for natives of the colonies in their own public service. At the end of the second world war, a Colonial Office White Paper went far towards admitting this indictment. There were, it said, 'potential candidates in the Colonies, both inside and outside the Civil Service, who have hitherto had no opportunity of acquiring the same standard of education as candidates from the United Kingdom or the Dominions'.[34] Over the next ten years £1 million would therefore be allocated by the British government to enable selected colonial candidates to receive professional and vocational training which would qualify them for appointment to the higher grades of the Colonial Service. It was, however, much later in the day than most people had yet begun to realize and especially in East and Central Africa the lack of qualified and experienced African civil servants today is perhaps the most immediate danger to the stability and growth of the new states emerging there.

Meanwhile all this reshaping of the Colonial Services mostly affected the younger men. What kind of people were those at the top, the Governors themselves, who remained at the decisive point in the making and application of policy? Leaving on one side the three 'fortress' colonies, Gibraltar, Malta, and Bermuda, where by long-standing arrangement the Governor was always a serving General, 103 men held office between 1919 and 1939 as Governors in the remaining thirty colonial administrations. Rather more than half (54) had actually begun their careers in the Colonial Service. Of these sixteen had joined as Eastern cadets, twenty had begun in tropical Africa (of whom seven had started in Kenya and five in Nigeria). Of the remaining eighteen, three had begun by getting a job on a Governor's personal staff as private secretary or A.D.C. Six others had begun as clerks in the West Indies, where three had been born, including Sir Donald Cameron who was certainly one of the two or three outstanding Governors of the period. Both these methods of entry were backdoors which the new system was virtually certain to close. Two more were men from the professional services, one doctor and one lawyer.

Of the forty-nine whose first jobs had not been in the Colonial Service, no less than twenty-eight had been army officers. Seven of these had found their way into the Colonial Service after military employment in a colony, six more came by way of the Indian army, while three had been secretaries of the Overseas Defence Committee. Of the twenty-one who had not begun as professional soldiers, seven came from the Home Civil Service (three from the Colonial Office itself and one each from the War Office, the Admiralty, the Treasury, and the Local Government Board. Two of these, incidentally, began in clerical not 'administrative' posts and one was a doctor). The Egyptian Civil Service supplied two, the Sudan Service and the Indian Civil Service one each, while two more were private secretaries to Dominion Governors-General. Another seven owed their connexion with the Empire to service in South Africa either in the British South Africa Company service, or in the Boer war or the 'reconstruction' period that followed it. In this, as in other ways, this sample reflected the Colonial Service of the period of expansion and much of the history of the Colonial Empire from the eighteen-eighties to the first world war. Although only fifty-five of the 103 were graduates (27 Oxford, 18 Cambridge, 5 Edinburgh, 2 London, 2 Dublin, and 1 unidentified) the rise of the university man even before the first world war is plain. Of the fifty-three who were first appointed to the public service (including the army) before 1900, nineteen were graduates. Of the forty-four appointed between 1900 and 1915, thirty-three were.

The complaint that Governors were too often chosen from outside the service was still voiced and even in this period twelve of the 103 who held office during the inter-war years were men whose first appointment in the Colonial Service was that of Governor. Of these, eight had begun as professional soldiers, one was a Cabinet Minister (Sir Herbert Samuel), one a trade unionist who after eighteen years as a Member of Parliament was made Governor of Tasmania and later of the Falklands, one was a Treasury official, and one (Sir Edward Grigg) had begun his career on the editorial staff of *The Times*. Five of the twelve had been Members of Parliament before their appointment and four were appointed to very minor posts, two to the Seychelles, one to St Helena, and one to the Falklands. Three went to Kenya, which had no wholly 'Colonial Service' Governor throughout this period. (Sir Robert Coryndon, who came nearest to it, had begun with the British South Africa Company and been Rhodes's private secretary.) Four more of the twelve were High Commissioners in that other trouble spot, Palestine, which also had only one 'Colonial Service' man between the wars. It was, perhaps, only fitting that the Treasury official should have gone straight to one of the plums of the service, Malaya.

The consistent appointment in Kenya and Palestine of men from outside the Service must suggest that Ministers doubted its capacity to supply those broader qualities of statesmanship which the reconciliation of the sharply conflicting objects of British policy in these two countries evidently demanded. If the Service in these years produced neither a Lyautey nor a Lugard, it had in Cameron, Hugh Clifford, and Guggisberg three remarkable Governors who each demonstrated sharply their conviction of the paramountcy of native interests as they understood them, Cameron in his sustained opposition to a settler-dominated Closer Union in East Africa, Clifford by his repeated rejection of Leverhulme's demand for large-scale concessions in Nigeria, and Guggisberg by his insistent conviction of African potential. The majority maintained a high average of commonsense practicality in administration. But exceptional qualities were needed to survive wholly unimpaired the autocratic isolation which the system still imposed on Governors. If very few reacted to the point of eccentricity, not many were entirely immune from a certain rigidity which was only in part a legacy from the pioneer days before the war and the sturdy individualism they had so often demanded.

Government in the Colonial Empire was bureaucratic government. Society and economy were shaped most powerfully by other agencies, native and immigrant. But the limits within which those agencies worked, narrow to the point of suffocation or wide to the point of neglect, depended, to an extent which it is now hard to imagine, on the bureaucracy, the hard core of that world apart that made up the Colonial Empire. For that bureaucracy, of course, the limits of manœuvre were set by the brute economic and social facts as it saw them in each territory and also by its own attempt to work out for itself some rationale of its own activities. In comparatively few territories—Ceylon, Kenya, Malta, and some of the West Indies—they were also set by the interests which found expression in local political institutions. But limits were also set by Parliament and the cluster of institutions—Ministers, Parties, and pressure groups—which centred in it.

Generalizations about the role of Parliament in the formulation of colonial policy in the inter-war years are exceptionally hazardous. The detailed research on which they must be based has yet to be done, and can, in any case, only be doubtfully conclusive until the public archives are open. Many critics have emphasized Parliament's limitations as an effective supervisor of the bureaucratic trustee; they have done little more than echo—although sometimes with a different purpose—what John Stuart Mill said a hundred years ago:

'To govern a country under responsibility to the people of *that* country, and to govern one country under responsibility to the people of another, are two very different things. What makes the excellence of the first is that freedom is preferable to despotism: but the last *is* despotism. The only choice the case admits, is a choice of despotisms: and it is not certain that the despotism of twenty millions is necessarily better than that of a few, or of one. But it is quite certain, that the despotism of those who neither hear, nor see, nor know anything about their subjects, has many chances of being worse than that of those who do. It is not usually thought that the immediate agents of authority govern better because they govern in the name of an absent master, and of one who has a thousand more pressing interests to attend to . . . The responsibility of the British rulers of India to the British nation is chiefly useful because, when any acts of the government are called in question, it ensures publicity and discussion . . . It is doubtless a useful restraint upon the immediate rulers that they can be put upon their defence, and that one or two of the jury will form an opinion worth having about their conduct, though that of the remainder will probably be several degrees worse than none. Such as it is, this is the amount of benefit to India, from the control exercised over the Indian government by the British Parliament and people.'[35]

Parliamentary intervention in the affairs of the Colonial Empire was limited, in the first place, for institutional reasons, rooted both in geography and history. It was rarely necessary for the Colonial Office to promote legislation in Parliament. Laws for the colonies were normally made separately by the legislators of each colony, even if, as in Gibraltar, the Governor was himself the legislature. Their constitutions were almost all laid down by executive instruments (Letters Patent or Orders in Council), for which no Parliamentary sanction was required. In all except five of them, the British government could legislate if need be by Order in Council. Their revenues were provided locally and their estimates required the Secretary of State's approval not that of Parliament. Of course, all these matters could be discussed, if members wished and the Whips could find time, but that was quite different from the normal position of the Home Departments in which if the government wanted any new legislation it had to find Parliamentary time. The only occasion on which an opportunity necessarily occurred to raise any colonial issue was the annual debate in Committee of Supply on the Colonial Office vote. This very fact meant that the Colonial Secretary usually opened the debate with a broad, if conveniently selective, survey of his Department's activities while others speakers each pursued the affairs of a particular territory in which they were interested. The occasion was accordingly ineffective for any sustained discussion of a major issue, or even for pressing home a minor one.

Secondly, Parliamentary intervention was limited not only because Parliament often had 'a thousand more pressing interests to attend to' but because not many members of either house had direct personal knowledge of, or interest in, the colonies. Both criticisms have perhaps been pressed too hard. Even if the attendance was small, a great deal of Parliamentary time was taken up by those colonial issues on which there was strong disagreement, most of all those which sharply focused the latent oppositions between the protective and the developmental aspect of trusteeship, the interests of the natives and those of immigrant enterprise: no one who has worked through the debates and questions on Kenya and closer union in East Africa or on Palestine could be in any doubt of that. Nor was intervention on colonial issues limited, as has often been alleged, to a very small group. During Amery's tenure of the Colonial Office between 1924 and 1929 something like a third of the members raised some colonial issue in the House of Commons, even if only by asking a single question.[36] On the other hand, most of the talking during the same period about the predominant issue of East Africa was done by a much smaller group, varying slightly from session to session, but usually between fifteen and twenty strong and divided between what might be called the 'Development' lobby and the 'African rights' lobby. Nor did colonial affairs make a poor showing by that other barometer of Parliamentary concerns, question time. A substantial proportion of the 'more than five hundred questions' put down to the Colonial Secretary in 1924 were no doubt concerned with relations with the Dominions. But in the 1929–30 session, 471 were put down for oral answer— only part of the total—a number exceeded only by the 493 on India and the 1,199 on foreign affairs.[37]

Parliament was not, however, well equipped to make effective use of the information available to it. In marked contrast to other colonial powers, the British published, either in the colonies or in London, an extraordinary amount of information about their activities. Commissions of inquiry were no doubt often a convenient device for shelving awkward decisions but their reports were usually substantial and informative. Annual Reports were sometimes amazingly revealing, sometimes discreetly obscure, often blandly complacent, but they were published not only for each territory but for almost every department of government in each territory, and on the whole maintained an honourable standard of accuracy. But to make full use of all this material, to probe its understatements and pursue the clues it often provided to problems it was careful not to underline, Parliament needed more than the amateur efforts of a handful of private members. Lacking any such instrument as a Standing Colonial Committee, empowered to examine officials on the basis of material the Colonial Office was required to put before it, Parliament was not equipped to supervise colonial administration in areas whose problems were not dramatized by the evident conflict of rival interests.[38] Even if it had been, it must be doubtful how far it would have been concerned to stimulate what was most lacking: a sense of urgency sustained by adequate resources. Through all the East African debates in the 'twenties, for example, almost nothing is said of Uganda and not much more of Tanganyika. Satisfied that African rights were not in jeopardy, their most vocal watchdogs in Parliament seem to have felt that the problems of those territories could safely be left to time and the officials. Little said in Parliament foreshadowed the series of disturbances in the West Indies in the mid-thirties. More than anything else the shock these administered to British complacency brought about the more vigorous and constructive phase of trusteeship signalized by the Colonial Development and Welfare Act of 1940, but delayed by the second world war until the end of colonial rule was almost in sight.

To assess the effectiveness of what Parliamentary intervention there was is more difficult. Except for the brief intervals of minority Labour government in 1924 and 1929 to 1931, Conservatives had an overall majority in every Parliament from 1919 to 1945. During most of the 'twenties the opposition was hopelessly divided between Labour and Liberals, while from

1931 to 1935 it was all but eliminated. Few policies actually put into effect throughout the inter-war years can therefore have been seriously unacceptable to most Conservatives.

In colonial affairs, the party's major preoccupation was economic development. The priorities as it saw them were clear: transport, especially railways, agricultural research to develop new crops and increase the yields of those already established, medical and educational advance as the means to increase the economic potential of native populations. If the emphasis was usually on European enterprise as the agency of development, this was also seen as the most effective method of raising the standard of the native peoples. Colonial development thus fell naturally into place in the wider aim of Empire Development, Empire Settlement, and greater Empire self-sufficiency to be brought about by Imperial Preference. But if for the more ardent proponents of this policy the strengthening of Empire was a deeply felt and indeed central objective, they remained a minority in the party and still more among its leadership. For a much larger group, the Empire served rather the function for which some of their successors have recently seemed to cast Europe: a natural solution to the long-term problems of the British economy. The General Election of 1923 convinced Baldwin that a General Tariff, the essential prerequisite of substantial Imperial Preference, was still a doubtful political asset in Britain and when at last Imperial Preference came in 1932 it was as a measure of economic first aid rather than the expression of any national conversion to the full-blooded doctrines of imperial self-sufficiency. It was indeed Amery's unyielding convictions on that issue which did most to limit his political influence and prevented his return to the Colonial Office in 1931.[39] Cunliffe Lister, who, after Amery, had the biggest impact and the longest term at the Colonial Office, was a convinced protectionist but of a more pragmatic cast of mind than Amery. On one occasion indeed he went so far as to tell the House 'my view of Imperial policy is that I want to get as much trade as I can'.[40]

The most vocal exponents in Parliament of economic development as the real issue in colonial policy were a small group of backbenchers led by Page Croft, secretary of the Empire Industries Association which Amery, Neville Chamberlain, and Lord Lloyd had founded in 1923 and which boasted 200 members in Parliament in 1930. But if the members of this group were strong supporters of the settler cause in Kenya and of European enterprise in general, British economic activities in the Colonial Empire as a whole were too diverse for the shriller insistence on European interests entirely to prevail even among Conservatives. They were the activities of traders more than planters, of planters more than manufacturers, with the outstanding exception of Manchester cotton, and of all of these more than of settlers, though the latter found vocal support through their close personal connexions in the Parliamentary party. Mining which, in conditions favourable to settlement, as in Rhodesia, strongly reinforces settler interests, was elsewhere important only in tropical territories like Malaya where it resembled rather a plantation than a settler structure. For traders, native production and native markets were often more important than European. In East Africa the Manchester cotton industry, through the Empire Cotton Growing Corporation which it largely financed, had indeed a major interest; but, paradoxically, it was Africans who grew the cotton and Indians, Manchester's growing competitors, who before long bought most of it.

Such diverse interests in colonial development found regular expression in Parliament though it was usually confined to specific points and involved a far larger number of members than the few but more continuously active supporters of the settlers in East and Central Africa. The spokesmen of these more diverse interests shaded into that body of opinion, not unrepresented in any party, which was less sure of the absolute necessity of European enterprise. It was, for instance, Sir Humphrey Leggett, the Chairman of the East African Section of the London Chamber of Commerce and of the British East Africa Corporation, a man with more than twenty years' experience in East Africa, and Lugard's 'close friend and ally' as Miss Perham calls him, who told the Joint Select Committee on Closer Union in East Africa in 1930 that 'Colonist' development in East Africa was 'more likely than not to result in failure',[41] that it was very likely to hinder plantation development as well as native development and that neither were essential to native development, citing African progress in Uganda and Tanganyika in support of these opinions.

Nor were Conservatives blind to the limitations of government loans and private investment as the sole sources of development finance to supplement colonial revenues. Milner demanded an Imperial Development Fund so that 'the poorer Colonies, which have no credit' might get the help of which they were the most in need.[42] Amery tried unsuccessfully to divert half of the £1 million a year that Malaya offered the navy in 1921 to a Colonial Development Fund to help the 'weaker brethren'.[43] When the British government declined to provide the new preferences it had promised at the Imperial Economic Conference in 1923 the £1 million which it was calculated they would have cost was made available to finance an Empire Marketing Board, freed from detailed Treasury control. As its chairman, Amery showed what could be done by using some of its funds to finance agricultural and scientific work in the Colonial Empire.[44] Although the party leaders declined to accept its conversion into a larger Empire Marketing and Development Fund their programme for the 1929 election included a Colonial Development Fund.[45]

But it was the Labour Party which won the election and produced the first Colonial Development Act, providing up

to £1 million a year. Presented as part of an emergency plan
to reduce British unemployment the Bill passed through all
stages in one week and without a division. The sum was small,
and the purposes for which it could be spent limited to aiding
and developing agriculture and industry in the Colonial
Empire and 'thereby promoting British industry'. When he
introduced the 1940 Act, the Secretary of State, Malcolm Mac-
Donald, claimed that the primary purpose of the earlier Act was
'not to help colonial development . . . but . . . to solve our own
unemployment problem'.[46] This had been repeated by many
authorities since but is not wholly justified: speakers in the 1929
debates were in fact preoccupied with colonial problems and
many sought assurances that the Act would be interpreted
widely and that larger sums would be found if they were needed.
Amery promised full Conservative support and questioned the
wisdom of a Development Committee composed entirely of
business men on which the Labour government rather eccen-
trically insisted.

The Labour Party on the other hand was, of course, the
heir to the humanitarian tradition, not only, as it were, by
direct descent but also by its absorption of many of the radicals,
as the fortunes of the Liberal Party declined. But particularly
in the first years after the war some of its left wing and especially
the Independent Labour Party, heirs rather of Hobson and
the Little Englanders than of Lenin, were prone to adopt the
attitude that Socialists could keep their hands clean only by
an early, if not an immediate, liquidation of Empire, a point
of view which shaded into the recurrent propaganda for
an internationalization of colonial responsibilities under the
League of Nations or, more practically, an extension of the
Mandate system to all colonies. In *Labour and the Nation* (1928)
these three approaches settled into a firm enunciation of the protective aspect of trusteeship, a more guarded aspiration towards the progressive development of self-government, and a

rather ambiguous reference to the extension of the Mandate system.

'The Labour Party views with grave concern the appalling evils produced by capitalist exploitation in certain of the tropical and sub-tropical parts of the British Commonwealth of Nations. It holds that the welfare of indigenous races, their economic prosperity, and their advancement in culture and civilization, must be the primary object of colonial administration, to which all other interests must be rigorously subordinated. It notes with satisfaction that, where that principle has been observed, primitive peoples have achieved, in a comparatively short time, results which decisively disprove the statement that they are incapable of social progress. . . .

'A Labour Government, therefore, will make no compromise with policies which aim at accelerating the economic development of backward areas by methods which undermine the independence, the social institutions and the *morale* of their inhabitants, and which thus are injurious both to them, and, ultimately, to the working classes of Europe. It will use every means in its power to protect them in the occupation and enjoyment of their land, to prevent absolutely forced labour whatever form it may assume, and to ensure that contracts between native workers and European employers are entered upon voluntarily and not under duress, that such contracts are subject to the approval of a public authority . . . It will encourage the development of the services concerned with health and education. Its policy will be based upon the firm conviction that all the dependencies of the Crown ought, as soon as possible, to become self-governing States. It will take steps, therefore, to transfer to the inhabitants of these countries, without distinction of race or colour, such measure of political responsibility as they are capable of exercising while imperial responsibility for their government will be maintained during the period preceding the establishment of democratic institutions. . . . It

E

will co-operate cordially with the Mandates Commission of the League of Nations, and will make every effort to strengthen and extend its authority.'[47]

The next pronouncement of Labour Party policy, made in 1933, insisted in greater detail on the dangers not only of the 'Capitalist Policy' of development but even of what it called the 'African policy'. The latter might, for example, lead to 'the establishment of a system of individual Native landlordism, which is as bad as white landlordism'. 'Socialisation and self-government' were defiantly asserted to be the 'immediate objectives' but colonies differ widely and 'any attempt to treat them in a uniform way'[48] in respect of either would be disastrous.

Until the later thirties the most vocal Labour spokesmen on colonial issues in Parliament belonged to a small group of about fifteen, including some Liberals, who were almost all closely connected with the Anti-Slavery and Aborigines Protection Society, an ancient but small non-party body. They did not oppose development but they distrusted its direction. Government revenue and loans were spent far too much, if not exclusively, to the advantage of settlers or European enterprise and large development projects, unless carefully controlled, would lead to forced labour, or the seizure of native land. Lord Olivier, one of the original Fabians, a former Colonial Office man and Governor of Jamaica, a representative member of this group, indeed elicited the weighty support of Lord Lugard, a Conservative so far as he had party affiliations, for the proposition that 'development if pushed forward too rapidly, is pernicious'. It was, many of this small but well-informed group felt, 'because of this idea that these regions must be developed as quickly as possible that we encounter all these tendencies towards forced labour and the doctrine that it is the duty of the native to work'.[49] But their influence in the Labour Party, though considerable, can be exaggerated. It was not from their ranks that Labour found its colonial ministers in

1924 or 1929, nor was their outlook represented by the report in which the Trade Union Congress, largely inspired by Bevin, recommended in 1930 'as full a development as possible of the economic relations between the constituent parts of the British Commonwealth'. Bevin indeed was the only member of the party the Labour government appointed to the Development Committee set up under the 1929 Act. The 'Native Rights' lobby, at least until the later 'thirties, depended for its not inconsiderable influence not so much on party support—no votes were likely to be won or lost on the issues it took up—but rather on its non-party character, its connexions with the churches and the missionary societies, and with sympathetic ex-officials, which enabled it to mobilize a substantial part of what is nowadays called the Establishment. In her life of Lugard, Margery Perham gives a classical account of how a pressure group of this kind operated in the campaign against settler control of Kenya and the Closer Union issue.[50]

When ten years later in 1943 the Labour Party issued a statement of its post-war aims in the colonies it was in fact confined to Africa and the Pacific.[51] 'For a considerable time to come these peoples', it affirmed, 'will not be ready for self-government, and European peoples and States must be responsible for the administration of their territories.' They must, of course, be regarded 'as a trust for the native inhabitants' and a primary object 'should always be to train the native inhabitants in every possible way so that they may be able in the shortest possible time to govern themselves'. But much more attention was given to proposals for specific improvements in education, health, labour supervision, producers' co-operatives, the elimination of racial discrimination except when designed to protect the natives in the ownership of land, and for economic development based on long-term government plans. These would require capital from outside sources, both by way of loans and free grants for which the 1940 Colonial

Development and Welfare Act already provided but the scale of the resources needed was emphasized. To supervise the administration of all colonies the party now called for an International Authority with equal representation of administering and non-administering powers, visiting missions, and the enforcement of a revised mandate code, including the Open Door in all colonies, i.e. the abolition of Imperial Preference, though exceptions might be permitted where the Permanent Court of International Justice (of all bodies!) was satisfied they were in the colony's interest.

Although this continued preoccupation with international supervision found no echo among Conservatives, the two parties had in fact moved much closer together. 'Vigorous State action to promote colonial development and welfare' had become 'the new orthodoxy'.[52] If Labour also accepted that in many territories the over-riding responsibility of the trustee would be needed 'for a considerable time to come' the Conservative Colonial Secretary in Churchill's wartime administration, Oliver Stanley, told Parliament that same year 'it is up to us . . . to ensure that as quickly as possible people are trained and equipped for eventual self-government'.[53] But time had not stood still while Britain had so laboriously worked out something of what trusteeship really meant. Now that she was at last ready for the task, the unchallenged authority of the inter-war years was no longer hers to command in most of the Colonial Empire.

NOTES TO CHAPTER II

[1] J. E. Flint, *Sir George Goldie and the Making of Nigeria* (London, 1960), p. 275.

[2] Sir R. Furse, *Aucuparius: Recollections of a Recruiting Officer* (London, 1962), p. 26.

[3] Sir D. Cameron, *op. cit.*, p. 255.

⁴ For the criticism, see Lugard, *op. cit.*, pp. 155–91, Cameron, *op. .cit.*, pp. 252–63, and, among later critics, two distinguished colonial administrators both of whom had also served in the Office, Sir Alan Burns, *Colonial Civil Servant* (London, 1949), pp. 155–76, and E. W. Evans, *The British Yoke* (London, 1949), pp. 75–76 and 112–16.

⁵ For the division of the Office in 1907, see Lord Elgin's despatch of 21 September 1907 (Cmd. 3795), and J. A. Cross, 'Whitehall and the Common-wealth', *Journal of Commonwealth Political Studies*, Vol. 2, No. 3 (1964), forth-coming. Business relating to the three High Commission Territories in South Africa and to Fiji and the Western Pacific remained with the Dominions division 'because of their proximity to autonomous communities'. See R. B. Pugh, 'The Colonial Office' in *Cambridge History of the British Empire*, Vol. III (Cambridge, 1959). Sir Cosmo Parkinson, *The Colonial Office from Within* (London, 1947), pp. 47–51, gives some account of the development of this early medical and scientific work.

⁶ Commons *Hansard*, 30 July 1919, c. 2174.

⁷ Milner, *op. cit.*, p. 177.

⁸ Sir S. Caine, 'Colonial Development: A British Contribution to World Progress', *Progress*, Vol. 47 (1957), p. 80, from which the figures are taken, except those which relate to Iraq and the 1929 colonial budgets which are mine.

⁹ *Report of a Committee on Research in the Colonies* (Cmd. 1472), 1921, p. 10.

¹⁰ Amery, *op. cit.*, p. 336. Pugh, *op. cit.*, p. 759.

¹¹ Sir James (later Lord) Stevenson, formerly of John Walker and Sons, the distillers.

¹² For the setting up of the Education Committee see R. Oliver, *The Mis-sionary Factor in East Africa* (London, 1952), pp. 263–71, and M. Perham, *Lugard: The Years of Authority* (London, 1960) pp. 657–61. For Vischer, see Sonia Graham's unpublished London Ph.D. thesis, 'A History of Education in relation to the development of the Protectorate of Northern Nigeria 1900–1919, with special reference to the work of Hanns Vischer'.

¹³ The Fisheries Adviser was financed from the funds of the 'Discovery' Committee (which administered a research programme in the Antarctic with funds derived from the whaling industry), while the Agricultural and Animal Health posts received some assistance from the Empire Marketing Board (see below, p. 55).

¹⁴ Besides those mentioned above (p. 31) the Research Committee appointed in 1919 maintained an increasingly shadowy existence until the early 'thirties. In association with the U.K. Medical Research Council, a Colonial Medical Research Committee was set up in 1927, taking over the management of the Tropical Diseases Fund (£2,000 per annum from 'Dominion and Colonial governments'). An Overseas Mechanical Transport Council was set up in 1928, half its cost being met by colonial governments and the rest by the Empire Marketing Board. After 1929 there was a lull in such developments, until the later 'thirties when the Colonial Forest Resources Development Department

(1935) and the Colonial Empire Marketing Board (1937) mark the beginnings of a new series, parallel to the enlarged conception of the role of government in colonial development.

[15] Burns, *op. cit.*, pp. 175–6.

[16] A good example is the development of the International Labour Conventions during the inter-war years, which could evidently not be dealt with at all conveniently on a 'geographical basis' and were handled by the General Department until hived off into the Social Services Department set up in 1938. (*Labour Supervision in the Colonial Empire 1937–1943* (Colonial No. 185, 1943), paras. 46–53, illustrates this development.)

[17] Earl of Swinton, *I Remember* (1948), pp. 65–68.

[18] Sir Cosmo Parkinson (1938–40; 1940–2). Lugard's assertion that between 1825 and 1921 'the post of permanent Under-Secretary has only been held for an aggregate of eighteen years by promotion from the office itself' (*op. cit.*, p. 157) is untrue however it is interpreted. Stephen (1836–47), Herbert (1871–92), Meade (1892–7), Wingfield (1897–1900), Anderson (1911–15), and Fiddes (1916–21) had all previously served in the Office although Herbert was an Assistant Under-Secretary only for one year, and Anderson had been away as Governor of the Straits Settlements for the period immediately preceding his term as P.U.S. Ommaney (1900–7) had been a Crown Agent since 1877, so he can hardly be regarded as an outsider, in the sense in which Merivale, Rogers, Hopwood, and even Herbert were.

[19] Amery, *op. cit.*, pp. 336–7.

[20] Colonial Office Conference 1927, *Summary of Proceedings* (Cmd. 2883), and Appendices (Cmd. 2884); Colonial Office Conference 1930, *Summary of Proceedings* (Cmd. 3628), Appendices (Cmd. 3629).

[21] *Report of a Committee on the System of Appointment in the Colonial Office and the Colonial Services* (Cmd. 3554), p. 40.

[22] *Ibid.*, p. 5.

[23] I have drawn heavily on Furse's own account in *Aucuparius: Recollections of a Recruiting Officer*, and on Sir C. Jeffries, *The Colonial Empire and Its Civil Service* (Cambridge, 1938). Since these lectures were given, an American scholar, R. Heussler, has published in *Yesterday's Rulers* (Oxford, 1963) an interesting assessment of the recruitment and training of colonial administrators since 1919. He emphasizes the 'elitist' presuppositions implicit in the selection criteria of the administrative service, which were strongly criticized in a contemporary Fabian Society report, *Downing Street and the Colonies* (London, 1942). His book is not, however, always reliable on detailed matters of fact.

[24] Recruitment for Ceylon was suspended between 1931 and 1935. In 1935–7 one-third of the vacancies were filled by Europeans selected in London. After 1937 no further European appointments were made. Sir C. Collins, *Public Administration in Ceylon* (London, 1951), p. 102.

[25] See, e.g. *Report of the Committee on the Staffing of the Agricultural Departments in the Colonies* (Cmd. 730), 1920; *Report of the Departmental Committee on*

Colonial Medical Services (Cmd. 939), 1920; *Agricultural Research and Adminis-tration in the Non-Self-Governing Dependencies* (Cmd. 2885), 1927; *Report of Committee on Colonial Scientific and Research Services* (included in Cmd. 2883), 1927; *Colonial Agricultural Service* (Cmd. 3049), 1928; *Colonial Veterinary Service* (Cmd. 3261), 1929.

[26] Furse, *op. cit.*, pp. 241–2.

[27] *Report of the Inter-Departmental Committee on Forestry Education* (Cmd. 1166), 1921; Furse, *op. cit.*, p. 77. *The Training of Candidates and Probationers for Appointment as Forest Officers in the Government Service* (Colonial No. 61), 1931, pp. 35–40. By then its income was £5,000 from colonial governments, £2,000 from the British government plus £2,200 for specific projects.

[28] Amery, *op. cit.*, p. 358.

[29] Professor (later Sir) Percy Nunn, Principal of the College, was a member of the Advisory Committee.

[30] *Post-War Training for the Colonial Service* (Colonial No. 198), 1946, p. 22.

[31] *Op. cit.*, p. 53. Cf. the Office memorandum for the Colonial Office Conference 1930: 'Clearly no obstacle must be created against the employment of locally domiciled persons in the service of their own country, and their pro-motion in that service. The Committee's proposals do not create any such obstacle.' Cmd. 3629, p. 161.

[32] Collins, *op. cit.*, pp. 99–102. Sir Cecil Clementi increased the number of Malays appointed to the Malay Civil Service for duty in the F.M.S., and also established a Straits Settlements Civil Service to provide some openings in that Colony.

[33] D. Kimble, *A Political History of Ghana 1850–1928* (Oxford, 1963), p. 122.

[34] *Organisation of the Colonial Service* (Colonial No. 197), 1946, p. 5.

[35] *Considerations on Representative Government* (World's Classics Edition), pp. 410–16.

[36] I am indebted to my colleague Mr E. A. Brett for the information that during the Conservative administration of 1924 to 1929 no less than 170 members of the House of Commons made some contribution on East African or general colonial policy, even if only by asking a single question.

[37] R. W. McCulloch, 'Question Time in the British House of Commons', *American Political Science Review*, Vol. 27 (1933), pp. 971–7.

[38] There were weighty arguments against any such Committee, especially that it raised 'issues of Parliamentary procedure and constitutional practice of a far reaching character' (Mr Chamberlain, Commons *Hansard*, 2 August 1939, c. 2369). See also Lord Hailey, *An African Survey* (London, 1938), pp. xxvii–xxviii, for a characteristically terse discussion of the issue.

[39] Amery, *op. cit.*, p. 511.

[40] Commons *Hansard*, 1 July 1932, c. 2211.

[41] Perham, *op. cit.*, p. 687. *Joint Committee on Closer Union in East Africa Vol. III Appendices* (H. of C. No. 156), 1931, pp. 45–46.

[42] Milner, *op. cit.*, p. 181.

[43] Amery, *op. cit.*, p. 198.

[44] *Ibid.*, p. 346 f. See also *Empire Marketing Board: Note on the Work and Finance of the Board* (Cmd. 4121), 1932.

[45] *The Times*, 19 April 1929.

[46] Commons *Hansard*, 21 May 1940, c. 45.

[47] *Labour and the Nation* (1928), p. 44.

[48] *The Colonial Empire* (1933), p. 4.

[49] *The Anti Slavery Reporter and Aborigines' Friend, Series V*, Vol. 18, p. 64.

[50] Perham, *op. cit.*, pp. 673–91.

[51] *The Colonies: The Labour Party's Post-War Policy for the African and Pacific Colonies* (1943), p. 2.

[52] Sir W. K. Hancock, *Wealth of Colonies* (Cambridge, 1950), p. 45.

[53] Commons *Hansard*, 13 July 1943, c. 49.

THE DILEMMAS OF TRUSTEESHIP

The government of dependencies 'whose population' was not 'in a sufficiently advanced state to be fitted for representative government' and which 'if held at all, must be governed by the dominant country, or by persons delegated for that purpose by it' was, Mill asserted, 'as legitimate as any other, if it is the one which in the existing state of civilization of the subject people, most facilitates their transition to a higher stage of improvement'.[1] For such government the ideal form was that of an enlightened bureaucratic despotism. 'We need not expect', Mill continued, 'to see that ideal realized; but unless some approach to it is, the rulers are guilty of a dereliction of the highest moral trust which can devolve upon a nation: and if they do not even aim at it, they are selfish usurpers'. In this Mill echoed Burke: 'all political power which is set over men . . . ought to be *some way or other* exercised for their benefit'. The realistic moderation with which these great men expressed the idea of trusteeship has been less remarked than the idea itself.

Nor were their arguments directed to justifying the seizure of power in territories hitherto free. It was the expansion of European, and the emergence of American, imperialism at the end of the nineteenth century which focused attention once again on that more intractable issue, in an era when, even in the jungle of sovereign states, naked force was still felt to need some justification. 'It is difficult for the strongest advocate of national rights to assert that the people in actual occupation or political control over a given area of the earth are entitled to do what they will with "their own", entirely disregarding the direct and indirect consequences of their actions upon the rest of the world. . . . There is nothing unworthy, quite the contrary, in the notion that nations which, through a more stimulative environment, have advanced further in certain arts of industry, politics, or morals, should communicate these to nations which from their circumstances were more backward, so as to aid them in developing alike the material resources of their land and the spiritual qualities of their people. Nor is it clear that in this work some . . "compulsion" is wholly illegitimate. Force is itself no remedy, coercion is not education, but it may be a prior condition to the operation of educative forces . . . it follows that civilized Governments *may* undertake the political and economic control of lower races . . . What, then, are the conditions which render it legitimate? They may be provisionally stated thus: Such interference . . . must be directed primarily to secure the safety and progress of the civilization of the world, and not the special interest of the interfering nation. Such interference must be attended by an improvement and elevation of the character of the people who are brought under this control. Lastly, the determination of the two preceding conditions must not be left to the arbitrary will or judgment of the interfering nation, but must proceed from some organized representation of civilized humanity.'[2]

J. A. Hobson, from whose famous (but, I suspect, little read) book *Imperialism* I have been quoting, did not, you will notice, contend that to be legitimate Imperial rule must benefit the 'lower races' alone or even that the advantages they secured from it must be the maximum possible but merely that their condition must be improved. But he added another condition which, on the face of it, has nothing to do with their advantage. This too is stated with studied moderation. Imperial rule is also to be directed 'primarily to secure the safety and the progress of . . . the world, and not the special interest of' the imperial power. It is not argued that this condition is necessary for the benefit of the subject people but as a rule for international policy. Hobson certainly did not 'expect to see' these ideals realized, or even approached. 'The true conditions for the exercise of such a "trust" ' were, he wrote, 'entirely lacking'.[3] His opinion was, of course, that the contemporary development of the advanced capitalist countries at the beginning of this century was such as entirely to preclude the possibility of colonial trusteeship.

Twenty years later Lugard restated in the *Dual Mandate* what had long been the official defence of British Imperialism. 'The tropics are the heritage of mankind, and neither, on the one hand, has the suzerain Power a right to their exclusive exploitation, nor, on the other hand, have the races which inhabit them a right to deny their bounties to those who need them. . . . The policy of the "open door", has two distinct though mutually dependent aspects—viz., equal opportunity to the commerce of other countries, and an unrestricted market to the native producer. The tropics can only be successfully developed if the interests of the controlling Power are identical with those of the natives of the country, and it seeks no individual advantage, and imposes no restriction for its own benefit.'[4] Like other Imperialists, Lugard believed passionately in his ideal and saw no reason why it should not, by and large, be realized. But the proclamation of the Dual Mandate received its classical expression, like many another doctrine of social and economic policy, just when the conditions which had made it seem plausible were beginning to disappear. Was the doctrine of trusteeship necessarily dependent on the conception of a self-regulating harmonization of interests which the classical theory of free competition assumed? It was one thing to claim that the Open Door was, as Hobson had implied, the necessary condition of international acquiescence in the powers that imperial states claimed for themselves over large areas of the world. It was surely quite another to claim that it was a sufficient condition that native interests would not be exploited. Open competition by traders of all nations would, the argument went, assure the colonial producers fair prices for their exports and equally assure colonial consumers fair prices for their imports. But what if colonial conditions were such that competition was more than usually imperfect? Both issues were sharply raised by the course of events in the inter-war years as we shall see. But let us for the moment put them on one side.

Was it not unlikley that, taking the sphere of colonial government as a whole, the interests of the colonial power should be *identical* with those of the natives? Trusteeship suffered greatly from the overstatement of self-justification. The aggregates with which it worked were sums which could not, in fact, be added up. Even in the strictly economic sphere, the techniques which might make it possible to calculate the share of national product that accrued to natives and non-natives, to residents in a colony and non-residents, had not yet been invented and, if they had been, sketchy colonial administrations had hardly begun, even at the end of the second war, to produce the data needed for such calculations.

How, again, could a balance be struck between the social changes that any economic development must bring and native satisfactions within their own social order? The ideas of Lugard and his followers brought this problem into much greater prominence just at a time when the easy assumption of the obvious superiority of Western civilization was sharply shaken by the first war, and the increasingly evident incapacity of the Western economic system to solve the problem of unemployment. They were soon reinforced by the much greater knowledge which anthropologists and administrators began to make available of the complex purposes which native social organization served. A large new area of uncertainty was thus added to the problem.

Let me illustrate this. Hobson had considered that 'the true "imperial" policy' was 'best illustrated' by Basutoland which had been rescued from the industrial exploiters, where the old political and economic institutions were preserved, the British authorities interfering as little as possible with native ways. Europeans were not allowed to hold land or to prospect for minerals and needed a licence even to open a store.[5] In 1935 a Commissioner sent out by the British government reported[6] —I quote Sir Keith Hancock's summary of his findings—that 'Economically there was a great deal to hope for from the agricultural and pastoral resources of the country and the intelligence of its people. But the resources had been squandered, and the intelligence left without guidance. The administration had done nothing effective to check erosion, which was occurring on a scale that threatened "the whole fabric of the soil". It had done nothing to check stock theft, which was occurring on a scale that threatened to undermine both the moral integrity and the economic productivity of the Basuto people. It had not even been effective in collecting the taxes that were its due. Basutoland suffered from a lack of governance which was sometimes dignified with the title of "indirect rule". Never since the British government first took to itself responsibility for Basutoland, Sir Alan Pim said, had it given the country rule of any sort, direct or indirect. Indirect rule meant the incorporation of Native institutions into a single system of government, under the "continuous guidance, supervision, and stimulus of European officers". It regarded Native institutions, not as an end, but as a means towards the development and welfare of the Native people to whom the institutions belonged. But in Basutoland the Chiefs of the family of Moshesh had been allowed to go their own irresponsible and increasingly prodigal way; there were two parallel sets of institutions in the country, and both of them were futile.' Sir Alan Pim also reported that more than 50 per cent of the adult male Basutos were at any one time normally absent, working on the farms and mines of the Union of South Africa, a figure, he pointed out, 'in striking contrast to the estimate made by the Belgian Congo Committee of 1924–5' in whose opinion 'not more than five per cent. could be absent for long periods, and an additional five per cent. within two days' journey, without definitely harmful effects'[7] to tribal life. Part of the remedy he proposed was that Basutoland should adopt the Nigerian system of native administration with its closer European control of native institutions and attempt to adapt them to the new needs of economic and social development as opposed to the almost complete absence of 'interference' with native society which Hobson had esteemed the ideal.

But in the home of the native administration system, in Nigeria itself, in areas where export crops were produced by African small-holders, a new problem was already posing the question of what was to be done to adapt Native Authorities to the needs of a society in which, as in Western Nigeria, economic growth had already by the mid-thirties produced in fair number new classes unknown to traditional society, cocoa brokers, traders, lorry and bus operators, farmers employing labour, school teachers, and was resulting in growing urban areas in which the coexistence of many different ethnic groups made the maintenance or extension of traditional native authority doubtfully effective. How far, in short, even in the most favourable circumstances, where large-scale European plantations or mines, let alone European settlement, did not exist, was it possible or desirable to try to maintain or adapt the native social system? What, in such circumstances, were 'native' interests and how, even if they could be ascertained, could they be reconciled with 'European' interests in the maintenance of law and order and the provision of social services especially those all-important but unpopular public health measures so vital to continued European activity as well as to the natives themselves. Nor, of course, was this a specifically African problem: it was indeed more sharply posed in Malaya where so many of the new forces were expressed in the activities of Chinese and Indian immigrants, the legacy of an earlier age which could not simply be expunged, and where the attempt to maintain the authority of the Sultans ran up against the paramount pressure for a greater degree of administrative unity which the development of the economy increasingly demanded.[8]

But if, even as formulated in the more extended version of the Dual Mandate, the principle of trusteeship thus did not provide any unambiguous answer to the actual problems of colonial government either in the economic or the wider social sphere, neither did it provide very specific guidance in the sphere of politics. It emphasized, to use Amery's words in his speech to the Colonial Office Conference in 1927, that 'the ultimate responsibility for the general governance of' the affairs of the Colonial Empire 'must, at any rate for any future that we need take into consideration here'[9] rest with the British government. This followed, conveniently enough, from the Dual Mandate itself: the responsibilities which the trustee had felt justified in assuming in the joint interests of the world and the colonial peoples evidently could not, on that basis, be laid aside, until the ward could reasonably be regarded as equipped to discharge them himself. But moreover, certain further deductions could be drawn. They have been most clearly formulated by John Plamenatz.[10] Fitness for self-government might be held to imply, first the ability to give modern trade and industry the security they need, second the ability to afford security of person and good government by the standards of western Europe, and third the ability to produce native rulers strong enough and responsible enough to respect international law. Mr Plamenatz points out that the first and third of these conditions require a strong government while the second requires in the broad sense constitutional government, not democracy or parliamentary government, but a government which respects the rules governing the exercise of power and where there is an independent judiciary with high professional standards. On the doctrine that the British were trustees for world interests, it could be inferred that their responsibilities could properly be handed over only if a native government had been brought into existence capable of satisfying at least the first condition, probably also the third, but conceivably the second as well.

A quite different criterion of that fitness for self-government which would justify the trustee in handing over to the ward could, however, be deduced from the second half of the Dual Mandate, the doctrine that the British were also trustees for the welfare of the native races. This might be defined as 'the ability to work the institutions that make democracy and freedom effective'.[11] The Labour Party was using this line of argument when—no doubt with the Kenya settlers' claims in mind—it said in its 1928 policy statement that 'imperial responsibility . . . will be maintained during the period preceding the establishment of democratic institutions'.[12] But though it was possible, it was evidently not necessary to take the view that democracy was the only form of government to which a proper regard for the welfare of the colonial peoples would allow the trustee to relinquish his responsibilities. In the political sphere, as in the economic and social spheres, the principle of trusteeship thus provided no unambiguous answer, still less did it help to prescribe the all-important intermediate steps.

Such light as, even in its Dual Mandate model, the torch of trusteeship could be made to yield thus seemed to illumine far more clearly one or two paths *not* to be followed rather than any definite road forward through the still largely unknown, extraordinarily varied and usually deceptive country which the application of Western technology, in however modest a form, the growth of the market, and research in the natural and social sciences, were just beginning to disclose in the Colonial Empire. The more thoroughgoing advocates of the principle of trustee- ship would never have allowed that it is only in a revolutionary phase, and then rather briefly, that general principles are at all seen as susceptible of complete and direct application in politics. In a well-established order, on the other hand, poli- tics are understood, though not always admitted, to call, in a necessarily imperfect world, for 'the endless composition of claims in conflict'.[13] Such an evolution in outlook was re- flected in the colonial policy of the Labour Party though not always in the views of its more thoroughgoing socialist sup- porters. Its first detailed pronouncement on African policy, in 1926, after remarking that 'Labour has hitherto naturally given little detailed attention to the Empire', continued 'the time may be not far distant when Labour will be called upon to assume responsibility for the government of the country',[14] a considera- tion which could be seen already at work in the party's in- creasingly cautious approach to self-government, which lasted until the end of the second world war.

Again, if brought to bear at all, the principle of trusteeship, like any other, had to be brought to bear in each territory on an historically determined situation, in which the actions of the past, however reprehensible the principles then at work, had created responsibilities which could not simply be liquidated. Many a harassed Colonial Secretary might have agreed that it would have been more convenient, as well as possibly more virtuous, if Indian or Chinese labour had never been brought to territories like Malaya, Fiji, Trinidad, or British Guiana, or if European settlement had not been officially encouraged in Kenya in 1903 or in Palestine after the first world war, or if Britain had not in Ceylon or Cyprus found herself in control of territories where, in a far more remote past, earlier colonizations had produced sizeable minorities, like the Ceylon Tamils or the Cypriot Turks, wholly distinct in language and culture from the majority of people. But, confronted with such situations, had not the imperial power responsibilities, not merely to the majority, or to those who could claim to be the indigenous people, but to *all* the inhabitants? This line of thought, as natural to the rulers of an old-established multi-national state as it has seemed to their critics inevitable in an Imperialist policy of 'divide and rule', appears again and again in their pronouncements of policy. It was the basis of the restatement of trusteeship implicit in the Report of the Joint Select Committee on Closer Union in East Africa. The famous declaration of 1923 that in Kenya 'the interests of the African natives must be paramount, and if and when those interests and the interests of the immigrant races should conflict, the former should prevail', meant, said the Joint Select Committee, 'no more than that the interests of the overwhelming majority of the indigenous population should not be subordinated to those of a minority belonging to another race, however important in itself'.[15] Similarly, in 1938, Malcolm MacDonald, then Colonial Secretary, rejected an opposition motion that the primary purpose of colonial policy should be the welfare and progress of the native inhabitants, claiming that it was, on the contrary, the welfare and progress of *all* the inhabitants, though, he went on, 'our first duty' was 'always' to the native inhabitants.[16]

If the principle of trusteeship was thus reduced to the exceedingly modest aim that imperial power must be, in Burke's words, *'some way or other* exercised for the benefit' of the colonial peoples, it has also to be recognized that, such as it was, it could in any event operate only within the fairly narrow, if fluctuating, limits defined by the strategic preoccupations of British statesmen, the economic pressures to which they responded, and the reluctance to surrender power from which they were by no means exempt, even if temperament and experience combined to give them a flexibility not often displayed by imperial rulers. Egypt, though it was never a colony and its independence had been unilaterally declared by Britain in 1922, most strikingly displays the distortion of trusteeship by defence, but Malta, Gibraltar, and Cyprus all illustrated how changing conceptions of strategic needs set limits for colonial policy makers.

It is essential to underline the limits which were set to any simple application of trusteeship by the facts of history, the imperatives of defence, and the more insidious pressures of British economic interest. It is only common sense to admit not only the ambiguities inherent in the idea of trusteeship itself, but also the uncertainties imposed by the likelihood of mistakes in estimating the consequences of policy which was certainly greater in the Colonial Empire than in more developed countries. But it is also necessary to allow that there was an area of decision in colonial policy in which the demands of trusteeship, if by no means always conceded, yet significantly affected the outcome. The greatest disservice which the too complacent reiteration of the professions of trusteeship has done to a true estimation of the late phase of British imperial rule is to have strengthened the counter myth which denies it any place at all.

It may now be more profitable to look a little more closely at some of the economic, social, and political dilemmas to which ambiguities, as well as conflicts of purpose and the limits of manœuvre, condemned the makers of colonial policy during the inter-war years. A brief glance at the end of the Open Door should begin by noticing that in the West Indies, Fiji, Cyprus, and Mauritius, Imperial Preference long preceded the Ottawa Conference of 1932, while in East Africa and in Nigeria and the Gold Coast it was never adopted apart from the quota regulation of textiles introduced in the two West African territories, as elsewhere, in 1936 against the Japanese. The major change in 1932 was the extension of Imperial Preference to Hong Kong, Ceylon, and Malaya. In the classical theory of trusteeship, we have seen, the Open Door fulfilled a double function: it ensured, it was claimed, the acquiescence of the rest of the world in British control of so large a part of the tropics and simultaneously ensured that the colonial peoples received fair treatment in world trade. Much attention was focused on the former issue in the 'thirties but, to those not committed to opposition to Imperial Preference on other grounds, its exploitation by the Fascist powers, themselves committed to the most extreme theories of economic self-sufficiency, could hardly supply convincing evidence that its contribution to the increasing international tension was more than marginal. Foreign acquiescence in Empire, as the French example earlier suggested, depended a great deal more on the realities of power than on economic policies as relatively insignificant as the proportion of world trade affected by British colonial preferences. That is not, of course, to deny that the economic policies of the 'thirties had *any* effect in contributing to international discord, but merely to attempt to see that effect in perspective.

More relevant to the preoccupations of trusteeship is the attempt to assess the consequences of the change in British commercial policy on the colonies themselves. The tariffs and still more the textile quotas imposed in the 'thirties aroused protests, not only in Britain, but in some colonies. Although in Ceylon the State Council, elected, let us remember, by universal adult suffrage, reluctantly accepted Imperial Preference on a temporary basis made permanent only in 1938, it altogether declined to impose quota restrictions against Japanese imports and this was done by British Order in Council. In the Straits Settlements the quotas were imposed by the official majority against the unanimous opposition of the unofficials. The policy was designed to restrict cheap imports and reduce consumption. How could this possibly be justified in countries where poverty was, even at best, the lot of almost all the inhabi-

tants? But if the case for free imports might seem straightforward, was it still true that colonial producers would get the
best price for their exports when able to sell them freely at world
prices settled by free competition? In a world like the world
after 1929 this seemed a distinctly uncertain blessing. The
Dominions, who were, after all, free to decide for themselves
where their own interest lay, thought otherwise. 'What they
wanted', Sir Keith Hancock wrote more than twenty years ago,
'was a shelter in British markets for their exports of food and
raw materials. They were prepared to pay for this boon by
giving increased shelter in their own markets to British exports
of manufactured goods.'[17] From the economic point of view,
this bargain was, in the judgement of that great scholar, 'not
precisely a mountain peak of human wisdom; but from the
moral point of view it could hardly be described as an abyss of
human depravity'. There was, of course, a great difference
between 'the voluntary give and take of self-governing nations
and the unilateral decisions' by which the trustee judged 'not
only its own interests, but those of its dependencies'. Britain
was ready to give the dependencies the same privileges as the
Dominions demanded. Was it wholly unreasonable to demand
from them, what the Dominions freely offered, some reciprocity? The story of Imperial Preference cannot, Hancock concluded, 'be told simply as a dirge for free trade and a lament
for departed virtue'. There was a sharing of favours and a
sharing of burdens. But here was, in fact, a striking illustration
of the inadequacy of that aggregate 'the interests of the colonies'
or even, 'the interests of the colony', as a tool—even of the most
primitive kind—in the analysis of policy.

Another scholar, Dr. F. V. Meyer, carried out just after the
second world war that detailed examination[18] of Imperial
Preference in the Colonial Empire which Hancock had suggested would certainly show that in the colonies, no less than
in the Dominions, interests were diverse and conflicting. He

concluded that the United Kingdom's contribution to certain colonies had been substantial. The preferences it granted on sugar, molasses, pineapples, bananas and citrus fruit, wines and tobacco were costly and of notable benefit to the producing colonies concerned, in particular the West Indies, Fiji, Mauritius, Cyprus, and Nyasaland. In return the United Kingdom had received preference in practically all the non-African colonies and also in the Gambia, Sierra Leone, Somaliland, and North-Western Rhodesia, and had also tried to benefit itself by imposing textile quotas in those colonies and in Nigeria and the Gold Coast. There was no doubt that these measures had resulted in increased proportions of colonial purchases from the Empire, but how much of that had been a net benefit to the United Kingdom was more problematical, in view of the possibility, which in textiles seemed almost certainty, that she had in consequence suffered from intensified foreign competition in non-colonial markets. In addition the textile preferences and quotas and the preference on boots and shoes had stimulated competition by low-cost Empire producers, notably India and Hong Kong. The United Kingdom, Dr Meyer pronounced, had on balance lost more from preferences accorded to the colonies than it gained from preferences in their markets. On the other hand the East African colonies which offered no preferences had gained to a minor extent from coffee and hard fibres preferences and Nyasaland to a substantial extent from that on tobacco. The West African colonies, especially Gambia and Sierra Leone, had on balance lost since their major products could not benefit from preferential treatment because Empire production exceeded Empire consumption. Ceylon and Malaya had also, on balance, lost while Malta lost without compensation. It was the sugar and banana colonies (the West Indies, Mauritius, and Fiji) and Cyprus and Nyasaland which (together with India) gained from the system.

more backward community should get 'a fair share from central funds during the present period of unequal racial needs and political representation'.[21] It took another seven years before the settlers would accept the income tax he also recommended to increase the revenue and distribute its incidence more fairly.

Where European enterprise took the form of plantations or mines, difficulty in securing adequate labour supplies, either because of the unwillingness of the existing population to engage in the work required or the lack of sufficiently large numbers in the area of the enterprise, had often led, before the first war, to the importation of labour, either by some special system of recruitment or under indenture. The labour in such cases was usually Indian as in Fiji, Ceylon, British Guiana or Mauritius, or, especially in Malaya, Chinese. The hostility of Indian opinion to the indenture system, which it considered nationally degrading, led to its suspension after the first war. But the social and political complexities which resulted cannot be ignored in considering the claims of immigrant enterprise to be complementary to native enterprise, especially as a considerable proportion invariably remained in the territory and eventually became a permanent element in the population. In such circumstances, the effects were in some cases similar to those so much feared by critics of the administration in Kenya. The native population, largely excluded from the developing modern sectors of the economy, tended to remain engaged mainly in traditional activities such as subsistence agriculture, or fishing, and economically relatively underdeveloped and weak even if, as in Fiji or Malaya, they retained their traditional social organization and a measure of political privilege, sheltered by the British administration. Apart from sisal in Tanganyika, plantations were not of very great importance in British tropical Africa, but mining, especially in Northern Rhodesia and in the West African territories, inevitably recruited its labour force from a wide area. In addition, the employment opportunities available in Southern Rhodesia and the Union of South Africa attracted large numbers of Africans from British territories further north, especially Nyasaland.

The regulation of labour recruitment was an important pre-occupation of colonial governments in the inter-war years and much was done to assist the migrant by the regulation of contracts, the limitation of the period of engagement, medical examination, the provision of transport, the development of recognized routes with rest camps, and arrangements for deferred pay and repatriation. The social effects of migrant labour in traditional society were more disruptive than was generally supposed. The theory that if migrants were absent only for limited periods these effects would be relatively unimportant proved erroneous. Rules of social life in the villages were greatly weakened and agricultural productivity seriously lowered. It was an interesting commentary on the effect of the continuous criticism of labour recruitment by European enterprise in East and Central Africa that virtually nothing was said about the hardships of the migrant or seasonal labour which sought work in the African cocoa farms of the Gold Coast, or on the African cotton plantations of Buganda, or even in the gold mines of the Gold Coast, or the iron ore mines of Sierra Leone, European enterprises though these were. The Colonial Office Labour Adviser reported in 1941 that, although in West Africa the position was 'theoretically admirable, with a flow of entirely free labour, unrecruited and untrammelled by any sort of contract', in practice the worker was '. . . in a far worse position than his brother in a country where adequate arrangements exist for the collection, transport, care, and subsequent repatriation of the worker'.[22]

Migrant, or more generally seasonal, labour was thus to be found wherever economic growth produced the stimulus of a sufficient demand. Intervention in the interests of that labour might be just as necessary, though evidently far more difficult, in areas of native as of immigrant enterprise. But, whatever the appropriate remedies might be, this example illustrated the comparative neglect of the possible complexities of positive trusteeship in countries like Uganda and British West Africa where its vocal watchdogs in Britain seem to have felt a once-for-all decision in favour of native interests had been taken. It might also suggest that in a larger perspective some at least of the problems associated with European settlement or enter-prise were problems inseparable from economic development of any kind which were merely thrown into prominence by the visibility of racial differences between employer and employed.

If production was in native hands, could it safely be assumed that unrestricted access to the world market would ensure that producers received the full competitive price? This issue was dramatically posed in 1937 when the Gold Coast cocoa far-mers successfully refused to sell their cocoa and imposed a boy-cott of European imports. The immediate cause of their pro-ducers' strike was, a Commission of Enquiry reported,[23] an agreement on the part of twelve of the thirteen European firms who together bought 98 per cent of the cocoa to share the market among themselves on the basis of past performance and to eliminate competition by a price based on the world price and fixed margins for freight and other costs. There was really nothing new in this, except the impressive unanimity of African reaction. The tendency to concentration among European firms had been a very well-marked feature of the West African economy for several decades; similar pooling agreements had been made on various occasions in the previous twenty years, nor had they been confined to cocoa; others had at various times been concluded for other crops. Even if, as the firms argued, they had in the previous seven years paid out for cocoa sums substantially larger than the sums due at world prices, it was not evident that the remedy they proposed was the right one; moreover, it might be that since an even smaller number of the same firms controlled by far the greater part of the import trade the losses they claimed to have made on their purchases of cocoa had in fact been recouped by profits on their sales of imports larger than would have been possible in a more competitive, let alone a perfectly competitive, economy. It is unnecessary to consider whether the conclusions reached by the Commission on the basis of its analysis of the cocoa trade were sound, or whether the measures actually adopted some years later by the British government in establishing publicly controlled buying monopolies for the major products were those best calculated to safeguard the interests of the producers. Both the analysis and the measures adopted have been severely criticized.[24] What is common ground is that, in West African conditions, competition in certain sectors of the economy was imperfect. Whether the remedy should be sought in public control of this major sector of the economy or in public action designed to promote a closer approximation to perfect competition has been the subject of as heated controversy in this context as in most others. What this example illustrated is that trusteeship, here as elsewhere, required, at the least, constant vigilance and greatly more economic competence than colonial governments or the Colonial Office possessed before the second world war.

And if it was not true that 'production by natives under European guidance' was in itself a sufficient condition of economic development free from serious exploitation, what was to be said of that other panacea, large-scale capital investment by European enterprise? There were many kinds of development which could only be achieved on this basis, whether it was straightforward private enterprise or as in the famous Gezira irrigation project in the Sudan one in which government, private enterprise, and native tenant farmers were combined in a single scheme in which the profits were shared on a basis prescribed in advance. In the Gezira project,[25] perhaps the most constructive development undertaken in any colonial country, the share of private enterprise which provided management and some capital over the twenty-five years between 1925 and 1950 totalled £16 million, that of the tenants in the same period totalled £40 million, and the average profit received by each tenancy in 1946 was £49. By 1950, admittedly a boom year, it was £281. In 1946 an economist made a pioneer investigation of the national income of Northern Rhodesia,[26] and calculated that the output of the highly successful mining industry of that country had a gross value of £14½ million. Only £6·5 million of this was however spent in Northern Rhodesia and of that the share of African employees was less than a fifth. Her calculations showed that £10·4 million of Nyasaland's territorial income of £13·8 million in 1948 was earned by Africans. In Northern Rhodesia, with an African population four-fifths that of Nyasaland, the total territorial income was £39 million but only £11·5 million was earned by Africans.[27] There were great problems about calculations of this kind, notably in the valuation of subsistence production; but it none the less seemed safe to assume that the benefits of the copper industry had not, at that stage, been shared to any significant extent by the African population as a whole.

But the most perplexing problem of colonial policy in the inter-war years was one in which not even the rough and ready calculus of economic aggregates, had it then been available, would have served to test the aims of policy. It was, paradoxically, the one in which the experts, both academic and official, tended to be most certain of the fundamental rightness of the dominant ideas. Yet it was also one in which no policy could rest, in the last analysis, on more than judgements of value made by the policy makers themselves. Was the task of trusteeship, so far as those narrow limits of history, power, and economic pressure might allow, one of transforming colonial society into a modern western civilization, however long that might take? Or was it to preserve, so far as might be, the traditional order of native society, purged of its grosser abuses, in Western eyes (cannibalism, for example) so that it might be enabled to survive until the native peoples were 'able to stand by themselves'? 'Indirect Rule'—it is time to give this school of thought the name by which, rather misleadingly, it was generally known—did not argue that the traditional institutions of native society should be preserved unchanged (as Hobson had gone far to imply) or that they could be left entirely free to make their own adaptation to the new demands which were bound to follow the imposition of colonial rule. The task was to assist them to make that adaptation. Changes so great that such an adaptation evidently could not be made must therefore not be introduced. Economic development and education should accordingly be promoted only so far as seemed likely to prove consistent with that over-riding purpose. It was for instance because the native social institutions whose disintegration they wished to prevent had developed in intimate relationship with an agricultural environment that advocates of indirect rule from Lugard onwards so strongly urged that native peasant production should be the basis of economic development. 'Indirect rule' called for a gradual blending of modern Western and traditional native elements without attempting to prescribe in advance what character the mixture should ultimately attain. It is difficult today to do justice to these ideas, when we can see so much more easily the inconsistencies, indeed the impossibility, of such a controlled social change in a world in which neither the speed nor the social consequences of economic growth—even by native peasant producers—could be foreseen once seriously begun.

Indirect rule had three major weaknesses. It demanded of the European agents of control an alert empiricism informed not only by conviction of the value to any people of its own social values and institutions but also by a detailed knowledge of those institutions and of the precise impact on them of the varied social and economic results of Western rule. Such knowledge, even in most favourable circumstances, they could never attain. Secondly, native social institutions, especially in Africa, varied greatly in the extent to which they could effectively be utilized even for the simplest purposes of administration, let alone as the chosen instruments of that social reintegration which the inroads of modernity were making desperately urgent in some areas while others even in the same territory seemed to have remained largely untouched by their impact. Changes which could readily be absorbed, for example by the great Moslem emirates of Northern Nigeria with their well-developed systems of local administration and taxation, could not possibly be accommodated by communities of a few thousand people with no central authority more elaborate than a gathering of family heads. Thirdly, even the largest and most highly organized native states were an uncertain basis on which to construct any institutions which looked like being able to support the management of the central services of the territories of which they now formed only a relatively small part. It was these two factors, the immense range of native societies which colonial rule brought within a single administrative unit and the territorial unevenness of the social change it induced, that proved incompatible with the ideas of indirect rule.

Local administration apart, it was in educational policy that those ideas had their greatest influence, assisted by a widespread anxiety to avoid reproducing what were considered the dangerous results of educational policy in India. Insistence on the use of native languages in the earlier years of schooling, attempts to give education a more practical bent, and a desire to see more attention given at the secondary stage to vocational rather than literary or general education all reflected this

approach. But, especially in Africa, other influences, of which
shortage of money was not the least important, resulted in a
policy of close co-operation in education with the missions,
which provided almost all primary, as well as many secondary,
schools and teacher training besides. Although their leading
authorities accepted a good deal of this general approach to
educational policy, there was a great variety in its actual application. Without the missions, practice might well have been
more influenced by hostility to 'literary' education and by some
of the more doctrinaire enthusiasts for its adaptation, not to the
developing needs of Africa, but to features of traditional society
destined to diminishing importance. But in their fundamental
approach, the educational policy makers were surely thinking
on the right lines, even if that approach was distorted by some
of the more conservative administrators and also by Africans
determined not to be fobbed off with what they deemed a
second best in education. The new independent states of Africa
and Asia, which are certainly not going to be replicas of any
Western country, are rediscovering the vital importance of
reshaping education to meet the actual needs of native
society.

To turn, finally, to the political implications of trusteeship.
In my first lecture, I claimed that British policy, as well as the
demands made on it by colonial spokesmen, had indeed been influenced by the existence of the Dominions. I believe this to have
been of crucial importance in determining the British habit of
mind as compared with that of other colonial powers. But too
much can easily be claimed for it and, especially by apologists
for British colonial policy after the second world war, it generally has been. British policy never, in the inter-war years or
earlier, contemplated the eventual incorporation of the colonial
territories in a Greater Britain. There was a general impression,
it can hardly be called more than that, that local participation in colonial government was desirable and could be pro-

gressively increased as capacity for such participation developed, which often meant as the pressure for it became too great to be conveniently resisted. If British policy was certainly not opposed in principle to any idea of eventual self-government it equally certainly did not during the inter-war years conceive it to be part of its duty 'officiously to strive' to bring self-government into existence. A substantial proportion of that relatively small group who were closely and actively concerned with colonial policy was wholly sceptical of any idea that, in the Colonial Empire, self-government was likely to be achieved by the development of parliamentary, still less democratic, institutions. To the people who had, after all, invented parliamentary government, the extent of political consensus that it requires for its continued existence was quite well understood. But with that understanding went a profound conviction that political development was not to be brought about by social engineering, by elaborate constitutional provisions supported by social planning. Rather, it must be an organic growth, fostered by habits of accommodation, which were taken to be the supreme art in politics. There resulted an assumption that piecemeal concessions of varying degrees of participation in government might be expected somehow to result in the development of political habits which could in the long run be translated into an institutional basis for self-government appropriate to the varying genius of the inhabitants of a given territory.

For all the scepticism of the professionals, British opinion, especially liberal opinion, continually underestimated the strength of feeling that representative institutions, however remote they might be from achieving responsible government, invariably aroused in communally divided countries. For all their experience in Ireland and India, they remained hopeful that experience would teach the habit of accommodation. Here too, history had imposed a limitation which the British never quite brought themselves to think of trying to remove. In virtually every territory a Legislative Council has been established at a time when the unofficials to be appointed to it were mostly members of the local British business and professional community. It might still have an official majority—almost all of them had during the inter-war years—but it had the functions and many of the ceremonial procedures of a parliament, and it was inevitable that, as a native educated and professional class emerged, its members too should seek representation in that legislature and look to its eventual development as a genuine local parliament. Convinced of the entire incompatibility of such a development with their ideals, the 'indirect rule' administrators concentrated on limiting the territorial scope of the Councils wherever possible and so missed the opportunity of reconciling the native authority system with the need for territorial political unity which might have been provided by arranging for Legislative Councils made up of representatives of the Native authorities. Far sighted in this as in most other things, Guggisberg arranged such a link in the Gold Coast Colony in 1925 but the only other territory in which anything similar was done was Fiji where it long survived as the basis of Fijian representation.

So long as Legislative Councils existed they were bound to suggest development by well-recognized stages—elected minority, unofficial majority, elected majority, responsible government. The combined effect of this fact and the habit of mind I have tried to describe was the gradual development in the inter-war years of the theory that while British overall responsibility would continue for an indefinite period, colonial governments would pass through progressive stages to eventual self-government. And although this did not necessarily imply parliamentary government, no alternative was suggested. As early as 1919 Amery had cautiously stated the progressive theory while regretting that the process must necessarily take a great deal longer than some members would like.[28] In 1938, Malcolm MacDonald enunciated it again to the House of Commons in a peroration[29] which emphasizes both the notion of organic growth and its exceedingly long-term character.

'The great purpose of the British Empire is the gradual spread of freedom among all His Majesty's subjects in whatever part of the world they live. That spread of freedom is a slow, evolutionary process. In some countries it is more rapid than in others. In some parts of the Empire, in the Dominions, that evolutionary process has been completed, it is finished. Inside the Colonial Empire the evolutionary process is going on all the time. In some colonies like Ceylon the gaining of freedom has already gone very far. In others it is necessarily a much slower process. It may take generations, or even centuries, for the peoples in some parts of the Colonial Empire to achieve self-government. But it is a major part of our policy, even among the most backward peoples of Africa, to teach them and to encourage them always to be able to stand a little more on their own feet.'

Mr MacDonald did not mention that in some colonies that evolutionary process had in fact, and quite recently, gone backwards. Malta which from 1919 to 1936 had had full internal self-government, and Cyprus, which had had an elected majority from 1925 to 1931, had both found themselves bundled unceremoniously from the front to the back of the procession. Was the whole progressive theory then simply a sham? Certainly, if with that theory in mind, and assuming the objective to have been democratic parliamentary government, one examines the history of most colonies which have now become independent, the answer must seem depressingly obvious. The truth, I suggest, is more complex. Among the remoter objects of policy was some form of self-government appropriate to the genius of the people, and the valid criticisms are that no alternative to a parliamentary form was ever clearly envisaged while the notion of organic growth facilitated many developments which were not only unlikely to promote a parliamentary form of government but even to bring into existence the national base needed for any kind of self-government.

The British habit of setting up each territory as a separate unit of administration and government, with its own budget, laws and public services, has unquestionably been a powerful factor in fostering colonial nationalism and also, where the unit was a suitable one to serve as the basis of a state, self-government of some kind. But another aspect of this habitual approach was a tendency to accept whatever units the British found themselves confronted with and to maintain them—even within a larger territory which for other purposes they administered as a single entity—without considering what effect maintaining such smaller units must necessarily have on the possible emergence of any unit suitable to provide the basis for a state of any kind. It was, for instance, initially convenient in Malaya nominally to govern through the Sultans and in consequence nine separate Malay States were retained in this small area.[30] The indirect rule system in Africa provides many similar examples in Uganda, Nigeria, and Ghana. Moreover, this tendency applied not only to territorial units, but to racial communities or minorities, which were themselves often treated as separate units for many purposes of government, as, for example, the Chinese Protectorate in the Straits Settlements whereby a special set of officials administered the Chinese through their own community leaders, or the Fijian administration in Fiji under which the affairs of Fijians were in almost all important matters in the hands of a separate organization of government, which resembled a state within a state. Arrangements of this kind may be the basis, for the community concerned, of some degree of self-government within a colonial system but they are not likely to promote any national self-government within the territory as a whole or the gradual development of a habit of accommodation between different communities which the idea of organic political growth demands. In saying this, I am not suggesting either that regional or communal loyalties in such territories are fictitious or that it is at all easy for a colonial ruler to reduce their force, but only that arrangements of this kind can hardly be regarded as exemplifying stages in any development towards self-government on a national basis in each territory, such as the progressive theory implied.

The problems of trusteeship were the problems of power, of the responsibilities of the strong towards the weak. The unequal distribution of political and economic power in the world, which was the fundamental basis of colonialism, has not been suddenly abolished by the accession of most colonies to political independence. The idea of trusteeship could not, any more than any other general principle, supply a clear and definite prescription of the proper role of a colonial power in the enormous variety of actual situations which confronted British rulers in the Colonial Empire. But whenever a serious and sustained attempt was made to bring it to bear on the actual circumstances of a particular territory it brought into much sharper relief specific problems inherent in such a relationship. With the end of the colonial era, it is for the rulers of the new independent states to judge what their responsibilities for the welfare of their own people require. But the rich and powerful countries of the world are not thereby absolved from any further responsibility towards those countries. Now, as earlier, their interest as well as their duty should impel them to seek to reduce the international tensions that result from these great disparities in wealth and power. In that stupendous task, the search for reciprocities of interest, which was at the heart of the trusteeship idea, remains more likely to provide a viable basis for the relationship between a rich and strong and a poor and weak country than the unmitigated national altruism, or national egotism which are too often proffered to us today as the only moral or rational bases of policy. Greatly changed though their terms have been by the disappearance of western European colonial rule, the dilemmas of trusteeship remain, as the young Churchill wrote of East Africa more than half a century ago, 'the problems of the world'.[31]

NOTES TO CHAPTER III

[1] Mill, *op. cit.*, pp. 408-9.

[2] J. A. Hobson, *Imperialism* (London, 1902). All quotations in the text are from the third edition (1938), pp. 225, 228-9, 232.

[3] *Ibid.*, p. 237.

[4] Lugard, *op cit.*, p. 61.

[5] Hobson, *op. cit.*, pp. 245-6.

[6] Sir W. K. Hancock, *Survey of British Commonwealth Affairs. II: Problems of Economic Policy 1918-1939, Part II* (London, 1942), pp. 141-2. The report so summarized is *Financial and Economic Position of Basutoland* (Cmd. 4907), 1935.

[7] Cmd. 4907, p. 34.

[8] The contemporary debate is summarized in L. A. Mills, *British Rule in Eastern Asia* (London, 1942), pp. 50-73.

[9] Cmd. 2884, pp. 4-5.

[10] *On Alien Rule and Self-Government* (London, 1960), pp. 38-55.

[11] *Ibid.*, p. 47.

[12] *Labour and the Nation*, p. 49.

[13] The phrase is Dr Kedourie's. See his *Nationalism* (London, 1960), p. 18.

[14] *The Empire in Africa: Labour's Policy* (1926), p. 7. Cited in R. Hinden, *Empire and After* (London, 1949), p. 119

[15] *Joint Committee on Closer Union in East Africa. Vol. I: Report* (H. of C. 156), 1931, pp. 29-31.

[16] Commons *Hansard*, 7 December 1938, c. 1246.

[17] Hancock, *op. cit.*, pp. 309-12.

[18] F. V. Meyer, *Britain's Colonies in World Trade* (London, 1948), pp. 120-8.

[19] *Despatch to the Governor of the East African Protectorate relating to Native Labour* (Cmd. 1509), 1921.

[20] *Report by . . . (Lord Moyne) on Certain Questions in Kenya* (Cmd. 4093), 1932.

[21] *Ibid.*, p. 43.

[22] *Labour Conditions in West Africa* (Cmd. 6277), 1941, p. 11.

[23] *Report of the Commission on the Marketing of West African Cocoa* (Cmd. 5845), 1938.

[24] P. T. Bauer, *West African Trade* (Cambridge, 1954), pp. 204–14 and 263–343.

[25] A. Gaitskell, *Gezira* (London, 1959), pp. 267–74.

[26] P. Deane, *Colonial Social Accounting* (Cambridge, 1953), p. 37.

[27] *Ibid.*, p. 214.

[28] Commons *Hansard,* 30 July 1919, c. 2176.

[29] Commons *Hansard,* 7 December 1938, c. 1248.

[30] I owe this illustration to T. H. Silcock, *The Commonwealth Economy of Southeast Asia* (Durham, North Carolina, 1959), p. 79.

[31] Sir W. S. Churchill, *My African Journey* (London, 1908, reprinted 1962), p. 44.

Date Due
